Coleridge's Meditative Art

by REEVE PARKER

In defining and illustrating the intricate and resourceful play of Coleridge's mind, Reeve Parker takes a fresh look at the meditative poems. He illuminates them through close readings and through references to and detailed commentary on passages from Coleridge's other poems, his notebooks, letters, lectures, and essays.

Although Professor Parker's emphasis throughout is on literary interpretation rather than on psychology, he explores the quality of Coleridge's and Wordsworth's relationship, offering new evidence on the nature and significance of their influence on each other. He gives full explications of five major meditative poems: "This Lime-Tree Bower My Prison," "Frost at Midnight," "Hymn Before Sun-rise in the Vale of Chamouny," "Dejection: An Ode," and "To William Wordsworth," devoting a separate chapter to each. These poems, he believes, are more than confessional in nature, and he argues that they reveal Coleridge as a far more subtle literary craftsman than has been generally recognized.

Challenging or going beyond traditional interpretations, this book is a sensitive and original contribution to the critical dialogue about Coleridge's art.

Coleridge's Meditative Art

REEVE PARKER is Associate Pr
fessor of English at Cornell Univ
sity. A graduate of Princeton U
versity and a Rhodes Schola
also holds an A.B. degree
Oxford University, and he re
his Ph.D. from Harvard Uni

Coleridge's Meditative Art

by REEVE PARKER

Cornell University Press | ITHACA AND LONDON

First published 1975 by Cornell University Press.
Published in the United Kingdom by Cornell University Press Ltd., 2-4 Brook Street, London W1Y 1AA.

International Standard Book Number 0-8014-0853-9
Library of Congress Catalog Card Number 74-25367

Printed in the United States of America by York Composition Co., Inc.

For my mother and in memory of my father

Contents

For meditation, I presume, is that act of the mind, by which it seeks *within* either the *law* of the phenomena, which it had *contemplated* without (*meditatio scientifica*), or semblances, symbols, and analogies, corresponsive to the same (*meditatio ethica*). At all events, therefore, it implies *thinking*, and tends to make the reader *think*, and whatever does this, does what in the present over-excited state of society is most wanted, though perhaps least desired. Between the *thinking* of a Harvey or Quarles, and the thinking of a Bacon or a Fenelon, many are the degrees of difference, and many the differences in degree of depth and originality; but not such as to fill up the chasm *in genere* between thinking and no-thinking, or to render the discrimination difficult for a man of ordinary understanding, not under the same contagion of vanity as the writer.

COLERIDGE (1821)

> Yea, he deserves to find himself deceived,
> Who seeks a heart in the unthinking man.
> Like shadows on a stream, the forms of life
> Impress their characters on the smooth forehead,
> Nought sinks into the bosom's silent depth:
> Quick sensibility of pain and pleasure
> Moves the light fluids lightly; but no soul
> Warmeth the inner frame.

SCHILLER, *The Death of Wallenstein* (I, vii, 42-9) tr Coleridge 1800. Reprinted as "Motto from Schiller" with Coleridge's "Meditative Poems in Blank Verse" in *Sibylline Leaves* (1817)

Preface

When Coleridge undertook in 1815, largely under financial pressure, the first edition of his collected poems, he put much energy and thought into its shape and presentation. What began as a preface, for example, grew into the *Biographia Literaria*, arguably the most influential critical essay in English. The result of his labors, *Sibylline Leaves* (1817), was a milestone in his life as well as a tombstone for his career as a poet. Though there were subsequent editions of the collection, their form never differed greatly from that of the first.

Common to all editions was a section called "Meditative Poems in Blank Verse," in which Coleridge grouped some of his best and most characteristic poems. Four of them, "Frost at Midnight," "This Lime-Tree Bower My Prison," "Hymn Before Sun-rise in the Vale of Chamouni," and "To William Wordsworth," along with "Dejection: An Ode," in many ways similar to them, are discussed at length in this book, each in a separate chapter. Each poem, taken by itself, has much artistic subtlety; my readings depart from, challenge, or extend previous interpretations in ways that I hope will encourage further discussion. Considered as a group, along with passages from other poems and from notebooks, letters, lectures, and essays useful in illuminating them, the poems also provide an avenue to the central activity and concern of Coleridge's mind, the process that he variously called "thinking" or "reflection" or "meditation" and valued as a source of consolation and comfort in a troubled life.[1]

In trying to recover the meaning of Coleridge's word "meditative," I am resisting what, following Coleridge's own usage in his early years, I would call "organic" tendencies in recent criticism.[2] Though no particular critic or school espouses an "organic" approach as such to the poems, the term is useful in describing assumptions that readers often bring to them, assumptions involving the nature and genesis of art. In one form, organicism tends toward biological metaphors for the creative process, metaphors that court an obscure naturalism. An example of such a metaphor, which has gained some currency, from one of the most judicious writers on Coleridge's art, is Albert Gérard's description of the movement of expansion and contraction in the meditative poems as revealing an "inner rhythm of systole and diastole [that] probably derives from one of the deepest urges in the romantic mind, . . . a structural rhythm to which . . . inspiration spontaneously shaped itself."[3] In another form, organicism assumes that the highest achievement of romantic poetry is the unmediated expression of felt experience, as though there were something discernible as "experience" prior to and independent of the language that calls it into being and to which that language, shunning artful elaboration, ought self-effacingly to return. Various readers, among them Humphry House and M. H. Abrams, have argued for seeing a more intricate art in the poems, in the contexts provided by Coleridge's other writings and by earlier descriptive and meditative traditions. This book is an attempt to extend and further substantiate their insights.[4]

In the *Biographia*, Coleridge challenged Wordsworth's argument for rejecting the language of art in favor of that of nature and spontaneity. As Abrams has summarized Coleridge's views, "The feelingful language and figures of a poet must differ from the spontaneous and feelingful language spoken sometimes by men in real life, in that the poet, after all, sets himself the artificial act of composing a *poem*, which is a conventional, metrical medium for producing foreseen effects."[5] However counter to modern poetics such a definition may run, our understanding of the meditative poems will be enhanced if we follow the lead of the *Biographia* and restore its balancing emphasis on artifice. To regard the poems instead as spontaneously shaped by the heart will be to misconstrue both their nature and his enterprise in composing them.

In his definitions of the imagination, Coleridge was concerned with the same play of mind that informs his own meditative poems. A fuller and closer appreciation of the art of those poems will help to refute the persistent argument that the poet and the philosopher were at odds in him, an argument that derives from naturalistic assumptions about poetry that he challenged: "He deserves to find himself deceived,/ Who seeks a heart in the unthinking man," begins Coleridge's motto to the meditative poems. With the continuing publication, in *The Collected Works of Samuel Taylor Coleridge* and *The Notebooks of Samuel Taylor Coleridge*, of hitherto unavailable speculative material, scholars will pay increased attention to his work as a scientific and religious thinker, and it will be useful to have as full a sense as possible of the highly playful cast of his intelligence, lest his exuberant verbal energies be thought to confound (as, indeed, he on occasion suspected they might) his efforts toward a comprehensive philosophical outlook. The essay that became the *Biographia* was begun as a preface to his collected poems, and it will be poetic justice now in more than one sense to turn the tables and read the meditative poems as an introduction to the complex and intimidating reaches of his prose.

Not everyone has admired the aspects of his mind I wish to focus on. Harriet Martineau saw in Coleridge the admonitory embodiment of a vice of intellect. Her spiritual anchorages as a Victorian differ in many ways from those of readers in the later twentieth century, but the hazards described in many recent judgments resemble shoals she charted in her eloquent indictment of his genius:

Those who feel as strongly as I do the irreverence and vanity of making the most solemn and sacred subjects an opportunity for intellectual self-indulgence, and cocoon-spinning out of one's own interior, will feel certain that the prophecied immortality of Coleridge will not be so much that of his writings as of himself, as an extreme specimen of the tendencies of our metaphysical period, which, being itself but a state of transition, can permit no immortality to its special products but as historical types of its characteristics and tendencies. . . . Coleridge appears to me to have been constitutionally defective in will, in conscientiousness and in apprehension of the real and true, while gifted or cursed with inordinate reflective and analogical faculties, as well as prodigious word power.[6]

At the risk of oversimplification, I take as my premise that what Martineau saw as vices were Coleridge's virtues, that the self-indulgent "cocoon-spinning" so distressing to her earnest sensibility was in fact just the salutary egotism Coleridge accurately saw from the mid-1790's on as the matrix of his meditative activity.

He seems always thus to stimulate controversy. And, not surprisingly, because criticism is rarely if ever capable of moral and intellectual disinterestedness, even the shrewdest judgments tend to reveal the proclivities of defenders and detractors alike. Coleridge himself, it is well known, sketched his own features into portraits he drew of others. But whatever else this study indicates of my own propensities, in offering an appreciation of the "inordinate reflective and analogical faculties" at work in his poems as an index of his genius, I am not interested in defending frivolity or suggesting that the personal qualities that exasperated those closest to Coleridge were in reality the traits of a maligned and misunderstood paragon. My purpose is to recover the intellectual and emotional activity that went into the making of some of his most successful poems and to see those poems clearly in the perspective of his interest in the cultivated art of meditation.

To illustrate the resourcefulness he was capable of, this study begins with a reading of "This Lime-Tree Bower My Prison" that finds Coleridge adapting, somewhat playfully, the mode of seventeenth-century meditation on the Book of Revelation. The second chapter, drawing on poems and prose of the 1790's and 1800's, is concerned with a more general description of what he called "intellectual activity" in the context of a theodicy for suffering; it argues a case for the substantial continuity of that context in his literary theory and practice. The subject of the third chapter is Coleridge's response, as recounted in the *Biographia* and as seen in his poem on Joan of Arc, to the provocative challenge Wordsworth's "Salisbury Plain" posed to his assumptions about the role of the imagination. Subsequent chapters deal with four poems that span the period 1798–1807 and suggest the range of his meditative art. In discussing "Frost at Midnight" and "Dejection: An Ode" I want to demonstrate not only how subtly they are wrought but also how each of them should be seen less as a merely autobiographical expression than as a dramatic projection of a meditative solution to distress. The same may be said of the chapters on the "Hymn Before Sunrise" and "To William Wordsworth," which, amplifying ideas broached earlier about Coleridge and Wordsworth, place those poems in a new light, as significant gestures of resistance, self-assertion, and generosity.

Most of the seventh chapter originally appeared in *Forms of Lyric: Selected Papers from the English Institute,* edited by Reuben Brower (New York: Columbia University Press, 1970), and, along with passages from the *Collected Letters of Samuel Taylor Coleridge,* edited by E. L. Griggs (6 vols; Oxford: The Clarendon Press, 1956–1971), is reprinted with permission. Each of the five poems discussed at length in this book is printed, for the reader's convenience, with the appropriate chapter; the texts are from E. H. Coleridge's edition of *The Complete Poetical Works of Samuel Taylor Coleridge* (2 vols; Oxford: The Clarendon Press, 1912). Like every other reader of Coleridge today, I owe particular thanks to Kathleen Coburn for the high scholarly standards and the usefulness of her edition of Coleridge's notebooks, and to her and her fellow editors for the excellence of the volumes of the *Collected Coleridge*.

My work on Coleridge began under David Perkins and Jerome Buckley at Harvard University, and I owe much to their thoughtful advice and judgment, and to that of W. J. Bate, at that stage. Among those who read all or part of the present text, I am most grateful for the criticism and suggestions of four people: M. H. Abrams, Ellen Lambert, Stephen M. Parrish, and especially Neil Hertz. Each of them will appreciate, as I do, how fully conventional statements of exoneration apply. I wish also to thank the Society for the Humanities and the administrators of the Clark Fund at Cornell University for grants to assist the completion of the book.

Reeve Parker

Ithaca, New York

1

Diseases into Pearls: "This Lime-Tree Bower My Prison" as Coleridgean Meditation

To the birth of the tree a prepared soil is as necessary as the falling seed. A Daniel was present; or the fatal characters in the banquet-hall of Balshazzar might have struck more terror, but would have been of no more import than the trail of a luminous worm. In the far greater number, indeed, of these asserted boons of chance, it is the accident that should be called the *condition*— and often not so much, but merely the *occasion*—while the proper cause of the invention is to be sought for in the co-existing state and previous habit of the observer's mind.

COLERIDGE (1821)

And I looked, and lo, a Lamb stood on the mount Sion, and with him an hundred forty and four thousand.

REVELATION 14 : 1

This Lime-Tree Bower My Prison

[Addressed to Charles Lamb, of the India House, London]

In the June of 1797 some long-expected friends paid a visit to the author's cottage; and on the morning of their arrival, he met with an accident, which disabled him from walking during the whole time of their stay. One evening, when they had left him for a few hours, he composed the following lines in the garden-bower.

Well, they are gone, and here must I remain,
This lime-tree bower my prison! I have lost
Beauties and feelings, such as would have been
Most sweet to my remembrance even when age
Had dimm'd mine eyes to blindness! They, meanwhile,   5
Friends, whom I never more may meet again,
On springy heath, along the hill-top edge,
Wander in gladness, and wind down, perchance,
To that still roaring dell, of which I told;
The roaring dell, o'erwooded, narrow, deep,   10
And only speckled by the mid-day sun;
Where its slim trunk the ash from rock to rock
Flings arching like a bridge;—that branchless ash,
Unsunn'd and damp, whose few poor yellow leaves
Ne'er tremble in the gale, yet tremble still,   15
Fann'd by the water-fall! and there my friends
Behold the dark green file of long lank weeds,
That all at once (a most fantastic sight!)
Still nod and drip beneath the dripping edge
Of the blue clay-stone.

                    Now, my friends emerge   20
Beneath the wide wide Heaven—and view again

The many-steepled tract magnificent
Of hilly fields and meadows, and the sea,
With some fair bark, perhaps, whose sails light up
The slip of smooth clear blue betwixt two Isles   25
Of purple shadow! Yes! they wander on
In gladness all; but thou, methinks, most glad,
My gentle-hearted Charles! for thou hast pined
And hunger'd after Nature, many a year,
In the great City pent, winning thy way   30
With sad yet patient soul, through evil and pain
And strange calamity! Ah! slowly sink
Behind the western ridge, thou glorious Sun!
Shine in the slant beams of the sinking orb,
Ye purple heath-flowers! richlier burn, ye clouds!   35
Live in the yellow light, ye distant groves!
And kindle, thou blue Ocean! So my friend
Struck with deep joy may stand, as I have stood,
Silent with swimming sense; yea, gazing round
On the wide landscape, gaze till all doth seem   40
Less gross than bodily; and of such hues
As veil the Almighty Spirit, when yet he makes
Spirits perceive his presence.

                               A delight
Comes sudden on my heart, and I am glad
As I myself were there! Nor in this bower,   45
This little lime-tree bower, have I not mark'd
Much that has sooth'd me. Pale beneath the blaze
Hung the transparent foliage; and I watch'd
Some broad and sunny leaf, and lov'd to see
The shadow of the leaf and stem above   50
Dappling its sunshine! And that walnut-tree
Was richly ting'd, and a deep radiance lay
Full on the ancient ivy, which usurps
Those fronting elms, and now, with blackest mass
Makes their dark branches gleam a lighter hue   55
Through the late twilight: and though now the bat
Wheels silent by, and not a swallow twitters,
Yet still the solitary humble-bee

Sings in the bean-flower! Henceforth I shall know
That Nature ne'er deserts the wise and pure;   60
No plot so narrow, be but Nature there,
No waste so vacant, but may well employ
Each faculty of sense, and keep the heart
Awake to Love and Beauty! and sometimes
'Tis well to be bereft of promis'd good,   65
That we may lift the soul, and contemplate
With lively joy the joys we cannot share.
My gentle-hearted Charles! when the last rook
Beat its straight path along the dusky air
Homewards, I blest it! deeming its black wing   70
(Now a dim speck, now vanishing in light)
Had cross'd the mighty Orb's dilated glory,
While thou stood'st gazing; or, when all was still,
Flew creeking o'er thy head, and had a charm
For thee, my gentle-hearted Charles, to whom   75
No sound is dissonant which tells of Life.

An accident occasioned "This Lime-Tree Bower My Prison," as perhaps every reader knows. In a letter to his brother-in-law Robert Southey, Coleridge wrote that on "the second day after Wordsworth came to me, dear Sara accidentally emptied a skillet of boiling milk on my foot, which confined me during the whole time of C. Lamb's stay & still prevents me from all *walks* longer than a furlong.—While Wordsworth, his Sister, & C. Lamb were out one evening;/ sitting in the arbour of T. Poole's garden, which communicates with mine, I wrote these lines, with which I am pleased." Inspiration may have come—as in Blake's *Milton*—through his foot, but we must seek the "coexisting state and previous habit" of Coleridge's mind to understand the proper cause and nature of one of his best "meditative poems in blank verse." To echo Coleridge's neoclassical usage in the first epigraph to this chapter, "This Lime-Tree Bower My Prison" is an "invention," and as such it makes an apt beginning for this book, providing a clear example of the subtlety of his meditative art.

Like many of his poems, it grew out of an interpenetration of reading and personal relationships. What the poet offers as a spontaneous monologue of immediate experience is informed by personal history and shaped by a significant literary consciousness. Though the poem has never lacked admirers, neither the extent of the personal experience involved nor the context of literary influence discernible in its language has been adequately described.

1

The poem was dedicated and parts of it addressed to Lamb, whom Coleridge in 1796 called his "dearest friend." Lamb's visit to Nether Stowey in July 1797, when the poem was composed, may be seen as the culmination of their friendship, which began years earlier in school at Christ's Hospital; certainly the poem in an important sense offers Coleridge's most considered definition of that friendship. From the beginning of their acquaintance, Lamb had been drawn to the brilliance displayed by the older Coleridge. Their schoolboy bond developed into fuller friendship later, in December and January 1794–1795, when Coleridge, with the heady vision of Pantisocracy dissipating and his relationships with Southey and the Fricker family degenerating, took refuge in London. As Lamb later fondly recalled, they spent long evenings at the Salutation and Cat in Newgate Market, talking metaphysics and poetry. But Coleridge's immediate past soon caught up with him; in mid-January Southey's vociferous importunities in support of the mute claims of Sarah Fricker prevailed, and Coleridge went guiltily west again, eventually to be married.

The friendship with Lamb had been for Coleridge a comfortable one, and for much of the next two years, they were in steady correspondence. Several of Lamb's letters—but only one by Coleridge, discussed below—survive, chiefly from May 1796 to January 1797, when the correspondence was at its peak. They permit a fairly clear view of the relationship.[1] Though exchange of domestic news on both sides was ample, the correspondence was largely literary and gossipy, with the focus on their own writings. As George Whalley has said, Lamb had a "warm affection and a deep and guileless admiration for Coleridge."[2] He typically reacted with diffidence to Coleridge's more vigorous critical intellect. His occasional negative comments about his friend's poems drew expansive, justifying rebuttals, to which he usually deferred gratefully. At one point, questions arose about "personal" (as distinct from epic) poems and about borrowings. Lamb was vexed when Coleridge, abusing his role as editor of the collection, *Poems on Various Subjects,* which included a few poems by Lamb, tampered with some of his lines. "I charge you, Col., spare my ewe lambs, and tho' a Gentleman may borrow six lines in an epic poem (I should have no objection to borrow 500 and without acknowledging) still in a Sonnet—a personal poem—I do not 'ask my friend the aiding verse.'" Though Lamb was a confirmed literary jester in conversation, letters, and essays, in his "personal" poems he prized sincerity, "things that come from the heart direct, not by the medium of the fancy." "I love my sonnets because they are the reflected images of my own feelings at different times."[3]

It is true that Lamb had extravagant praise for the Miltonic loftiness of Coleridge's "Religious Musings" and for the opening lines of the section he contributed to Southey's epic, *Joan of Arc.* His enthusiasm for these efforts at the sublime was welcome, perhaps enhancing Coleridge's respect for the acumen of this friend. Lamb's "*taste & judgment,*" he said, he saw reason to think "more correct & philosophical than my own, which yet I place pretty high."[4] But though Lamb urged Coleridge to explore "the loftier walks of Pindus" as his proper region, he was also constantly critical of what he called "elaborateness" and artifice. At one point, in November 1796, partly sensing the contradiction in his metaphor, he advised him thus: "Cultivate simplicity, Coleridge; or rather, I should say, banish elaborateness; for simplicity springs spontaneous from the heart, and carries into daylight its own modest buds, and genuine, sweet, and clear flowers of expression. I allow no hot-beds in the gardens of Parnassus."[5] Or again, "I hate made-dishes at the muses' banquet." What emerges from all of Lamb's amiable, preceptorial fussiness is that, while he supported Coleridge's attempts at epic sublimity, his steady emphasis on tenderness, "sincerity," and simplicity in more "personal" verse proposed a decorum for such writing that would have cramped Coleridge's inventive energies.

Still, in the summer of 1796, when Coleridge was settled with his wife in Bristol, he missed Lamb's company. His open estrangement from Southey had effectively dissolved that literary bond. True, there was Wordsworth, whom Coleridge had met the previous autumn (when he apparently heard an early version of "Salisbury Plain") and with whom he seems to have been in correspondence, but it was still a year before the Wordsworths' arrival at Alfoxden would bring Coleridge the opportunity for an intercourse fuller and more stimulating than any he had ever known. So he sent off the first of a number of invitations urging Lamb to come west on vacation. Lamb was tempted, but he demurred throughout the summer. He cited vexing circumstances: an ill brother and the demands of his employer at India House. And perhaps unstated along with the reasons openly offered was a common-sense awareness that Coleridge's marriage had altered the conditions which earlier had fostered their relationship. Could Lamb, whose urbane spirits bubbled among London's ample amusements, really have enjoyed the prospect of two weeks cooped up in a cottage with a friend whose wife he had never met and about whose marriage he had reasons to be uneasy? Even on a lark?

Then, in September 1796, an appalling calamity occurred. Lamb's sister Mary, in a fit of lunacy, knifed her mother to death and wounded her father. To Charles fell the burden of burying his mother, defending Mary against threatened criminal proceedings, and holding the remains of the family together. A few days after the stabbing he wrote to Coleridge, with notable composure charging him not to "think of coming to me" and asking instead what he felt Coleridge alone among his friends could provide: "Write,—as religious a letter as possible—."[6]

Coleridge's immediate response was a remarkably eloquent letter of consolation, which we shall consider more fully later.

To Lamb it was an "inestimable treasure" and alone of the many letters Coleridge wrote him in 1796–1797 survived his subsequent shifts among London lodgings. In the letter Coleridge also renewed his invitation: "I wish above measure to have you for a little while here; no visitants shall blow on the nakedness of your feelings; you shall be quiet, and your spirit may be healed. I see no possible objection, unless your father's helplessness prevent you. . . . . I charge you, if by any means it be possible, come to me."[7] But neither friend visited the other, though they continued to correspond into the winter. Under the emotional weight of the calamity, Lamb was of a mind to abandon the "idle trade of versifying," but he resumed almost at once his literary precepts, telling Coleridge he valued his personal poems as he valued Rousseau's *Confessions*, for "the same frankness, the same openness of heart, the same disclosure of all the most hidden and delicate affections of the mind."

But if Lamb conceived of artifice as inimical to such pastoral openness—and again and again this was the burden of his gentle strictures—one can imagine how inadequately such a prescription would have accommodated Coleridge's literary sensibility. Whatever the reason, early in 1797, some time after he had moved to Nether Stowey, Coleridge's side of the correspondence lagged. By the end of March, Wordsworth had supplanted Lamb as the critic and friend to whom Coleridge most eagerly turned. (Lamb's later coolness toward the poems of the man whom in 1800 he referred to with undisguised wryness as Coleridge's "god" is the more understandable in this context of rivalry for Coleridge's allegiance. Perhaps he even felt that Wordsworth was encouraging Coleridge in the very tendencies he had tried to check. That is a possible inference from the way he disparaged the second [1800] edition of *Lyrical Ballads:* "It too artfully aims at simplicity.")[8] In April Lamb complained about Coleridge's silence. Then, in June, when Coleridge was doubtless guilty about neglecting a friend and hopeful of reassuring him with a display of generous hospitality—such improvised bursts to forestall the loss of any good opinion were frequent with him—he wrote another letter urging Lamb to Stowey. Lamb, whose own domestic circumstances were more stable, was again teased with the prospect of resuming the friendship he had so cherished. But he was still doubtful, if not evasive. "It depends on fifty things, besides the expense, which is not nothing." This time, however, hope seems to have won out, for in three weeks he arrived.

During his week at Stowey, Lamb met Sarah, Tom Poole, and Coleridge's new friends the Wordsworths, also visitors, who soon leased the nearby estate at Alfoxden. Given the recent lapse in their correspondence and Lamb's resultant apprehensions about Coleridge's waning interest, one can imagine how inhibiting Lamb must have found that whole new world. (He later apologized to Coleridge for being "sulky" in the company.) Perhaps wishing to establish his credentials in such a brotherhood, he expressed particular enthusiasm for Wordsworth's recitation of *"that inscription!"*—the poem published a year later in *Lyrical Ballads* as "Lines Left upon a Seat in a Yew-Tree"—and afterward asked Coleridge to copy it for him, "if you think Wordsworth has no objection." As many readers have noted, "This Lime-Tree Bower My Prison" has marked affinities with Wordsworth's inscription. Was Coleridge, already in rivalry with his new poet-friend, competing for Lamb's admiration? At any rate, all indications are that the visit brought out Lamb's diffidence. He even left behind his great-coat, "in the oblivious state the mind is thrown into at parting."[9]

Not much else is known or can reasonably be inferred about Lamb's stay, beyond the account Coleridge supplied in his matter-of-fact headnote to the poem: "In the June of 1797 some long-expected friends paid a visit to the author's cottage; and on the morning of their arrival, he met with an accident,

which disabled him from walking during the whole time of
their stay. One evening, when they had left him for a few
hours, he composed the following lines in the garden-bower."

2

Partly, no doubt, because of the documentary elaborateness
of both that note and the subtitle of the poem ("Addressed to
Charles Lamb, of the India House, London"), partly because
of the steady attention within the poem itself to the author's
predicament and to the details of local topography, and partly
because of the prominent colloquial effects ("Well, they are
gone, and here must I remain,/This lime-tree bower my
prison!"), the poem has seemed to many readers just the sort
of "personal" poem Lamb had so often urged Coleridge to
cultivate. Though Coleridge could easily have disabused Lamb
of that impression, he apparently never did, even when Lamb
(of all people) finally complained in 1800 of the embarrassment of being addressed as "my gentle-hearted Charles":

For God's sake (I never was more serious) don't make me ridicu-
lous any more by terming me gentle-hearted in print, or do it
in better verses. It did well enough five [sic] years ago when I
came to see you, and was moral coxcomb enough at the time
you wrote the lines, to feed upon such epithets; but, besides that,
the meaning of gentle is equivocal at best, and almost always
means poor-spirited; the very quality of gentleness is abhorrent
to such vile trumpetings. My *sentiment* is long since vanished. I
hope my *virtues* have done *sucking*. I can scarce think but you
meant it in joke. I hope you did, for I should be ashamed to believe that you could think to gratify me by such praise, fit only
to be a cordial to some green-sick sonneteer.[10]

In our own time, the poem has usually been read as a signal
achievement in a genial meditative style. Hailed for its spontaneous, organic structure, for the remarkable achievement of
a mind overhearing itself, and for its fluent record of naturally
developing thought, it has been read as a "conversation" poem
and cited as the first full emergence of a relaxed style that

profoundly influenced Wordsworth and, through him, much later English poetry. At the same time, readers have wished to account for and thus emphasize its naturalistic mode without falling into the trap of calling it automatic art. Donald Davie's frequently quoted analysis of the syntax of the poem comes perhaps closest to that fallacy when he argues that it "acts out, in its own developing structure, the development of feeling behind it."[11] But even such a theory of affective mimesis is insufficient, for the poem is more than a deft rendering of thought and feeling in process, of the mind moving spontaneously from solipsistic preoccupation with melancholy to the release of assertive joy.

Coleridge's mind provided the structure of the poem, it is true, but (to adapt one of his favorite Kantian distinctions) in a constitutive rather than merely regulative sense. R. A. Durr, in an excellent essay on the essentially religious nature of the poem, contends that "This Lime-Tree Bower My Prison" embodies a recurrent pattern in Coleridge's poetry in which "initial disharmony between man and nature [is] resolved through the imaginative act of empathic identification with an 'object,' whereupon the poem returns to the opening scene transformed." This pattern reflects "the spiritual action of transcending the morbid condition of the alienated Soul through realization of—'seeing'—the all-encompassment of the Life of God."[12] Implicitly informed by a characteristically unobtrusive analogical gesture, Coleridge's poem brings to a culmination the major phase of his relationship to Lamb. That gesture, and the structure dependent upon it, are fully discernible, I think, in the light of the shaping influence, on both consolatory letter and poem, of the Christian meditative tradition Coleridge encountered in extensive reading of seventeenth-century Puritan and Anglican writers. The case for a close link between Coleridge and that tradition can also be made on other grounds, but "This Lime-Tree Bower My Prison" reveals how imaginative that link could be.

For interpreting Coleridge's poem, the salient text in that

tradition is Richard Baxter's *The Saints' Everlasting Rest*. My guess is that Coleridge knew this treatise well in 1796 when Lamb suffered his calamity and that Baxter's formulations and examples of the art of Christian meditation, or ones very like his, were centrally operative in Coleridge's imagination when he addressed himself to his friend, both in the letter Lamb treasured and in the poem that finally exasperated him. What follows is in part an attempt to supply the ground on which this conjecture is based and to anticipate its problematic aspects. But, more important, the notion that Coleridge was offering Lamb (and himself) a consolation based in essentially Christian tradition can be used to frame an interpretation of "This Lime-Tree Bower My Prison" that will illuminate anew the analogical nature of Coleridge's poetic mind.

Though Baxter was one of the seventeenth-century religious thinkers whom he read closely, no proof exists that Coleridge had read *The Saints' Everlasting Rest* by 1796.[13] Baxter's treatise on meditation, the earliest of a number of English vernacular adaptations of the discipline so important to continental Roman Catholic thought after Loyola, did have an extraordinary circulation, however, going through perhaps two dozen editions in the century and a half following its original publication in 1650, and one might reasonably suppose that Coleridge knew it as an undergraduate at Cambridge or even as a schoolboy. In November 1796, little over a month after his "religious" letter to Lamb, Coleridge wrote to Thomas Poole that he "did not particularly admire Rosseau—Bishop Taylor, Old Baxter, David Hartley & the Bishop of Cloyne are *my men*," an allusion whose familiarity one might naturally guess to be based in part in acquaintance with Baxter's most widely known work.[14] The argument for the influence of *Saints' Rest* on Coleridge's letter and poem remains conjectural, based on affinities discussed below. Though what follows makes a case for that specific influence, the more important consideration is that Baxter's treatise represents a tradition of meditative Christian consolation Coleridge knew intimately, even if through other examples.[15]

Baxter contends in *The Saints' Everlasting Rest* that the practice of meditative exercises in this world can raise the soul's powers to full affective awareness of the joys awaiting it in the "rest," or celestial afterlife. The essence of his argument, as well as the source for his chief rhetorical device, is the belief that the huge gap between the pains and pleasures of the world and the circumstances of that rest can be bridged only by employing the mind in the "set and solemn" art of meditation. Baxter's ultimate sanction (and repeatedly invoked inspiration) for his vision of the world beyond is the Book of Revelation, the text Coleridge himself pointedly imitated in *Religious Musings* (1796). Saint John's apocalytic prophecy is, I think, also Coleridge's ultimate model in "This Lime-Tree Bower My Prison," and Baxter's treatise (or another like it) mediated that visionary scriptural narrative in his mind as he shaped and defined his relationship with Charles Lamb. The tradition embodied in *Saints' Rest*, in other words, provides an indispensable analogical context in which to read his first fully realized meditative poem.

A Puritan struggling with the problem of election, Baxter was nevertheless, as Louis Martz has emphasized, no dour Calvinist austerely repudiating the world's charms.[16] While acknowledging in *Saints' Rest* the limitations of the mortal nature to which the soul was bound, he urges the Christian to employ his faculties of mind and body in this life in an endeavor to know the next. To attain a fully felt conception of the eternal rest enjoyed by the elected saints, Baxter advocates meditation on the experience of the sensuous world. As a Puritan in mid-seventeenth-century anti-Romish England prudently might, he invokes the authority of the New Testament for thus enlisting the senses in spiritual struggle: "And it is very considerable, how the Holy Ghost doth condescend in the phrase of Scripture, in bringing things down to the reach of sense; how He sets forth the excellencies of spiritual things in words that are borrowed from the objects of sense."[17]

Not surprisingly, Baxter is at some pains to avoid charges of papist indulgence in sensuousness: "No, not that we should take the Spirit's figurative expressions to be meant according to strict propriety; or have fleshly conceivings of spiritual things, so as to believe them to be such indeed; but thus to think, that to conceive or speak of them in strict propriety is utterly beyond our reach and capacity; and therefore, we must conceive of them as we are able" (359–360). In this head-and-heart philosophy, meditation is more than "the bare thinking on truths and the rolling of them in the understanding and memory": "This is the great task in hand, and this is the work that I would set thee on; to get these truths from thy head to thy heart, and that all the sermons which thou hast heard of heaven, and all the notions that thou hast conceived of this rest, may be turned into the blood and spirits of affection, and thou mayest feel them revive thee, and warm thee at the heart, and mayest so think of heaven as heaven should be thought on" (334).

Coleridge's consolatory letter of 1796 and the poem that followed ten months later share with *Saints' Rest* enough particular expressions to suggest that Baxter's mode of Christian meditative exercise crucially influenced Coleridge's response to Lamb's crisis. Stylistically, the letter is unlike any other he wrote during the Nether Stowey years. More measured and deliberate in syntax, more solemn in the tone of address, less effusive and hectic in manner, it offered just what Lamb seemed to need: comfort and consolation ministered by one whose own voice was confident in the rhythms of faith. Normally Coleridge's letters are uneven, desultory, and impulsive, revealing a mind prolific in communicative energies but frustrated in its need for a sense of more intimate, face-to-face conversation, where the response of the auditor could be anticipated, gauged, and checked. (He had written to Poole, four days earlier: "And I have much, very much, to say to

axter's influence—or for that of a similarly spe-
n Coleridge's response to Lamb's calamity can-
, be made with only these two passages in his
less, just such a meeting, as that found in *Saints'*
gic of theodicy and the art of meditation seems
uppermost in Coleridge's mind when Lamb ap-
religious a letter as possible." Substantiation of
must come through a reading of the poem as

not the voice Coleridge wrote in was Baxter's,
the putative resemblances to Baxter were "con-
iberate, his letter to Lamb is a stronger espousal
Christian theodicy than is found elsewhere in the
tarian pronouncements that are Coleridge's wont
Perhaps he felt that Lamb's crisis called not for
etapolitics or for abstruse Coleridgean musings
entary and fervently articulate doctrine. What-
e's intentions, Lamb found it possible despite his
aps even as a diversion from it—twice within the
o take Coleridge to task for Trinitarian opinions
ous and blasphemous than expected from the
speculative professions during their earlier ac-
ad been so decidedly Socinian.[21]

ave to do here with what W. J. Bate, discussing
ater philosophical and critical plagiarisms, calls
ss," with Coleridge slipping into the precisely
rmulations of another mind because of a hesitant
to the particular doctrinal positions involved. In
ts, Bate contends, Coleridge serves as an "usher
could not feel completely free to advance him-
iously, Coleridge did not feel for the Old Baxter
e of "my men" the uneasy ambivalence that so
red in his attitudes to, say, Kant and Schelling,
obviously, nothing usefully called plagiarism is
th Baxter. Bate's acute remarks relate to his investi-

you—& consult with you about—for my heart is heavy . . .
and my feelings are so dim & huddled, that tho' I can, I am
sure, communicate them to you by my looks & broken sentences, I scarcely know how to convey them in a letter.")[18]
Here, then, is the letter to Lamb:

Your letter, my friend, struck me with a mighty horror. It rushed
upon me and stupefied my feelings. You bid me write you a
religious letter. I am not a man who would attempt to insult the
greatness of your anguish by any other consolation. Heaven
knows that in the easiest fortunes there is much dissatisfaction
and weariness of spirit; much that calls for the exercise of patience and resignation; but in storms like these, that shake the
dwelling and make the heart tremble, there is no middle way
between despair and the yielding up of the whole spirit unto the
guidance of faith. And surely it is a matter of joy that your
faith in Jesus has been preserved; the Comforter that should re-
lieve you is not far from you. But as you are a Christian, in the
name of that Saviour, who was filled with bitterness and made
drunken with wormwood, I conjure you to have recourse in
frequent prayer to "his God and your God;" the God of mer-
cies, and father of all comfort. Your poor father is, I hope, almost senseless of the calamity; the unconscious instrument of
Divine Providence knows it not, and your mother is in heaven.
It is sweet to be roused from a frightful dream by the song of
birds and the gladsome rays of the morning. Ah, how infinitely
more sweet to be awakened from the blackness and amazement
of a sudden horror by the glories of God manifest and the hallelujahs of angels.

As to what regards yourself, I approve altogether of your
abandoning what you justly call vanities. I look upon you as a
man called by sorrow and anguish and a strange desolation of
hopes into quietness, and a soul set apart and made peculiar to
God! We cannot arrive at any portion of heavenly bliss without
in some measure imitating Christ; and they arrive at the largest
inheritance who imitate the most difficult parts of his character,
and, bowed down and crushed underfoot, cry in fulness of faith,
"Father, thy will be done."

I wish above measure to have you for a little while here; no visitants shall blow on the nakedness of your feelings; you shall be quiet, and your spirit may be healed. I see no possible objection, unless your father's helplessness prevent you, and unless you are necessary to him. If this be not the case, I charge you write me that you will come.

I charge you, my dearest friend, not to dare to encourage gloom or despair. You are a temporary sharer in human miseries that you may be an eternal partaker of the Divine nature. I charge you, if by any means it be possible, come to me.[19]

It would perhaps be sufficient to attribute Coleridge's altered style to the occasion, to see such solicitude and measured solemnity as tailored to Lamb's needs at a time of calamity, and to leave the matter at that. None of the consolation he offers is surprising for a Christian skilled in Scripture and possessed of traditional arguments against despair. Surely, for Lamb, what made the letter an inestimable treasure was less any doctrinal argument or inventive eloquence in itself than that such doctrine and eloquence came from Coleridge, before whose personality and intelligence he was so diffident and impressionable.

Two passages, however, seem close enough to the rhetorical mode of some characteristic parts of Baxter's *Saints' Rest* to suggest a more than coincidental likeness. The first resembles a trope of comparison recurring idiosyncratically in Baxter's treatise as a continual rhetorical substantiation of his theme about gaining a felt sense of what is in store for the elect Christian. This frequent trope is one of the clearest hallmarks of Baxter's genial, hortatory style in *Saints' Rest*. Here are two examples—there are many others—comparing earthly delights to eternal:

What delight hath the taste in some pleasant fruit, in some well relished meats, and in divers junkets? Oh, what delight then must my soul needs have in feeding upon Christ the living bread, and in eating with Him at His table in His Kingdom!   [364]

How delightful are pleasing odours to our smell! How delightful is perfect music to the ear! How delightful are beauteous sights

to the eye, such as
contrived buildings, l
gardens stored with
ers; or pleasant mea
think every time thou
smell hath the precic
of our glorified Savio
of all His saints, whic
odour and perfume!

Here again is the con

It is sweet to be rous
birds and the gladsom
more sweet to be awa
the hallelujahs of angel

A second passage in th
ter, though less closel
the congruence betwee
grieving friend and ar
ment. Baxter is concer
in furthering the soul's
of eternity but also wit
tial affliction on earth:

If our dear Lord did not
sleep out our lives, and l
sometimes deny us an ir
because he hath separate
promised; as it is said of th

Coleridge offers this sim

I look upon you as a ma
strange desolation of hop
and made peculiar to God
heavenly bliss without in s
arrive at the largest inher
parts of his character, and,
cry in fulness of faith, "Fat

The case of B
cific source—o
not, obviously
letter; nonethe
Rest, of the lo
to have been
pealed for "as
this argument
well.

Whether o
and whether
scious" or del
of consoling (
generally Un
at this time.
Priestleyan m
but for elem
ever Coleridg
grief—or per
next month t
more idolatr
friend whose
quaintance h

We may
Coleridge's
"vicariousne
orthodox fo
commitment
such momer
for what he
self."[22] Obv
he called o
plainly figu
and, just a
involved wi

gation of the psychological context of such literary transactions. If Coleridge was in any sense miming Baxterian or some comparable Anglican or Puritan theodicy in his consolations to Lamb, we are then dealing in the letter, and still more so in "This Lime-Tree Bower My Prison," with an area of literary playfulness difficult to chart, an area where the striking aptness of a distinct voice (distinct from Coleridge's customary epistolary voice) provides the informing instrument for a process of analogical thinking that culminates in one of his most successful meditative poems. No doubt such playfulness would itself have significant psychological aspects. The voluble urgings and uncomplicated theology of *Saints' Rest* may have had for Coleridge, to the extent that he was shaken (or, in sympathy, wished to be shaken) by Lamb's distress, a comforting resonance with the orthodoxies promulgated (according to his memory) in his Ottery St. Mary childhood, in effect elegizing an old, lost faith rather than formulating a new.

3

Whatever its psychological genesis, Coleridge's interest in such consolation appears to have led him to seek in the circumstances of Lamb's visit to Stowey ten months later a more elaborate fulfillment of the analogy urged when he wrote in his letter, "We cannot arrive at any portion of heavenly bliss without in some measure imitating Christ." If, as I suspect, in shaping his poem Coleridge drew on a climactic passage in *The Saints' Everlasting Rest,* or on similar material in another meditative text, significant (though ultimately unanswerable) questions arise about the extent to which the experience depicted in the poem as if it were generated spontaneously out of unanticipated melancholy was in reality something the "coexisting state and previous habit" of his analogical mind had virtually rehearsed for the sake of the poem itself.

The climactic passage Coleridge seems to have had in mind occurs in the final book of Baxter's work and constitutes, as he says, "the main thing . . . aimed at when I set upon this work," illustrative directions for meditating (or, as he variously calls it, "cogitating," "considering," "thinking"). It is in a sense the heart of Baxter's treatise, an example of how to "meditate on the joys above, think on them boldly as Scripture hath expressed them; bring down thy conceivings to the reach of sense." For the paradigm of the affecting joy the mind should seek in meditative exercise, Baxter turns to the fullest account in Scripture of the saints' rest, the Book of Revelation. As the one canonical work of explicitly visionary Christian apocalypse, Revelation quite naturally provides much of the language by which, throughout his treatise, he depicts the nature of the life to come. Baxter urges his Christian reader to place himself in the situation of John of Patmos and to "think of Christ as in our nature glorified; think of our fellow-saints as men there perfected; think of the city and state as the spirit hath expressed it." The passage conflates a number of passages from Revelation and other New Testament texts in an eloquent rendition of his central themes:

Suppose thou wert now beholding this city of God; and that thou hadst been companion with John in his survey of its glory; and hadst seen the thrones, the majesty, the heavenly hosts, the shining splendor which he saw. Draw as strong suppositions as may be from thy sense for the helping of thy affections. It is lawful to suppose we did see for the present that which God hath in prophecies revealed, and which we must really see in more unspeakable brightness before long. Suppose therefore with thyself thou hadst been that apostle's fellow-traveller into the celestial kingdom, and that thou hadst seen all the saints in their white robes, with palms in their hands; suppose thou hadst heard those songs of Moses and of the Lamb; or didst even now hear them praising and glorifying the living God; if thou hadst seen these things indeed, in what rapture wouldst thou have been! And the more seriously thou puttest this supposition to thyself, the more will the meditation elevate thy heart. I would not have thee, as the Papists, draw them in pictures, nor use mysterious significant ceremonies to represent them. This, as it is a course forbidden by God, so it would but seduce and draw down thy heart; but get the liveliest picture of them in thy mind that possibly thou canst; meditate of them, as if thou were all the while beholding them, and as if thou were even hearing the hallelujahs, while thou art thinking of them; till thou canst say, "Methinks I see a glimpse of the glory; methinks I hear the shouts of joy and praise; methinks I even stand by Abraham and David, Peter and Paul, and more of these triumphing souls! Methinks I even see the Son of God appearing in the clouds, and the world standing at His bar to receive their doom; methinks I even hear Him say, 'Come ye blessed of My Father!' and even see them go rejoicing into the joy of their Lord!" My very dreams of these things have deeply affected me; and should not these just suppositions affect me much more? What if I had seen with Paul those unutterable things, should not I have been exalted (and that perhaps above measure) as well as he? What if I had stood in the room of Stephen, and seen heaven opened and Christ sitting at the right hand of God? Surely that one sight was worth the suffering his storm of stones. Oh, that I might but see what he did see, though I also suffered what he did suffer! What if I had seen such a sight as Micaiah saw; "The Lord sitting upon His throne, and all the hosts of heaven standing on His right hand and on His left." Why, these men of God did see such things, and I shall shortly see far more than ever they saw, "till they were loosed from this flesh, as I must be." And thus you see how the familiar conceiving of the state of blessedness, as the Spirit hath in a condescending language expressed it, and our strong raising of suppositions from our bodily senses, will further our affections in this heavenly work.   [361–362]

As already suggested, this passage in *Saints' Rest* may have anchored the analogical interplay between Coleridge's poem and Revelation. The unannounced structural premise of his poem would then be an analogy between the afflicted poet, lamed by the "accident" and confined to his bower, and Baxter's earth-bound meditator. Both captives are able to free their spirits, Baxter's by drawing on his familiarity with the celestial landscape envisioned in the Book of Scripture, Coleridge through imagining the joys of Lamb and the Wordsworths as they wander the terrain of the Quantock Hills, a familiar stretch in his Book of Nature. In what would by such a reading become the pervasive metaphor of the poem, Coleridge's departed friends, rejoicing in the landscape as they emerge "beneath the wide wide Heaven" and behold the splendors of the late evening light, would correspond to the risen Christ and the saints before the Almighty's throne:

> Yes! they wander on
> In gladness all; but thou, methinks, most glad,
> My gentle-hearted Charles! . . .
> Ah! slowly sink
> Behind the western ridge, thou glorious Sun!
> Shine in the slant beams of the sinking orb,
> Ye purple-heath-flowers! richlier burn, ye clouds!
> Live in the yellow light, ye distant groves!
> And kindle, thou blue Ocean! So my friend
> Struck with deep joy may stand, as I have stood,
> Silent with swimming sense; yea, gazing round
> On the wide landscape, gaze till all doth seem
> Less gross than bodily; and of such hues
> As veil the Almighty Spirit, when yet he makes
> Spirits perceive his presence.

The affective response that is Baxter's meditative goal ("My very dreams of these things have deeply affected me, and should not these just suppositions affect me much more?") has a close analogue in Coleridge's lines, following the passage just quoted:

> A delight
> Comes sudden on my heart, and I am glad
> As I myself were there!

What then follows is a description of the bower itself as a rediscovered *locus amoenus*, a description leading to a *sententia* that, in diction and in argument, might easily be versified Baxter:

> Henceforth I shall know
> That Nature ne'er deserts the wise and pure;

No plot so narrow, be but Nature there,
No waste so vacant, but may well employ
Each faculty of sense, and keep the heart
Awake to Love and Beauty! and sometimes
'Tis well to be bereft of promis'd good,
That we may lift the soul, and contemplate
With lively joy the joys we cannot share.[23]

It will already have occurred to some readers that the *imitatio Christi* trope, if seen in the poem as well as in the consolatory letter, almost certainly presupposes a sly pun on Lamb's name, a pun that would have originated in (because it could hardly have escaped) the schoolboy wit of a Grecian at Christ's Hospital. The pun itself occurs twice in Coleridge's later correspondence.[24] On this point it is worth mentioning that an incidental aspect of Baxter's extensive dependence on the diction of Revelation in *Saints' Rest* is his habitual and (among seventeenth-century Puritan divines) virtually idiosyncratic use of John's designation of Christ as the Lamb. Given Charles Lamb's own notorious punning and Coleridge's fondness for wordplay, the idea that there may have been a very verbal wit in the conception and writing of both poem and letter, a wit fostering a train of fanciful analogy between Lamb and Christ, does not seem extravagant.

Corroborative evidence for this suggestion, with a bearing on Coleridge's poem, turns up in a letter he wrote to Benjamin Flower (a friend from Cambridge days, publisher of Coleridge's and Southey's *The Fall of Robespierre*, and editor of *The Cambridge Intelligencer*) in December 1796. The long opening paragraph, consoling Flower at the death of his father, is filled with what I have called Baxterian theodicy ("pray to God that he may give you a sanctified use of your Affliction")[25] and with echoes of Revelation and Job: "But God hath been merciful to us, and strengthened our eyes thro' faith, and Hope may cast her anchor in a certain bottom, and the young and old may rejoice before God and the Lamb,

weeping as tho' they wept not." Appealing to his own experience of suffering, Coleridge declares, "I have known
affliction, yea, my friend! I have been myself sorely afflicted,
and have rolled my dreary eye from earth to Heaven, and
found no comfort, till it pleased the Unimaginable High &
Lofty One to make my Heart more tender in regard of religious feelings." Then, concluding the paragraph without
transition, *he recapitulates Lamb's calamity* (apparently alluded to by him or Flower in an earlier letter): "The young
Lady, who in a fit of frenzy killed her own mother, was the
Sister of my dearest Friend, and herself dear to me as an only
Sister. She is recovered, and is acquainted with what she has
done, and is very calm. She was a truly pious young woman;
and her Brother, whose soul is almost wrapped up in her, hath
had his heart purified by this horror of desolation, and pros-
trates his Spirit at the throne of God in believing Silence. The
Terrors of the Almighty are the whirlwind, the earthquake,
and the Fire that precede the still small voice of his Love."[26]
The context of personal affliction, the unnamed reference to
Lamb, and the citation of the language of Revelation ("may
rejoice before God and the Lamb") anticipate aspects of the
poem Coleridge wrote the following summer.

   Various other expressions and motifs in Baxter and Coleridge support an interpretation of the poem as drawing on
Revelation to urge covertly the imitation of Christ. The opening lines of the poem, so frequently remarked for their colloquial syntax and tone, are an example:

> Well! they are gone, and here must I remain,
> This lime-tree bower my prison! I have lost
> Beauties and feelings, such as would have been
> Most sweet to my remembrance even when age
> Had dimm'd mine eyes to blindness!

The genial extravagance of this opening prison metaphor can
with some plausibility be seen merely as the fanciful musing
of a mind "overhearing itself" and nervously confronting its

melancholy. In Baxter, however, the figure of the Christian as a prisoner of this world recurs literally dozens of times:

> Take a poor Christian. . . . his heart is set on God, he hath chosen Him for his portion, his thoughts are on eternity, his desires there, his dwelling there; he cries out, Oh, that I were there! he takes that day for a time of imprisonment wherein he hath not taken one refreshing view of eternity; I had rather die in this man's condition and have my soul in his soul's case.   [249]

> Christ and faith are both spiritual, and therefore prisons and banishments cannot hinder their intercourse. Even when persecution and fear hath shut the doors, Christ can come in, and stand in the midst, and say to His disciples, "Peace be unto you." And Paul and Silas can be in heaven, even when they are locked up in the inner prison, and their bodies scourged, and their feet in the stocks.   [276]

The possibility of a play between Baxter's scriptural illustration here (from Acts 16:24, a prominent text in *Saints' Rest*) and the wry hyperbole Coleridge makes of the accident to his foot is more likely considering the version of the first lines he sent to Southey in July 1797:

> Well, they are gone, and here must I remain,
> Lam'd by the scathe of fire, lonely and faint,
> This lime-tree bower my prison!

Here the mock-heroic heightening may have seemed in its excess to jeopardize the fine balance of colloquial jocularity and uneasy dejection Coleridge wished to project; hence the second line was dropped.[27] But without reference to a typological structure supported by an apocalyptic framework, the hyperbolic despair retained by Coleridge in the sixth line, "Friends, whom I never more may see again," seems, in R. A. Durr's words, peculiar and unwarranted.[28] Such a structure and an explicit moral judgment on such despondency over loss are available in Baxter:

And if we lose creatures or means, doth it not trouble us more

than our loss of God? If we lose but a friend, or health, &c., all
the town will hear of it. . . . Thus it is apparent we exceedingly
make the creature our rest. Is it not enough that they are sweet
delights and refreshing helps in our way to heaven; but they
must also be made our heaven itself? . . . If we love our friend
we love his company; his presence is comfortable; his absence is
troublesome. When he goes from us we desire his return; when he
comes to us we entertain him with welcome and gladness; when
he dies we mourn and usually over-mourn. . . . If I be deprived
of my bosom-friend methinks I am as a man in the wilderness,
solitary and disconsolate; and is my absence from God no part of
my trouble, and yet can I take Him for my chiefest friend?
[191–212 *passim*][29]

If we bear in mind the analogy between absent friends and
"departed" friends (or, as the Baxterian analogy with Revelation suggests, departed saints), the poet's desolate lament over
lost beauties and feelings indicates a spirit mistaken in its
earthly attachments.[30]

>   I have lost
> Beauties and feelings, such as would have been
> Most sweet to my remembrance even when age
> Had dimm'd mine eyes to blindness!

Again, Baxter points the moral here. After a long summary of
the pleasures of the senses awaiting the soul in heaven, not
among the Quantocks, of "walks and prospects in the city of
God, and the *beauties* and delights in the celestial paradise
. . . and the delight of the sense of *feeling*," he admonishes
his reader thus: "If thou be a Christian indeed, I know thou
hast, if not in thy book yet certainly in thy heart, a great many
precious favours upon record; the very *remembrance* and re-
hearsal of them is *sweet*; how much more *sweet* was the actual
enjoyment!" (365, 371; emphasis added).

Once the dimensions of such an "allegorical" reading are
allowed, the possibility of regarding the poem as merely the
recorded expression of a spontaneous melancholy slips away.
If Coleridge was as familiar with Baxter as his *"my men"* im-

plies, then the walk of Charles Lamb and the Wordsworths
may even have been fancifully anticipated as a type of Baxter's eloquent metaphor of meditation:

Meditation has a large field to walk in. . . . It is not a walk from
mountains to valleys, from sea to land, from kingdom to kingdom, from planet to planet, but it is a walk from mountains and
valleys to the holy Mount Zion; from sea and land to the land of
the living; from the kingdoms of this world, to the kingdom of
saints; from earth to heaven; from time to eternity. It is a walking upon sun and moon and stars; it is a walk in the garden and
paradise of God.   [337]

The most remarkable passage in Coleridge's poetic imagining of that walk is the account of the "still roaring dell" into
which Lamb and the Wordsworths descend. It grew from the
three and a half lines in the 1797 draft version to eleven when
"This Lime-Tree Bower My Prison" was published in 1800:

> The roaring dell, o'erwooded, narrow, deep,
> And only speckled by the mid-day sun;
> Where its slim trunk the ash from rock to rock
> Flings arching like a bridge;—that branchless ash,
> Unsunn'd and damp, whose few poor yellow leaves
> Ne'er tremble in the gale, yet tremble still,
> Fann'd by the water-fall! and there my friends
> Behold the dark green file of long lank weeds,
> That all at once (a most fantastic sight!)
> Still nod and drip beneath the dripping edge
> Of the blue clay-stone.

This important passage might be regarded as an example of
Coleridgean naturalism, reflecting the systolic movement of
Coleridge's imagination, as though his brooding, melancholy
mind, passively borne along by the pulse of memory, sur-
renders the essential character of mind, conscious will.[31] But
such a reading would neglect the *emblematic* elements of the
landscape and risk reducing the poet's imaginative activity to
a muscular reflex.

But seen as imaginative topography, the oxymoronic descrip-

tion of the dell is a mutated, infernal form of the "sweet re-
cess," or *locus amoenus*. Though without announced typology
and in a distinctly minor key, it anticipates Wordsworth's description of the "narrow chasm" in the Simplon Pass episode
of *The Prelude*.[32] The oppressive elemental paradoxes, the
foreboding gloom, and the surreal movements of the dripping
weeds constitute "a most fantastic sight!" the imagining of
which generates in the poet the sublime response he simultaneously attributes to his wandering friends. The incantatory,
incremental verse conjures up the dell as a haunting presence;
the reader can imagine the mind's eye of the poet rapt in its
own recollection. (A variant of the dell in Coleridge's Gothic
drama *Osorio* [composed March–October 1797] is the "still
groaning well," the nightmare abyss that Ferdinand in his suicidal despair calls a "hellish pit.")[33] And like the stranger on
the hearth in "Frost at Midnight," the dell thus reimagined
works on the poet's mind to tease it into thought, however
melancholy. (In a prototypical fragment Coleridge said he
wrote at nineteen, the figure of Melancholy, "her folded arms
wrapping her tattered pall," reclines in a like setting:

> And still as pass'd the flagging sea-gale weak,
> The long lank leaf bow'd fluttering o'er her cheek.)[34]

The typical Coleridgean plight in the meditative poems is
just this vexed and thoughtful melancholy, self-indulgent yet
active of mind. Alahadra, the heroine of *Osorio*, is caught in
a vignette reflective of this psychological condition as she
moves through the landscape, unswerving from her resolve to
avenge her murdered husband:

> Yet each strange object fix'd her eye: for grief
> Doth love to dally with fantastic shapes,
> And smiling, like a sickly moralist,
> Gives some resemblance of her own concerns
> To the straws of chance, and things inanimate.

The typological context of these "concerns" helps to distin-
guish the Coleridgean meditator from more conventional fig-

ures of morbid sensibility. Melancholy is, to be sure, a "sickly" condition—we have seen the inordinate despair of the lime-tree prisoner—but for the mind schooled in habits of Christian meditation, the visionary dallying of grief is no merely private, idiosyncratic indulgence. So the imprisoned poet's grief toys with the remembered "shapes" of the dell, interpreting it by his own mood, "echo or mirror seeking of itself." What is rendered, however, reflects no simply existential imaginative pathos at work; in the implicit typology of the poem, the "narrow, deep" dell, "unsunn'd and damp," into which his friends descend, is an emblem of the grave and underworld, their winding journey through its preternatural gloom the type of an eschatological descent prior to salvation. Again, Baxter's directions for meditation provide an interesting congruence with Coleridge's account of the hellish pit:

First, therefore, admonish thy heart of its own inward neglects and contempts, and then of the neglects and trespasses in thy practice against this blessed state of rest. Set home these several admonitions to the quick. Take thy heart as to the brink of the bottomless pit, force it to look in, threaten thyself with the threatenings of the Word; tell it of the torments that it draweth upon itself; tell it what joys it is madly rejecting.   [352]

(Baxter's "bottomless pit" itself derives from Revelation 9:1ff. His adaptation of that detail is a good instance of how his treatise may have served to mediate the apocalyptic narrative for Coleridge's landscape meditation.)

The more one considers the various ways in which the passage describing the dell reaches out to other passages in Coleridge, some earlier, some later, the less substantial and consequential becomes any "actual," accidental experience Coleridge may have had in his bower (if he ever sat there, brooding in melancholy). What becomes correspondingly more important is the play of Coleridge's verbal imagination among the constructs of an ongoing literary creativity. His fidelity as a poet is less to an accurate rendering of the mind's momentary encounters with a landscape as observed *natura naturata* than to a perceiving of such moments in the contexts provided by a mind richly disposed toward wordplay and analogical powers.

The play of the meditative mind was, for Coleridge, hardly facetious activity. To discover aspects of eternity in Lamb's walk through the Quantock hills was not to give rein to a fanciful and trivial propensity for quaint resemblance and far-sought patterns. Readers of his poems have generally under-estimated the extent to which for him such play was compat-ible with—in fact essential to—fully serious thinking about the nature of reality and the extent to which those explorations necessarily proceeded by means of symbol and analogy. "I seem to myself to behold," he wrote in 1816, "in the quiet objects, on which I am gazing, more than an arbitrary illus-tration, more than a mere *simile*, the work of my own Fancy![35] Or, as he argued three years later, meditation, dis-tinct from nondiscursive contemplation, had for its province "the interpretation of the Facts of Nature and History by the Ideas." Its concern was to discover the "fittest organs of Communication by the symbolic use of the Understanding, which is the function of the Imagination."[36]

But the crucial premise in his theory of meditation (often overlooked in efforts to claim Coleridge as a progenitor of modern poetic consciousness) is one that puts him in the posi-tion of reaching back to medieval assumptions about religious correspondences and forward to some modern symbolist claims, the premise that natural phenomena and the human intellect are analogs of each other. To argue that such a prem-ise is compatible with contemporary existential thought is to neglect Coleridge's frequent contention that, as he put it in *The Statesman's Manual*, the appeal of such analogy is to a mutual basis of mind and nature in a transcendent ontology. Both mind and nature are symbols, consubstantial in their manifestation of the creative energy of God. Take away that consubstantial base and nature becomes a "heap of little things" to the mind. The eighteenth century had pursued its enlightened psychological investigations in the belief that, just as Newton had demonstrated the coherence of the external, "physical" world, so might one likewise discover the coherence of the mind; but for Coleridge the pursuit was misguided because it ignored the common ground of nature and mind in One Life. Analogy, ultimately conceived in terms of Christian emblemism, provided the grammar for the language of symbols.

4

Though the chief analogy Coleridge quietly prepared for his friend Lamb in "This Lime-Tree Bower My Prison" may have been an essentially Baxterian theodicy based on the *imitatio Christi* motif, the language of the poem establishes a complicated interplay with other poems as well. An example is the recapitulation of Lamb's calamity:

> Yes! they wander on
> In gladness all; but thou, methinks, most glad,
> My gentle-hearted Charles! for thou has pined
> And hunger'd after Nature, many a year,
> In the great City pent, winning thy way
> With sad yet patient soul, through evil and pain
> And strange calamity!

The idea of the notoriously urbane Lamb, who ridiculed rural enthusiasms, pining and hungering after Nature while "pent" in London, would have amused Coleridge's contemporaries and may in part have been offered thus mischievously; or, one might hear these lines simply as extravagant sentimentality, bordering on the disingenuous. But comedy and extravagance in Coleridge seldom occur without what he called "a body of thought," and the lines also recall the simile in *Paradise Lost* amplifying Satan's reaction to Eve on finding her alone and unsupported in her garden:

> Much he the place admired, the person more.
> As one who long in populous city pent,
> Where houses thick and sewers annoy the air,

> Forth issuing on a summer's morn to breathe
> Among the pleasant villages and farms
> Adjoined, from each thing met conceives delight,
> The smell of grain, or tedded grass, or kine,
> Or dairy, each rural sight, each rural sound;
> If chance with nymph-like step fair virgin pass,
> What pleasing seemed, for her now pleases more,
> She most, and in her look sums all delight.   [IX, 444–454]

The comic incongruity of this Lamb-Satan analogy serves Coleridge's larger, "serious" purpose in the poem. He would have read Milton's emphasis on the sensuous delight in Satan's response to Eve as a calculated ambiguity, its apparent innocence tinged with suggestion of the fallen dalliance to come. Similarly, for Lamb to delight in the merely terrestrial pleasures of the rural landscape would be to find in nature only a heap of little things, no matter how pastoral and unlustful the taste aroused. To hunger after such a nature would be to repudiate the more strenuous *imitatio* Coleridge was urging upon him. So for "gentle-hearted Charles" the way won, "with sad yet patient soul, through evil and pain / And strange calamity," must be the way of the Christian through earthly affliction to a landscape seen through sacramental vision.

When Lamb read "This Lime-Tree Bower My Prison," he may also have recognized in these lines a glance toward a passage in the verses Coleridge had contributed to Southey's *Joan of Arc*, a passage Lamb had singled out for special praise. It had been reworked in the separate, fuller version of his *Joan of Arc* material Coleridge had planned to publish that spring as *Visions of the Maid of Orleans* (a venture, Lamb complained, that entailed some egregious lapses of stylistic decorum), which I discuss in Chapter 3. The lines argue the power of superstitious fancy to unsensualize the savage mind by giving it new delights, entailing, in Lamb's enthusiastic words of the previous February, "the subserviency of Pagan worship and Pagan faith to the introduction of a purer and more perfect religion, which you so elegantly describe as winning with gradual steps her difficult way northward from Bethabra."[37]

> Wild phantasies! yet wise,
> On the victorious goodness of high God
> Teaching reliance, and medicinal hope,
> Till from Bethabra northward, heavenly Truth
> With gradual steps, winning her difficult way,
> Transfer their rude faith perfected and pure.

But did Lamb also know—and not bother to remark—that Coleridge's inspiration for these lines was in *Paradise Regained?* Milton's narrative of the wilderness temptation of Christ was a poem both Coleridge and Wordsworth admired and drew upon more than once. The analogy between the trials endured by Lamb in the great City and the testing (and proving) of Christ's messianic identity gave Coleridge an apt vehicle for the lesson of imitation his poem so unobtrusively inculcates.

> Meanwhile the Son of God, who yet some days
> Lodged in Bethabara where John baptized,
> Musing and much revolving in his breast
> How best the mighty work he might begin
> Of saviour to mankind. . . .
> And looking round on every side beheld
> A pathless desert, dusk with horrid shades;
> The way he came not having marked, return
> Was difficult, by human steps untrod;
> And he still on was led.   [I, 183–186, 295–299]

And this analogy with the proving of Christ's identity also helps prepare for the moment in "This Lime-Tree Bower My Prison" when the landscape of Lamb's walk is infused with transcendent illumination:

> Ah! slowly sink
> Behind the western ridge, thou glorious Sun!
> Shine in the slant beams of the sinking orb,
> Ye purple heath-flowers! richlier burn, ye clouds!

> Live in the yellow light, ye distant groves!
> And kindle, thou blue Ocean! So my friend
> Struck with deep joy may stand, as I have stood,
> Silent with swimming sense; yea, gazing round
> On the wide landscape, gaze till all doth seem
> Less gross than bodily; and of such hues
> As veil the Almighty Spirit, when yet he makes
> Spirits perceive his presence.

The latter part of this passage is Coleridge's rejoinder to the solipsistic pathos Wordsworth depicted in a passage in "Lines Left upon a Seat in a Yew-Tree" that employs the same "gaze . . . gaze" rhetorical figure. Perhaps Coleridge was drawn to mimic his friend's trope out of a sense of rivalry that, as suggested earlier, Lamb's enthusiasm for Wordsworth's "Inscription" intensified; but the response is also characteristic of his voice in the literary dialogue he and Wordsworth sustained in a number of other poems, some examples of which are discussed in Chapter 3. In this instance, Wordsworth's lines sketch the plight of a morbid solitary who in his self-indulged melancholy vexes himself to an utter and fatal despair:

> —Stranger! these gloomy boughs
> Had charms for him; and here he loved to sit,
> His only visitants a straggling sheep,
> The stone-chat, or the glancing sand-piper:
> And on these barren rocks, with fern and heath,
> And juniper and thistle, sprinkled o'er,
> Fixing his downcast eye, he many an hour
> A morbid pleasure nourished, tracing here
> An emblem of his own unfruitful life:
> And, lifting up his head, he then would gaze
> On the more distant scene,—how lovely 'tis
> Thou seest—and he would gaze till it became
> Far lovelier, and his heart could not sustain
> The beauty, still more beauteous! Nor, that time,
> When nature had subdued him to herself,
> Would he forget those Beings to whose minds
> Warm from the labours of benevolence

> The world, and human life, appeared a scene
> Of kindred loveliness: then he would sigh,
> Inly disturbed, to think that others felt
> What he must never feel: and so, lost Man!
> On visionary views would fancy feed,
> Till his eye streamed with tears. In this deep vale
> He died,—this seat his only monument.[38]

(Wordsworth, as Coleridge would have known, probably had in mind the many instances in *Paradise Lost* when "gazing" is associated with Satanic proclivity for envious rapture: for example, *PL* III, 613, 671; IV, 351, 356; IX, 524, 535, 539, 578, 611.)

The similarities of the Wordsworth and Coleridge situations, however, serve to highlight crucial differences. Both solitaries find resemblances to their own melancholy concerns in the immediate landscape, and for both the scene in the distance offers a contrasting loveliness. But Coleridge's poet relies on his mind's eye to make present to him what he is absent from, and that very reliance generates the "release" which turns his prison into a sacramental paradise. Wordsworth's brooder achieves no such release, his dejection giving way only to envy of others and more isolated despair, until he ends as the text for a sermon on pride, contempt, and the need for self-respect. "Subdued" in his solitude by nature, he is "inly disturbed to think that others felt / What he must never feel," a despair like that Coleridge's prisoner voices at the outset: "Friends, whom I never more may see again." Similarly, the gloomy boughs of his circling yew "bower" have "charms" for Wordsworth's "lost man," but charms that only nourish and intensify his proud self-pity. For Coleridge, and for "my gentle-hearted Charles, to whom / No sound is dissonant which tells of Life," even such a traditional harbinger of evil and ruin as the rook, like the water-snakes in the poem Coleridge was about to write, has a liberating "charm."

The poem relies, then, on a skein of allusions by means of which Coleridge conducts his argument. Such allusive tech-

nique is not unique to this poem. He was extensively dependent on Milton and Wordsworth, partly for psychological
reasons considered in subsequent chapters. Their poems provide in this case instrumental voices that help shape the occasion of his accident and Lamb's walk into types of the mind's
struggle for access to eternity. Such allusive play is central in
Coleridge's art. In a sense his poem was written for a very re-
stricted audience—"Addressed to Charles Lamb" indeed—
rather than a more general readership. But in a more important sense the question is not properly one of audience at all,
but of our coming to terms with a creative intelligence gifted
with a strong analogical bent. More than anything else, the
play of that intelligence is the focus of this book.

6

The meditative resolution to distress worked out in "This
Lime-Tree Bower" became an absorbing poetic interest for
Coleridge, not only in poems like "Frost at Midnight" and
"Fears in Solitude," but in later, more comprehensive plans
for series and collections of poems. His notebooks for the
years 1803–1805, for example, frequently mention a projected
work called "Comforts and Consolations," which seems eventually to have evolved into his 1809 periodical, *The Friend.*
Of relevance here are remarks during the fall and winter of
1803–1804 when he was first entertaining the idea of the project. He became intensely interested in what he called "the
comforts to be derived from generalization & the natural
Tendency to generalize which Sickness & indeed all Adversity
generates," apparently as the result of a specific experience
that served, in retrospect, as an epiphany:

In extreme low Spirits, indeed it was downright despondency, as
I was eating my morsel heartlessly, I thought of my Teeth of
Teeth in general—the Tongue—& the manifest *means & ends* in
nature / I cannot express what a manly comfort & religious re-

solves I derived from it—It was in the last Days of August, 1803—
I wish, I had preserved the very Day & hour.[39]

In early 1804, while setting his mind toward a rest cure in
Sicily, he wrote his friend George Beaumont about the project, characteristically exaggerating his progress but describing
the work in fuller detail:

I have now completed my materials (and three months will en-
able me to send them to the Press) for a work, the contents of
which you will conjecture from the Title—"Consolations &
Comforts from the exercise & right application of the Reason,
the Imagination, and the Moral Feelings." The "Consolations"
are addressed to all in adversity, sickness, or distress of mind /
the first part entirely practical—the second in which I consider
distress of mind from gloomy Speculation will, of course, be
speculative, & will contain a new Theodicee, & what will perhaps
appear to many a new Basis of Morals / the "Comforts" are
addressed to the Happy & Prosperous, attempting to open to
them new & perhaps better—at all events, more numerous & more
various Sources of Enjoyment.—Of this work every page has &
will come from my Heart's Heart—.[40]

This "new Theodicee," in appealing to those in adversity,
sickness, or distress of mind, perpetuates the concerns of "This
Lime-Tree Bower My Prison," written almost seven years
earlier. More important, both poem and prospectus anticipate
the kind of assertion Coleridge was making over a decade
later, when he was not only collecting his "Meditative Poems
in Blank Verse" for *Sibylline Leaves,* but also arriving at some
of his most explicit formulations of the relationship of the
meditative—or imaginative—mind to nature, in works such as
The Statesman's Manual, Biographia Literaria, and the brief
essays on aesthetics, "On Poesy or Art," and "On the Principles of Genial Criticism." Those formulations share an episte-
mology based upon enlightened egotism, a self-awareness developed out of the power of reflective generalization:

That, which we find in ourselves, is . . . the substance and life of *all* our knowledge. Without this latent presence of the "I am," all modes of existence in the external world would flit before us as colored shadows, with no greater depth, root, or fixture, than the image of a rock hath in a gliding stream or the rain-bow on a fast-sailing rain-storm.[41]

But the most arresting evidence that "This Lime-Tree Bower My Prison" anticipates the major elements of Coleridge's long-term interest in the process of meditation can be found in two little-known letters "To a Junior Soph" that appeared in *Blackwood's Magazine* in 1821. They contain his most expansive account of the power of meditation, which is seen chiefly as a power in adversity by which we may turn "diseases into pearls," just as "the cutting and irritating grain of sand, which by accident or incaution has got within the shell, incites the living inmate to secrete from its own resources the means of coating the intrusive substance." The *Blackwood's* letters urge the habit of meditation "as a source of support and consolation in circumstances under which we might otherwise sink back on ourselves, and for want of colloquy with our thoughts, with the objects and presentations of the *inner sense*, lie listening to the fretful *ticking* of our sensations." One passage is of special interest. After he traces, in the opening of the second letter, Wordsworth's peculiar leavening influence to an ability to discern the presence of the high in the humble, he turns to another illustration of meditative genius, one that in context with Wordsworth seems at first incongruous, the achievement of his patrons' father, Josiah Wedgwood, in bringing the art of pottery to its "demonstrably highest perfection." What is startling about Coleridge's illustration is that his account of Wedgwood's achievement is virtually a return to the narrative plan of "This Lime-Tree Bower My Prison":

In his early manhood, an obstinate and harassing complaint confined him to his room for more than two years; and to this apparent calamity Mr. Wedgwood was wont to attribute his after unprecedented success. For a while, as was natural, the sense of thus losing the prime and vigor of his life and faculties, preyed on his mind incessantly—aggravated, no doubt, by the thought of what he should have been doing this hour and this had he not been thus severely visited. Then, what he should like to take in hand: and lastly, what it was desirable to do, and how far it might be done, till generalizing more and more, the mind began to feed on the thoughts, which, at their first evolution (in their *larva* state, may I say?), had preyed on the mind. We imagine the presence of what we desire in the very act of regretting its absence, nay, *in order* to regret it the more livelily; but while, with a strange wilfulness, we are thus engendering grief on grief, nature makes use of the product to cheat us into comfort and exertion. The positive shapings, though but of the fancy, will sooner or later displace the mere knowledge of the negative. All activity is in itself pleasure; and according to the nature, powers, and previous habits of the sufferer, the activity of the fancy will call the other faculties of the soul into action. The self-contemplative power becomes meditative, and the mind begins to play the geometrician with its own thoughts—abstracting from them the accidental and individual, till a new and unfailing source of employment, the best and surest nepenthe of solitary pain, is opened out in the habit of seeking the principle and ultimate aim in the most imperfect productions of art, in the least attractive products of nature; of beholding the possible in the real; of detecting the essential form in the intentional; above all, in the collation and constructive imagining of the outward shapes and material forces that shall best express the essential form, in its co-incidence with the idea, or realize most adequately that power, which is one with its correspondent knowledge, as the revealing body with its indwelling soul.[42]

Juxtaposing this sketch of the metaphysical genesis of Wedgwood pottery, the notations about "Comforts and Consolations," and "This Lime-Tree Bower My Prison" in one sense confirms the portrait of Coleridge we have had from his own day to the present, a man fascinated by affliction and melancholy and virtually compulsive in his persuasion (hope?) that out of the circumstances of loss and dejection, properly "used," might come the release from selfish isolation to gen-

erative, harmonious joy. It is a portrait of a man whose steady
predicament is failure and frustration and whose steady resort
is to the possibility of a future resurgence, a man whose consolation and release are in the other, the unreal, the home projected into the future out of a sense of its absence in the present. From a psychoanalytic perspective, this is the important
Coleridge, and he looms in the shadows of literary history as
he did for Harriet Martineau, an admonishing specter of a life
foolishly deviant from liberal skepticism, right reason, and
humanistic acceptance of a flawed situation.

But another figure also emerges, a man whose medium was
words and whose confidence (scarcely warranted, it seems)
was in the power of verbal play to "call the soul into action"
and thus, through meditative exertion, to liberate it from the
"bad Passions" into an apprehension of self. This process, beginning in a "strange wilfulness" but depending for its success on a combination of deliberateness and habit, he described
at various times and in various contexts as a "new Theodicee"
or, more modestly, as a means of easing distress from affliction
or loss. As recorded by his nephew in *Table Talk*, Coleridge
late in life said that

Elegy is the form of poetry natural to the reflective mind. It
may treat of any subject, but it must treat of no subject *for itself;*
but always and exclusively with reference to the poet himself.
As he will feel regret for the past and desire for the future, so
sorrow and love become the principal themes of elegy. Elegy presents everything as lost and gone, or absent and future.[43]

The remark provides a Coleridgean adjustment to Charles
Lamb's insistence on the virtues of the "personal" poem.
Meditation functions as a "soother of absence" (the title Coleridge proposed in 1802 for a long topographical poem, then
for a series of poems he mentioned in a number of later notebook entries), "the sweetest nepenthe of solitary pain." The
poet in his lime-tree bower regrets the absence of Lamb and
the Wordsworths and broods on their imagined experience,

"engendering grief upon grief." But because of the "nature, powers, and previous habits of the sufferer," the accidental circumstances of his absent friends' evening walk are shaped, under the influence of what I have called a Baxterian sense of Scripture, into a poem that, in the process of drawing on the background of his relationship with Lamb, seeks the "essential" form of that relationship in the Book of Revelation. The form is defined in terms of an ideal that transcends place and time, or rather substitutes for the sense of loss and incompleteness an apprehension of sacramental mutuality, of participation in a harmonious world of reciprocal blessings, substitutes for the flux of time the stasis of eternity. With a wilfulness akin to Alahadra's in *Osorio* and to the brooding poet's in "Frost at Midnght" and "Dejection: An Ode," the poet is overwhelmed by self-induced despair, but at the same time the activity engendered draws what was only implicit in the initial description of the bower and dell into generalized precept:

> No plot so narrow, be but Nature there,
> No waste so vacant, but may well employ
> Each faculty of sense, and keep the heart
> Awake to Love and Beauty!

With this Baxterian employment, even the prison of the bower "soothes" as the eye seeks the principle among the "accidents" of his surroundings:

> Pale beneath the blaze
> Hung the transparent foliage; and I watched
> Some broad and sunny leaf, and lov'd to see
> The shadow of the leaf and stem above
> Dappling its sunshine! And that walnut-tree
> Was richly ting'd, and a deep radiance lay
> Full on the ancient ivy, which usurps
> Those fronting elms, and now, with blackest mass
> Makes their dark branches gleam a lighter hue
> Through the late twilight: and though now the bat

> Wheels silent by, and not a swallow twitters,
> Yet still the solitary humble-bee
> Sings in the bean-flower!

What is the "principle" here? Partly it is that of the coda to "Frost at Midnight," with nature seen under the aspect of its reciprocal energies, light and shadow especially engaged in rituals of benevolence that present paradisal antitypes to the fantastic interplay of demonic energy in the dell. The "dappling" of the sunshine on the broad leaf is a shielding effect by the leaf above to mitigate the blaze of the midday and afternoon sun, and the transparence of the leaves, like the translucence of symbols that for Coleridge allowed the universal to "shine through" the particular, permits the onlooker to perceive the blaze in its lenient, merciful aspect: the prison becomes a house of mercy, not vengeance, a place where the all-mightiness of the Divine Spirit is veiled in that benign condescension that alone makes it available as a blessing to the prisoner. Even the "usurpation" of the elms by the ivy, an act of parasitical encroachment, becomes to the meditative eye, in the late twilight, an effect of benevolence, the ivy's blackness paradoxically brightening the darkness of the elms' branches, lending a setting for their otherwise unappreciated hue. Emerging now from his burden of dejection, the poet finds amid the trappings of melancholy conventional in eighteenth-century landscape art ("the bat / Wheels silent by, and not a swallow twitters") a genial, companionable counterpart for his own solitary, singing self.[44]

In the final image, the poet sees a rook crossing the dilated glory of the setting sun and imagines it seen also by his "gentle-hearted Charles." The image is often compared to that of the water-snakes in "The Rime of the Ancient Mariner": each provides an occasion for a blessing that redounds with grace upon the blesser.

> My gentle-hearted Charles! when the last rook
> Beat its straight path along the dusky air

Homewards, I blest it! deeming its black wing
(Now a dim speck, now vanishing in light)
Had crossed the mighty Orb's dilated glory,
While thou stood'st gazing; or, when all was still,
Flew creeking o'er thy head, and had a charm
For thee, my gentle-hearted Charles, to whom
No sound is dissonant which tells of Life.

Here the rook is also the focus for the meditative eye playfully seeking the "ultimate aim . . . in the least attractive
products of nature." The shapings of that "inward" eye are
intricate. First, and most evident, the bird constitutes a unify-
ing presence: until it appears in the dusky air, the poet has
"seen" only his own surroundings and has been forced to the
resort of memory to imagine Lamb's view; now he actually
has a glimpse of something Lamb may also see. (The image of
the moon in the earliest draft of "Dejection," seen by both the
poet and his "Lady," functions in a similar way.) Second, the
rook beating "its straight path . . . Homewards" offers a
pointed contrast to the "wandering" and "winding" of Lamb
and his companions, as they progressed by chance in their ex-
cursion through the Quantock landscape. Its flight becomes
an emblem for his absent friend's direct and purposeful journey "Homewards" and a prompting for him so to return: seeing it, knowing it as a herald of nightfall, Charles will hasten
back to Stowey. But the image of the black rook, like the
raven a traditional harbinger of dusky death, has associations
of meaning that reinforce the analogies with the Book of Revelation we have so far been intent upon. Only under the proleptic dispensation governing that scriptural text can the darkness of this "least attractive product of nature" be seen to have
a "charm" for Lamb.[45] The "creeking" of its wings rightly has
such a charm only if that ominous, dissonant sound tells of
"Life." (Coleridge in a note exultingly cites a passage from
Bartram describing a similar circumstance in the flight of the
Savanna Crane: "shafts and webs [of their wings] upon one
another creek as the joints or working of a vessel in a tem-

pestuous sea." As usual with Coleridge, such detail is not simply trivial zoology; the creeking is an emblem of Lamb's own difficult, Christ-like progress: "winning thy way / With sad and patient soul, through evil and pain / And strange calamity!").

At one level, of course, "Life" is simply the "living things" of the world, those creatures we are admonished to love in "The Ancient Mariner." But "Life" in this poem is also the "Life" to come, whose echo and mirror are the "One Life" of this world, *natura naturans*. Only the armed vision can see the apparent prophet of calamity as in truth the herald of providential affliction. In this case Revelation 19:17–18 may be an apposite text:

And I saw an angel standing in the sun; and he cried with a loud voice saying to all the fowls that fly in the midst of heaven, Come and gather yourselves together unto the supper of the great God; that ye may eat the flesh of kings, and the flesh of captains, and the flesh of mighty men, and the flesh of horses, and of them that sit on them, and the flesh of all men, both free and bond, both small and great.

In addition, the final image of Coleridge's poem presents a landscape experience met in several other poems as well, that of a sound heard when and because all else is still. Such sound, which elsewhere he calls the "dear undersong in clamor's hour," surprises by its revelation of normally unapprehended process.[46] Awareness of that undersong comes as a sacramental reassurance, a sign of ultimate, inward grace: here, the merging of poet and Charles Lamb in a simultaneous imitation of Christ.[47] The "charm" of the bird is emblematic of victory over morbid desolation, the main argument of the entire meditative poem.

2

Coleridge and "Intellectual Activity"

Hartley was ousted by Berkeley, Berkeley by Spinoza, and Spinoza by Plato; when I last saw him Jacob Behmen had some chance of coming in. The truth is that he plays with systems, and any nonsense will serve him for a text from which he can deduce something new and surprising.

SOUTHEY (1808)

Southey's impatient caricature reduces the history of Coleridge's mind to a vindictive epigram we can readily dismiss. But even less exasperated students of Coleridge's thought sometimes tend to see the poems as part of an hypostasized intellectual development, reflecting his allegiance to one or another system of psychology and metaphysics. The meditative poems especially have supplied evidence for reconstructing his intellectual life, and an important tradition of Coleridge criticism has found the poems interesting chiefly as expressions of the poet's philosophic outlook.

Coleridge himself, it might be said, invited such an approach by insisting repeatedly that poetry worthy of the name have a "body of thought" and by urging Wordsworth to write the first genuinely "philosophical poem." If that last phrase is construed to indicate verse embodying a system of metaphysics, then, so the inference would run, his own poems may be seen as attempts at a similar enterprise. There are, moreover, moments in the poems, such as the lines in later versions of "The Eolian Harp" celebrating "the one Life within us and abroad / Which meets all motion and becomes its soul," that might suggest an argumentative didacticism or even sententiousness expressive of a rationally defined metaphysical system. In "Dejection: An Ode," for example, the impassioned "O Lady! we receive but what we give, / And in our life alone does Nature live" may be heard as a repudiation of Lockean empirical theory for the sake of something closer to projectivist idealism.

It would be wrong to deny that Coleridge's voracious scholasticism left traces in his poems or that verse was frequently for him an instrument of philosophic expression. But we should avoid quarrying the poems and prose writings for comments to fit, like counters, into an abstract scheme of philosophic development if in that process important elements of tone and context are neglected. The intricate analogical ingenuity and allusive literary wit of "This Lime-Tree Bower My Prison" are integral to the meaning of that poem; when, therefore, in a letter to Southey Coleridge glosses a passage with the note "You remember, I am a *Berkleian*," his playful pedanticism should not authorize a reading of the poem that is, in effect, only a nice elaboration of the remark, as though the whole were a philosophic manifesto. Particularly with the letters, we should not anaesthetize ourselves to Coleridge's exuberance, which often spills over into facetious self-parody: "I am a compleat Necessitarian—and understand the subject as well almost as Hartley himself—but I go farther than Hartley and believe the corporeality of *thought*—namely that it is motion—."[1]

On the other hand, it would also be a mistake to focus merely on the relaxed, colloquial quality of the meditative poems—the quality generally implied by calling them "conversation" poems—as though the obtrusive assertions in them (for example, "to whom no sound is dissonant which tells of Life") were extraneous to what deserves the attention of readers. The poems are not "personal" statements, nor should we imagine that in them we come to know, as one writer has put it, "a particular kind of personality that we value."[2] Behind that term "personality" (a term Coleridge rejected as having anything to do with the proper business of poetry) is a biographical fallacy, the assumption that the poem reveals an intimate psychological configuration of the man, that it expresses "the humanity of the man." Poetry for Coleridge was never a confessional activity. The job for the reader of the poems is to steer his course between, on the one hand, simply sifting them for clues in order to chart Coleridge's philosophic allegiances—noting shifts, apostasies, and anticipations—and, on the other, reading them as experiments in personal voice, attempts at imitating an intimate, colloquial candor in a style that transcends or even supersedes thought. To deviate from that course in either direction is to confuse art with academic philosophy or with life. The best general commentaries of the recent past have achieved such a course, though there is still no sufficiently detailed and comprehensive estimate of the poems or of the view they permit of the activity of Coleridge's mind.

One other preliminary point can be made. With Coleridge, as with all writers of genuinely religious temperament, while sectarian commitments can provide occasions and contexts for exploring metaphysical and theological questions of consequence, such allegiances tend to be only the outcroppings of more substantial aspects of mind. In the poems we have access to those more substantial aspects, but we risk identifying the outcroppings with the more substantial traits if we are content with an approach to the poetry that aims chiefly at analyzing the sectarian positions involved. With "This Lime-Tree Bower My Prison," for example, while the poet's urging upon Charles Lamb and himself of an imitation of Christ, through what I have proposed to call Baxterian meditation, is crucial to an understanding of the poem, its importance should also be seen in the context of the analogical play of mind it reveals. The tone of the poem—what might be called the quiet gaiety implicit in its analogical wit—is integral to its nature and meaning. As with his letters and notebooks, an indispensable touchstone for interpreting the poems is a sense of Coleridge's style, of the art that has gone into their making.

Because of the risk of disproportionate emphasis on metaphysical allegiances discernible in his poems, it is worth recalling that in both *his* theoretical and practical criticism Coleridge saw the immediacy of pleasure as the proper and definitive characteristic of poetry. (As he explained in the

Biographia, the value of meter in verse is in producing in the reader the pleasurable responses of excitement, gratification, and surprise.) Too often, I suspect, we neglect his emphasis on pleasure out of uncertainty whether it is compatible with what we conceive to be the higher seriousness of literary art. When we come upon it, Coleridge's playfulness may present something of a critical embarrassment to us, so that we seek an explanation in some psychological idiosyncrasy, as Samuel Johnson was inclined to regret Shakespeare's weakness for quibbles, though in Coleridge the weakness may seem a more telling indisposition, symptomatic of his undisciplined, recalcitrant psyche. But for Coleridge as well as Shakespeare (and more overtly playful writers like Byron and Joyce) the relation of wit and punning to the nature and function of analogy, metaphor, and moralizing in poetic expression is more significant and complex than for some other writers, say Wordsworth or Yeats. (In this regard, it helps to think of Coleridge in the tradition of the seventeenth-century poets he read with such pleasure, especially Donne and Herbert.)[3] My aim in this chapter and the next is to extend the ideas put forward in discussing "This Lime-Tree Bower My Prison" by a more general description and analysis of the play of Coleridge's mind and thereby to create a basis from which to consider, in succeeding chapters, four more of his most significant and interesting meditative poems.

1

The word "play" invites misconstruction. As a term to describe imaginative activity, it is not to be thought antithetical to seriousness, as casual usage often implies. It is, on the contrary, the most suggestive term for the kind of meditative activity Coleridge's poems exhibit, pointing to the openness to heuristic analogical associations that characterizes his most effective writing in verse or prose. To readers interested chiefly in philosophic, psychological, or political argument, the playfulness of his poems and essays will seem distracting or self-indulgent, hardly the essential process of his thinking. But the immediate freedom of play, relative to the ulterior concern of the writer, corresponds to the pleasure for the reader that Coleridge called "the *immediate* object" of the poem. That poetry and philosophy—or poetry and politics—are not identical is a truth we all know but are likely to forget. Coleridge's critical theories, which figure largely in my account of the play of his mind throughout this book, are valuable reminders of the signal importance of pleasure in the experience of literature. As he wrote in the *Biographia:*

The reader should be carried forward, not merely or chiefly by the mechanical impulse of curiosity, or by a restless desire to arrive at the final solution; but by the pleasurable activity of mind excited by the attractions of the journey itself. Like the motion of a serpent, which the Egyptians made the emblem of intellectual power; or like the path of sound through the air; at every step he pauses and half recedes, and from the retrogressive movement collects the force which again carries him onward. "Praecipitandus est *liber* spiritus," says Petronius Arbiter most happily. The epithet, *liber*, here balances the preceding verb; and it is not easy to conceive more meaning condensed in fewer words.[4]

This "pleasurable activity of mind," largely self-sufficing and free of the restless need for immediate, final solutions, characterizes Coleridge's writing and is a recurring focus in discussions of the nature of genius throughout his life. The emphasis is clear as early as 1795 in the distinction he drew between literary or speculative aptitude and practical political capacity. One of his Bristol lectures contains this account of the shortcomings, as an effective politician, of the Girondist leader Brissot:

The Girondists, who were the first republicans in power, were men of enlarged views and great literary attainments; but they seem to have been deficient in that vigour and daring activity which circumstances made necessary. Men of genius are rarely either prompt in action or consistent in general conduct: their early habits have been those of contemplative indolence; and the day-dreams, with which they have been accustomed to amuse their solitude, adapt them for splendid speculation, not temperate and practicable counsels. Brissot, the leader of the Gironde party, is entitled to the character of a virtuous man, and an eloquent speaker; but he was rather a sublime visionary, than a quick-eyed politician; and his excellences equally with his faults rendered him unfit for the helm, in the stormy hour of Revolution.[5]

The analysis here makes a telling self-portrait, one that belongs in the gallery with those Coleridge sketched of Milton and Hamlet. Undoubtedly he was drawn to Brissot as a man of sympathetic temperament. His own venture into practical political journalism, *The Watchman*, suffered from the deficiencies he traced in Brissot; and as an attempt to educate an extensive readership in the west of England in viewpoints on foreign and domestic issues opposing those promulgated by Pitt's government, it was hardly successful.

The elegiac account of the Girondists may be compared to a better known passage Coleridge wrote twenty years later when, taking up in the *Biographia* the question of "the supposed irritability of men of genius," he offered a distinction between "absolute" and "commanding" genius:

Where the ideas are vivid, and there exists an endless power of combining and modifying them, the feelings and affections blend more easily and intimately with these ideal creations than with the objects of the senses; the mind is affected by thoughts, rather than by things; and only then feels the requisite interest even for the most important events and accidents, when by means of meditation they have passed into *thoughts*. The sanity of the mind is between superstition with fanaticism on the one hand, and enthusiasm with indifference and a diseased slowness to action on the other. For the conceptions of the mind may be so vivid and adequate, as to preclude that impulse to the realizing of them, which is strongest and most restless in those who . . . want something of the creative, and self-sufficing power of absolute *Genius*. For this reason therefore, they are men of *commanding genius*. While the former rest content between thought and reality, as it were in an intermundim of which their own living spirit supplies the *substance*, and their imagination the ever-varying *form;* the latter must impress their preconceptions on the world without, in order to present them back to their own view with the satisfying degree of clearness, distinctness, and individuality.[6]

The restlessness of the commanding genius is like that of the reader (in the other passage just cited from the *Biographia*) who desires only "to arrive at the final solution." While Brissot exemplified the visionary genius Coleridge most identified with, Napoleon was beyond question the contemporary whose commanding genius—though failing in breadth and literary attainment—he saw as a powerful threat to the world. (In *The Friend* Coleridge called him a "mad realizer of mad dreams" and likened him to a Tartar despot.) "In times of tumult," he wrote in the *Biographia*, such men are "destined to come forth as the shaping spirit of Ruin, to destroy the wisdom of ages in order to substitute the fancies of a day, and to change kings and kingdoms, as the wind shifts and shapes the clouds."[7]

No doubt, as tradition has it, Coleridge was more conservative politically in 1815 than twenty years before and perhaps therefore more inclined to see figures like Napoleon as agents of destruction, but the sense of a distinction between literary and political activity was there in 1795. Likewise, it would be a mistake to argue, on the basis of recurring millennial language in early poems like "Religious Musings" and "Visions of the Maid of Orleans" (the latter by 1817 given the more "political" title, "The Destiny of Nations"), that Coleridge was ever a serious believer in millennial politics. As I hope to prove through illustrations below, the vividness of such language attracted Coleridge: "The mind is affected by thoughts, rather than by things."[8] Though he was, apparently, extensively involved in Jacobin politics and radical dissent at Cambridge, we should not imagine that he was frustrated into poetry by the failure of practical political expectations. The idea of the political enthusiast hurt into song by the course of events in England and revolutionary France is without foundation because it neglects the essentially poetic nature of the visionary genius as Coleridge consistently defined it.

Given Coleridge's celebration of the "pleasurable activity of mind excited by the attractions of the journey itself" and his repudiation of a restless desire to arrive at the final solution, one of the ironies of English criticism is surely that Keats, in a remark that has enjoyed wide currency because of its connection with his much admired comments about "negative capability," should have—by way of contrasting him with Shakespeare—accused Coleridge of letting go by "a fine isolated Verisimilitude" because of "an irritable reaching after fact and reason." For Coleridge the verisimilitudes were consubstantial means for attaining facts and reasons made thereby more lively. Keats's Coleridge has been perpetuated by many readers in the twentieth century whose impressions have been formed largely by the poems of mystery, "The Rime of the Ancient Mariner," "Kubla Khan," and "Christabel," and whose premises derive in part from imagist poetics and criticism. As J. L. Lowes showed so effectively in *The Road to Xanadu*, Coleridge's ability to absorb and recast images from far-flung and disparate sources was astonishing, perhaps unmatched by that of any poet before or since. But the chief impression left by Lowes's work is of a profoundly resourceful unconsciousness pursuing ends that remain largely inaccessible to interpretative commentary and scholarship. This impression ought to be complemented, if not largely supplanted, by emphasis on the continuities, the recurrences, and the patterns in Coleridge's writings as expressions of the realm of conscious intellect and intention. (I am not here directly concerned with an idiosyncrasy all students of Coleridge's letters have noticed, his tendency to repeat *verbatim*, to different correspondents, elaborate sentences and even paragraphs, though that tendency has more significance for an understanding of how his mind worked generally than would be suggested by merely psychopathological analyses.)

Coleridge's thinking was naturally poetic. Analogical and metaphorical play, frequently involving exploratory modulations of images that recur in poem, essay, notebook, or letter, dominates the movement of thought. True, he never abandoned what he on occasion disparagingly called "abstruse research"; but, though much popular and scholarly opinion holds otherwise, his natural mode was not in processes of abstract, speculative thought. (To realize this may help illuminate the impulse behind his frequent plagiarizing of philosophic terms and arguments.) With Coleridge more often than with any other major English critic, speculative insights characteristically veer off into figurative language. He saw a danger in this tendency, engagingly misdiagnosing his case: "My illustrations swallow up my thesis."

The "endless power of combining and modifying" vivid ideas that constitutes the largely disinterested playfulness of Coleridge's mind, even in his more "serious" and "involved" moments as a political journalist and poet in the mid-1790's, is illustrated in a complex of recurring images and themes involving Revelation, questions of theodicy, and the psychology of melancholy. We have already seen the prominence of such images and themes in "This Lime-Tree Bower My Prison," where they clearly derive in part from Scripture and, as I have argued, from seventeenth-century religious prose, perhaps Baxter. There are various other indications in his writing that his interest in such language was, as he said of Brissot, that of a sublime visionary.

One of his major undertakings in the winter of 1795–1796 was "Religious Musings," published the following April, a poem on which, as he confided to various correspondents at the time, he built all his "poetical credit."[9] Its subtitle ("A Desultory Poem, Written on the Christmas Eve of 1794"), though misleading about the date and duration of composition, points to the tradition Coleridge was extending, epitomized chiefly by Milton's "On the Morning of Christ's Nativity." Like Milton's, Coleridge's nativity poem draws extensively on the narrative apocalypse of St. John: in effect it is an attempt to depict the state of contemporary society under the aspect of Revelation. Profuse in topical allusions, chiefly to woes, domestic and foreign, resulting from the war with France, the poem depicts such contemporary evils as the necessary, providential prelude to a sequence of millennium, final destruction, and ultimate redemption by God, whose throne "forth flashing unimaginable day / Wraps in one blaze earth, heaven and deepest Hell." At the millennium, when the meek and faithful inherit the kingdoms of the world, "each heart / Self-governed," the politics of inequality and strife will vanish in a communist society, with all enjoying equally

> Such delights
> As float to earth, permitted visitants!
> When on some solemn Jubilee of Saints
> The sapphire-blazing gates of Paradise
> Are thrown wide open, and thence voyage forth
> Detachments wild of seraph-warbled airs,
> And odours snatched from beds of Amaranth,
> And they, that from the crystal river of life
> Spring up on freshened wing, ambrosial gales!
> The favoured good man in his lonely walk
> Perceives them, and his silent spirit drinks
> Strange bliss which he shall recognise in heaven.
>
> [343–354]

The heaven thus tasted by the "favored good man" is an early version of that imagined for Charles Lamb, another walker, in "This Lime-Tree Bower My Prison." (Perhaps the memory that Lamb had warmly encouraged the epic grandeur of "Religious Musings" figured in Coleridge's pleasure in recapitulating its visionary context in the poem addressed to him.) But of more immediate interest here are the affinities these lines have with the paradisal imagery in another poem Coleridge published in the 1796 collection, "The Eolian Harp," where the description of the lute concludes in an extended analogy:

> And now, its strings
> Boldlier swept, the long sequacious notes
> Over delicious surges sink and rise,
> Such a soft floating witchery of sound
> As twilight Elfins make, when they at eve
> Voyage on gentle gales from Fairy-Land,
> Where Melodies round honey-dropping flowers,
> Footless and wild, like birds of Paradise,
> Nor pause, nor perch, hovering on untam'd wing!

What link, deliberate or in some way subliminal, might there have been in Coleridge's mind between the sensuous fantasy here generated in his lover-poet and the vision, in "Religious Musings," of a millennial society emerging in the wake of the upheaval in France? Readers have frequently felt a disjunction between the ecstatic flight of this fantasy (which culminates in the well known "one Life" passage, added in 1817) and what Humphry House called the "governessy" reproach of Sara, "Meek Daughter in the family of Christ!" in the concluding lines. The contexts of Christian judgment and redemption informing the similar "Religious Musings" passage suggest a greater coherence between this paradisal fantasy and the basis for Sara's pensive orthodoxy. In the light of the more prominently scriptural inspiration of the nativity poem, the poet's exotic reverie in "The Eolian Harp" can take on more apocalyptic connotations. Sara's reproof would be directed then not at this flight of lyric millennialism, with which it is compatible, but at the more presumptuously dogmatic pantheism of the succeeding lines, in which the poet imagines his own brain, "indolent and passive," surrendering itself like the lute to the random gales of "idle flitting phantasies":

> And what if all of animated nature
> Be but organic Harps diversely fram'd,
> That tremble into thought, as o'er them sweeps
> Plastic and vast, one intellectual breeze,
> At once the Soul of each, and God of all?

(As suggested earlier, the word "organic" probably carries here none of the honorific meaning with which later readers of romantic literature endow it; how could it, after the reductive "but"?) The affinities of expression between the earlier reverie and the "Religious Musings" millennialism can thus sharpen the sense of the descent that takes place to these unregenerate shapings.

Of still further interest for understanding the play of Coleridge's mind is imagery similar to that in the "Eolian Harp" and the "Religious Musings" passages that occurs in the fragment of verse he included in the *Watchman* essay (25 March 1796) "On the Slave Trade" as part of a brooding polemic on the problem of evil. I have already cited this visionary landscape in connection with the apocalyptic aspects of the final lines of "This Lime-Tree Bower My Prison":

In my calmer moments I have the firmest Faith that all things work together for Good. But alas! It seems a long and dark Process.

> The early Year's fast-flying Vapours stray
> In shadowing Trains across the orb of Day:
> And we, poor Insects of a few short Hours,
>   Deem it a world of Gloom.
> Were it not better hope a nobler doom
> Proud to believe, that with more active powers
> On rapid many-coloured Wing
> We thro' one bright perpetual Spring
> Shall hover round the Fruits and Flowers
> Screen'd by those Clouds & cherish'd by those Showers![10]

What can be said about the play of mind that returns to this imagery so readily? We ordinarily assume that, whatever subconscious forces may influence choice of theme or, through elaborate symbolic disguises, rehearse conflicts and improvise solutions, expressions that seem to derive to a substantial extent from artful consciousness have an appropriateness measured by their function in the individual poem. They are realized to the extent that they participate in the structure of meaning defined by the single poem. These examples in Coleridge's writing present an opportunity to observe a different poetic situation, where the context of the particular expression or complex of expressions is something like an unactualized ideal poem, itself uncomposed, that nevertheless sustains for the mind of the poet a strong fascination, exercises upon it a pleasurable sway. Under that sway, the poet is in an important sense thrall to the activity of creation. The words "sway" and "thrall' suggest an experience of obsessive imprisonment or ecstatic rapture (and perhaps Coleridge's 1817 title, *Sibylline Leaves*, plays at that possibility); in his own analysis of the psychology of creation, as we shall see, Coleridge emphasized the vividness of the ideas and the gratification offered by the endless power of combining and modifying them. The paradox here is that, for all his insistence on the free play of the mind, pleasure comes to act as a determinist element, even an immediate cause, of that activity.

In fact, as a student of what he called "intellectual activity," Coleridge again and again explored such a determinist perspective. In letters, notebook entries, and prefaces he speaks of the "laws" of human nature. The notebooks of 1802–1804, for example, which reflect an intense period of self-observation, record instances of "hints" about such activity, glimpses of personal behavior generalized into patterns of mental processes analyzed for causal relationships:

A really important Hint suggested itself to me, as I was falling into my first Sleep—the effect of the posture of the Body, *open mouth* for instance, on first Dreams—& perhaps on all. White teeth in behind an open mouth of a dim face—/ My Mind is not vigorous enough to pursue it—but I see, that it leads to a development of the effects of continued Indistinctness of *Impressions* on the Imagination according to the laws of Likeness & what ever that may solve itself into.[11]

His interest in the "laws" of human nature may well derive from his early interest in associationist psychology, but along with what might be called his Hartleyan determinism goes an equally Hartleyan confidence in the providential ordering of human experience. He avowed such a providential determinism for thinking in his essay on the slave trade, which was in part an attempt to arrive at a theodicy for the most glaringly barbarous institution of his day:

I have the firmest Faith, that the final cause of all evils in the moral and natural world is to awaken intellectual activity. Man, a vicious and discontented *Animal*, by his vices and his discontent is urged to develop the powers of the Creator, and by new combinations of those powers to imitate his creativeness. And from such enlargement of mind Benevolence will necessarily follow; Benevolence which may be defined "Natural Sympathy made permanent by an acquired Conviction, that the Interests of each and of all are one and the same," or in fewer words, "Natural Sympathy made permanent by enlightened Selfishness." In my calmer moments I have the firmest Faith that all things work together for Good. But alas! it seems a long and a dark Process.[12]

For Coleridge, this was no idle journalistic flourish. It would be difficult to find a comparable passage bringing together more aspects of the mind discernible in the meditative poems: the generation of creative powers out of discontent, the sense of a creative harmony with the divine, and the flow of benevolence from expanded self-awareness. Already, in fact, by March 1796 here is a seminal formulation of the famous definitions of the primary and secondary imaginations in chapter 13 of the *Biographia*. ("The primary Imagination I hold to be the living Power and prime Agent of all human Perception, and as a repetition in the finite mind of the eternal act of creation in the infinite I AM.") His confidence in his ability, given the time and propitious circumstances, to unravel the mysteries of man's determinist yet heuristic psyche fluctuated, and his confidence in the capacity of man to imitate God's powers faltered, but he persisted in thinking that the only comprehensive determinism was in a universal theodicy.

Pleasure is the element linking Coleridge's theories of determinist psychology with the free play of mind among similitudes and analogies that characterizes his best writing. At almost the same time that he was articulating a theodicy to comprehend the slave trade he wrote a preface to a collection of poems that described the agency of pleasure in moving the mind from morbid absorption in its own melancholy suffering to enlightened egotism. Noteworthy here is emphasis on the determinist nature of the process: in the aftermath of acute suffering, the mind turning for consolation to the "employment" of describing its suffering:

Why . . . write Sonnets or Monodies? Because they give me pleasure when perhaps nothing else could. After the more violent emotions of Sorrow, the mind demands solace and can find it in employment alone; but full of its late sufferings it can endure no employment not connected with those sufferings. Forcibly to turn away our attention to other subjects is a painful and in general an unavailing effort. . . .

The communicativeness of our nature leads us to describe our own sorrows; in the endeavour to describe them intellectual activity is exerted; and by a benevolent law of our nature from intellectual activity a pleasure results which is gradually associated and mingles as a corrective with the painful subject of the description.[13]

This analysis closely resembles the account of habitual meditation that Coleridge offered to the undergraduate at Cambridge in 1821, an account in which, as we have seen, his reconstruction of Josiah Wedgwood's imaginative breakthrough in the technical arts of pottery closely resembles his own poetic rendering of a meditative experience in "This Lime-Tree Bower My Prison."[14] The 1796 preface is apologetic in function and, to some extent, in tone; perhaps partly as a result it is assertive and vague ("intellectual activity is exerted"), and it attributes, in a laconic, veiling gesture, to simply a "benevolent law of our nature" the process by which such intellectual activity generates pleasure. But despite the cautious, aphoristic style, the argument is central to the experience typically projected in his meditative poems, as we shall see. And in the context of the argument from theodicy, the awakening of "intellectual activity" is the final cause of suffering; it has itself a final cause in the generation of benevolence, a condition of permanent sympathy.

The 1796 preface and the slave-trade essay announce a theory of the mind that Coleridge continued to shape and elaborate. Recalling his contention that the awakening of intellectual activity is "the final cause of all evils in the moral and natural world," we can see the continuity of his interest in the suffering mind in a letter ten years later to Thomas Clarkson, a letter I shall return to in discussing his last major meditative poem, "To William Wordsworth":

With a certain degree of satisfaction to my own mind I can define the human Soul to be that class of Being, as far as we are permitted to know, the first and lowest of that Class, which is endued with a reflex consciousness of its own continuousness, and the great end and purpose of all its energies and sufferings is the growth of that reflex consciousness.[15]

2

The play of Coleridge's mind among images of distress and salvation can be seen in many poems of the 1790's. Two passages, from "Religious Musings" and "The Nightingale," have interesting affinities. In the first, an allegorical sketch envisions the haven from terror provided by religious devotion:

> God's altar grasping with an eager hand
> Fear, the wild-visag'd, pale, eye-starting wretch,
> Sure-refug'd hears his hot pursuing fiends
> Yell at vain distance. Soon refresh'd from Heaven

He calms the throb and tempest of his heart.
His countenance settles; a soft solemn bliss
Swims in his eye—his swimming eye uprais'd:
And Faith's whole armour glitters on his limbs!
And thus transfigured with a dreadless awe,
A solemn hush of soul, meek he beholds
All things of terrible seeming: yea, unmoved
Views e'en the immitigable ministers
That shower down vengeance on these latter days.

[68–80]

It is a lurid, gothic passage, one Coleridge perhaps had in mind when in 1797 he acknowledged a "general turgidness" in the poem. But for all the lumbering allegorical machinery, the transfiguration described anticipates the moment two years later in "The Nightingale," when the poet's child awoke

In most distressful mood (some inward pain
Had made up that strange thing, an infant's dream—)
I hurried with him to our orchard-plot,
And he beheld the moon, and, hushed at once,
Suspends his sobs, and laughs most silently,
While his fair eyes, that swam with undropped tears,
Did glitter in the yellow moon-beam! Well!—
It is a father's tale.[16]

Kenneth Burke calls such recurring images and situations "clusters" and sees them as indispensable for appreciating Coleridge's motives as a writer. A critic of signal importance for understanding Coleridge, he contends that by probing such clusters to discover "what kinds of acts and images and personalities and situations go with his notions of heroism, villainy, consolation, despair, etc.," one can disclose a "structure of motivation" at work. Burke readily discerns the kinds of structural analogues that permit a synoptic view of Coleridge as a writer unburdening himself. The concept of a "burden" that weighs upon the poet and, like a refrain, is in a symbolic relationship to his style is part of Burke's view that art is produced for purposes of comfort, as part of the consolation of philosophy. "It is undertaken as *equipment for living*, as a ritualistic way of arming us to confront perplexities and risks. It would protect us."[17] The aptness of Burke's approach to Coleridge ought to be a matter of general assent. Among major English writers is it not Coleridge preeminently who worked out of suffering and took suffering, in one attenuated form or another, as the avowed "motive" of his writing? Simply running through our minds a number of Coleridge titles, published or projected, makes Burke's point about "equipment for living" emphatically clear: *The Watchman, Comforts and Consolations, Soother of Absence, The Friend, The Statesman's Manual, Aids to Reflection*. The "prospectus" to *The Friend* advertises a journal dealing with "Sources of Consolation to the afflicted in Misfortune, or Disease, or Dejection of Mind, from the Exertion and right Application of the Reason, the Imagination, and the moral Sense."[18]

Burke's emphasis on the writer's burden seems the worthier of Coleridge; it springs, apparently, from the recognition that Coleridge's plight, whatever its idiosyncratic lineaments (upon which other critics so often dwell), reflects more general human tendencies. I would suggest, however, that especially in Coleridge's case the functionalist analysis Burke presents (which he seems to have derived in part from Malinowskian revisions of Freudian oedipal theory) is only part of the story. It implies that the positive form taken by the consolation Coleridge offers can be adequately explained by reference to the problem. But with Burke the conception of the problem remains essentially humanistic, positivistic, and skeptical, exactly what Coleridge himself, throughout his life, castigated as a "Laodicean self-confidence" in the power of unaided human reason. Burke sees the dramatic action in the poems as symbolic of conflict in Coleridge's mind; religious images and arguments, for example, represent one or another categorical problem in terms of which the conflict can be discussed: aesthetic, marital, political, narcotic, metaphysical. Prayer, about which Burke has a great deal to say, is seen always from the humanist's viewpoint, as performing a therapeutic function for the burdened mind. The "Ode to the Departing Year" is a "prophecy on two levels, ostensibly about political trends, implicitly about the course of internal psychological events that culminate in 'Dejection.' " The category of "religious" events is missing, and the traditional apocalyptic mode of the prophecy by-passed entirely. "The Eolian Harp" has a style symbolic—one might say symptomatic—of a marital burden (whether in his soaring flights of aesthetic and metaphysical imagination the husband will dissolve into a unitary philosopher, his wife excluded and abandoned) rather than an attempt to use the marital relationship as an analogy for the poet's sense of self and of God.

Suggesting the limitations of a functionalist approach conceived primarily along such post-Freudian lines highlights the dilemma we are in when interpreting the achievement of a writer like Coleridge, the context of whose work is so patently and avowedly religious. Plainly it will not do to submit passively to his perspective and write a "criticism" that simply reshuffles, while acquiescing entirely in, his "grammar" (Burke's convenient term); though the grammar of his religious language is sufficiently complicated to deserve synoptic handling, that approach would be essentially uncritical. Needed is a critical approach whose generalizations, in providing an intelligible structure for the poems, do not thereby obscure or neglect evident aspects of them.

It will help now to return to the lines cited earlier from "Religious Musings," about the wretch whose eager grasp of God's altar allows him to calm the "throb and tempest" of his heart. About the time he was finishing this poem, Coleridge used the same phrase in a *Watchman* review of Edmund Burke's "Letter to a Noble Lord." Lamenting the "woeful inferiority" and "fanaticism" of the letter, he drew a subjunctive sketch of Burke that resembles the self-portrait in the preface to *Poems on Various Subjects* (see above, p. 77) and to the gentle-hearted Charles Lamb of "This Lime-Tree Bower My Prison":

Alas! we fear that this Sun of Genius is well nigh extinguished: a few bright spots linger on its orb, but scarcely larger or more numerous than the dark *maculae* visible on it in the hour of its strength and effulgence. A tender and pleasing melancholy pervades those passages in which he alludes to his Son; and renders the fierceness and vulgarity of the rest more wonderful. It might have been expected, that domestic calamity would have softened his heart, and by occupying it with private and lonely feelings, have precluded the throb and tempest of political fanaticism.[19]

In a sonnet on Burke (published December 1794) Coleridge had hailed him as "Son of Genius." The playful shift to "Sun" suggests an imaginative toying with the possibilities of such apocalyptic imagery as he had used in "Religious Musings" and was to use in "This Lime-Tree Bower My Prison" and "Ode to the Departing Year." Heard also in the first sentence is the idiosyncratic and unmistakable hunting down of a Coleridgean metaphor. The illustration may not, as he put it, "swallow up" his thesis about Burke, but it bids fair to take on a metaphoric life of its own, free of its tenor: for a moment the reader is caught in that surprisingly sustained figure of the solar eclipse. The pursuit of political polemic becomes an occasion for exploring the pleasures of metaphor. The language here also points to Coleridge's involvement with what Kenneth Burke calls burdens, especially a brooding wistfulness about "private and lonely feelings" and their conflict with the cruder harshness of politics. But that very language itself indicates, I believe, that his concern was in part reinforced—perhaps even created—by his ready verbal gifts. The discussion of Burke is set out in language that reveals an interplay with expressions used in other contexts; we are left to consider if that discussion can be adequately understood apart from those contexts. The more we encounter this phenomenon in Coleridge the more it seems that writing for him was an activity approaching free play. It might be reductive to invoke Oscar Wilde's sly aphorism that "life imitates art," to argue that the world comes to have meaning for Coleridge insofar as he can see it in terms of expressions that are preliminary to or independent of his experience of it, and yet one is drawn to such formulations in trying to describe the process. In this case we can suggest that insofar as the pleasure he felt in his portrait, in "Religious Musings," of the allegorical Fear, its throb and tempest calmed, was in his mind as he wrote of Burke, he was recreating Burke through that medium of language, fashioning a Burke that derives as much from that language as vice-versa. Such is his enjoyment of that recreation that the "real" Burke may be momentarily obscured. Seven years later, describing to George Beaumont the eager politics of young men, he offered two optical analogies:

For what is the nature & the beauty of Youth? Is it not this—to know what is right in the abstract, by a living feeling, by an intuition of the uncorrupted Heart? To body forth this abstract right in beautiful Forms? And lastly to project this phantom-world into the world of Reality, like a catoptrical mirror? Say rather, to make ideas & realities stand side by side, the one as vivid as the other, even as I have often seen in a natural well of translucent water the *reflections* of the lank weeds, that hung down from its sides, standing upright, and like Substances, among the substantial waterplants, that were growing on the bottom.[20]

The "living" feeling and the "vivid" ideas anticipate the account of "absolute genius" in the *Biographia*. May we say that for Coleridge the politics of youth was poetry? His figure of the catoptrical mirror involves the same process of projecting a vivid phantom exemplified in the *Watchman* review of Burke, where the life of the passage cited above is in the solar metaphor. Similarly, the vividness of the ideas standing side by side with realities is itself epitomized in the vividness of Coleridge's language as he describes the lank weeds reflected in the well's translucent water. Who, encountering such reflections in a well, would not be quickened by his memory of the pleasurable cadences of that subtly elaborate metaphor? As we shall see in the next chapter, it is just this power of vivid language to recreate, to make anew, the familiar world of everyday reality that Coleridge celebrated in Wordsworth's exemplary "gift of spreading the . . . depth and height of the ideal world around forms, incidents, and situations, of which, for the common view, custom had bedimmed all the lustre."[21]

Certainly in the subjunctive account of Edmund Burke's "private and lonely feelings" after the "domestic calamity" of losing his son we can recognize the hand of the poet who six months later envisioned in his "personal" friend Charles Lamb, reeling from the calamity of his sister's homicidal derangement, the need for a haven where, as he said, "no visitants shall blow on the nakedness of your feelings." At about the same time, in introducing a "sheet of sonnets" assembled from various authors, to be circulated with copies of William Bowles' 1794 sonnets, he argued that the sonnet required the "development of some lonely feeling, by whatever cause it may have been excited." He then continued:

Those Sonnets appear to me the most exquisite, in which moral Sentiments, Affections, or Feelings, are deduced from, and associated with, the scenery of Nature. Such compositions generate a habit of thought highly favourable to delicacy of character. They create a sweet and indissoluble union between the intellectual and the material world.[22]

Through these quotations from prefaces and letters we can recover the notably consistent fabric of speculative generalization Coleridge was weaving out of the materials of his own poetic experience. As generalizations they suggest his later, more complex definitions of the imagination as literary activity. But my chief interest here is in seeing how, as arguments drawn from his own experience as an imaginative writer, they can lead us back to a more refined sense of his poetry as a compensatory "communication of sorrows" and as an assertion of identity uniquely developed in the poetic process. The imaginative writer is no polemicist for any body of doctrine or opinion. Coleridge believed that the meditative poet—like the "writer of Sonnets and Monodies" of the 1796 preface—wrote out of an egotist's compulsion for comfort and consolation; but he also believed that successful poetry transcended, if only for the moment, the context of such compulsion, and that the assertion of self it proceeded toward was a liberated creativity, a pleasurable activity despite its genesis in pain, a playfulness of mind that insulated the poet from the intrusion of the mundane reality of distress.

3

One of the most explicitly "political" poems Coleridge wrote was "Fire, Famine, and Slaughter: A War Eclogue," published anonymously in the *Morning Post* (8 January 1798). A wry, apocalyptic *jeu d'esprit*, it satirizes Pitt's hand in the foreign and domestic calamities of the war with France. The poem did not apparently loom large in Coleridge's mind then, nor perhaps would it have later except for an incident, probably in 1803, which prompted Coleridge several years thereafter, when he republished the poem in *Sibylline Leaves*, to compose an "apologetic preface." Walter Scott had recited the poem to a gathering at William Sotheby's that included the still anonymous author:

This he could do with the better grace, being known to have ever been not only a firm and active Anti-Jacobin and Anti-Gallican, but likewise a zealous admirer of Mr. Pitt, both as a good man and a great statesman. As a poet exclusively, he had been amused with the Eclogue; as a poet he recited it; and in a spirit which made it evident that he would have read and repeated it with the same pleasure had his own name been attached to the imaginary object or agent.[23]

Following Scott's recitation, Sotheby expressed dismay at the atrocious sentiments of the poem, whereupon, according to his preface, Coleridge spoke at length, less in defense of the poem's sentiments than in explanation of the "mood of mind and the general state of sensations" in which he wrote "such vivid and fantastic images." What he said, as he later recalled it, relates to our discussion of his "intellectual activity." Such a mood and state, he argued, were hardly likely to co-exist with "that gloomy and deliberate ferocity which a serious wish to realize such images would pre-suppose":

Prospects of pain and evil to others, and in general all deep feelings of revenge, are commonly expressed in a few words, ironically tame, and mild. The mind under so direful and fiend-like an influence seems to take a morbid pleasure in contrasting the intensity of its wishes and feelings with the slightness or levity of the expressions by which they are hinted; and indeed feelings so intense and solitary, if they were not precluded (as in almost all cases they would be) by a constitutional activity of fancy and association, and by the specific joyousness combined with it, would assuredly themselves preclude such activity. Passion, in its own quality, is the antagonist of action; though in an ordinary and natural degree the former alternates with the latter, and thereby revives and strengthens it. But the more intense and insane the passion is, the fewer and the more fixed are the correspondent forms and notions. A rooted hatred, an inveterate thirst of revenge, is a sort of madness, and still eddies round its favourite object, and exercises as it were a perpetual tautology of mind in thoughts and words which admit of no adequate substitutes.[24]

Like many distinctions Coleridge offers, this analysis of passion is complicated. The "action" he opposes to passion is not in this case the fulfillment of wish in deed but the activity of thought. His distinction is between passion that both releases thought and is sustained reciprocally by it and the deeper passion that permits only obsessive utterance. The conception in the apologetic preface—which amounts to a defense of poetry—is of a passionate poet lifted beyond pragmatic fixation in the situation that occasioned the feeling. Such, at any rate, is the gist of the self-portrait he went on to include:

The writer [of "Fire, Famine, and Slaughter"] must have been some man of warm feelings and active fancy; . . . he had painted to himself the circumstances that accompany war in so many vivid and yet fantastic forms, as proved that neither the images nor the feelings were the result of observation, or in any way derived from realities. I should judge that they were the product of his own seething imagination, and therefore impregnated with that pleasurable exultation which is experienced in all energetic exertion of intellectual power; that in the same mood he had generalized the causes of the war, and then personified the abstract and christened it by the name [Pitt] which he had been accustomed to hear most often associated with its management and measures.[25]

Whether or not we agree with Coleridge that this preface was his "happiest effort in prose composition," and whether we are inclined to accept, from a man whose politics had shifted, such a convenient exculpation from the charge of atrocious sentiments against Pitt, the preface clearly insists on the tenuousness with which successful poetic expression relates to nonliterary feeling and intention. He insists, not really on the unique or esoteric quality of poetry, not that poetry is divorced from life, or even irrelevant to everyday concerns, but on its natural affinity with what he called in the *Biographia* "the principles of grammar, logic, and psychology" and on the pleasure naturally resulting from "all energetic exertion of intellectual power." There is a distinction, in other words, between the specifically poetic pleasure he calls "joyousness" and the morbid satisfaction derived by the perversely vengeful sensibility. If as seems likely the preface was written in 1815, it provides further evidence of the striking long-term continuity in Coleridge's theoretical articulation of the poetic process. (Compare, for example, the language of the last paragraph quoted from the 1796 preface, page 77 above.)

   In the same year as the "Fire, Famine, and Slaughter" incident at Sotheby's, Coleridge wrote to his aristocratic friends the Beaumonts and, prompted by the execution of the Irish patriot Robert Emmet to a retrospective apostasy of his own Jacobin sympathies, recalled the frequent conflict between his pacifist principles and his writings and speeches. His account, even allowing for the special pleading his titled audience might have elicited, confirms his readiness to acknowledge how divergent the genuine interests of politics and the essentially literary activities of writing and speaking in public could be:

Tho' I detested Revolutions in my calmer moments . . . and tho' even to extravagance I always supported the Doctrine of absolute unequivocal non-resistance—yet with an ebullient Fancy, a flowing Utterance, a light & dancing Heart, & a disposition to catch fire by the very rapidity of my own motion, & to speak vehemently from mere verbal associations, choosing sentences & sentiments for the very reason, that would have made me recoil with a dying away of the Heart & an unutterable Horror from the actions expressed in such sentences & sentiments—namely, because they were wild, & original, & vehement & fantastic!—I aided the Jacobins, by witty sarcasms & subtle reasonings & declamations full of genuine feeling against all Rulers & against all established Forms! Speaking in public at Bristol I adverted to a public Supper which had been given by Lord —— I forget his name, in honour of a victory gained by the Austrians, & after a turbid Stream of wild Eloquence, I said—"This is a true Lord's Supper in the communion of Darkness! This is a Eucharist of Hell! A sacrament of Misery!—Over each morsel & each Drop of which the Spirit of some murdered Innocent cries aloud to God, This is *my* Body! & this is my Blood!"[26]

The proclivities for wordplay and analogy so excitedly aroused here figure centrally in the subtler art of his meditative poems. Much of my emphasis in this chapter has been on the extent to which, in formulating theories about the imagination, he focused on those proclivities and on the self-sufficiency of the poet's excitement. His disposition to catch fire by the very rapidity of his own motion, if it could lead him to speak vehemently from mere verbal association, also determined the shape his poems took:

Where there exists that degree of genius and talent which entitles a writer to aim at the honors of a poet, the very *act* of poetic composition *itself* is, and is *allowed* to imply and to produce, an unusual state of excitement, which of course justifies and demands a correspondent difference of language, as truly, though not perhaps in as marked a degree, as the excitement of love, fear, rage, or jealousy. The vividness of the descriptions or declamations in DONNE or DRYDEN is as much and as often derived from the force and fervor of the describer, as from the reflections, forms, or incidents, which constitute their subject and materials. The wheels take fire from the mere rapidity of their motion.[27]

Given the elusive goal of such generalizing—the activity of the imagination itself—it is to be expected that the best discussions of his poems will often settle for secondary matters of theme and artistry. My purpose here is to remind us that at least momentarily, with the aid of his own comments, we may be able to sharpen our perception of his analogical imagination. Wordplay with Coleridge is a window or (to use his figure) a catoptrical mirror on the activity of his mind. On occasion, he defended wordplay and the pleasures associated with it for himself and others, and an 1805 notebook fragment, which in both its tentativeness and its vividness makes an appropriate end to this discussion, once more permits us to glimpse in the sketch of another his own self-portrait:

Learnt not always, *at all*, & seldom *harshly* to chide, those conceits of words which are analogous to sudden fleeting affinities of mind / even as in a dance touch & join & off again, & rejoin your partner that leads down with you the whole dance spite of these occasional off-starts, all still not merely conform to, but of, and in, & forming, the delicious harmony—Shakespeare is not a 1000th part so faulty as the 000 believe him.[28]

3

Wordsworth and Coleridge: Visions of the Ideal World

Last, and pre-eminently, I challenge for this poet the gift of
IMAGINATION in the highest and strictest sense of the word.
. . . In imaginative power, he stands nearest of all modern
writers to Shakespeare and Milton; and yet in a kind perfectly
unborrowed and his own.

COLERIDGE (c. 1815)

Coleridge's ideas about "intellectual activity," as we have seen, involved a complicated context of progress, by means of analogical awareness, from distress to ease, from suffering to convalescence, the whole viewed as a new kind of theodicy. While the ultimate sanction for this theodicy, as for all theodicies, was God's Providence, the intermediate instrument was the playful imagination operating through a process of associative language. His theories seem in large measure to have been derived inductively, from watching his own poetic activity, if the impression generated by the 1796 preface is accurate. That would confirm the overwhelming impression given by the notebooks that his insights were generally won through a process of inveterate self-observation or, as he said of Shakespeare, meditative observation.

1

In the *Biographia Literaria*, Coleridge recalled an experience he regarded as a significant instance of just such an inductive discovery. If his memory served him well twenty years later, Wordsworth's recitation of "Salisbury Plain" early in their acquaintance had a profound impact on his thoughts about poetry and the nature of the imagination. The excellence of that poem, he declared, was instrumental in leading him, for the first time, to the conclusion that "fancy and imagination were two distinct and widely different faculties." Despite the importance of such a claim, there has been little discussion of Coleridge's interest in "Salisbury

Plain," and readers who know the poem only in its later published form, *Guilt and Sorrow; or, Incidents upon Salisbury Plain*—generally thought to be an inferior version—must find Coleridge's enthusiasm curious, his memory perhaps colored by his understandable admiration for Wordsworth's later achievements. Still, the definitiveness of his remarks about the poem he heard (probably in September 1795) cannot be easily dismissed:

I was in my twenty-fourth year, when I had the happiness of knowing Mr. Wordsworth personally, and while memory lasts, I shall hardly forget the sudden effect produced on my mind, by his recitation of a manuscript poem, which still remains unpublished, . . . I did not perceive anything particular in the mere style of the poem alluded to during its recitation, except indeed such difference as was not separable from the thought and manner; and the Spenserian stanza, which always, more or less, recalls to the reader's mind Spenser's own style, would doubtless have authorized, in my then opinion, a more frequent descent to the phrases of ordinary life, than could without an ill effect have been hazarded in the heroic couplet. It was not however the freedom from false taste, whether as to common defects, or to those more properly his own, which made so unusual an impression on my feelings immediately, and subsequently on my judgment. It was the union of deep feeling with profound thought; the fine balance of truth in observing, with the imaginative faculty in modifying the objects observed; and above all the original gift of spreading the tone, the *atmosphere*, and with it the depth and height of the ideal world around forms, incidents, and situations, of which, for the common view, custom had bedimmed all the lustre, had dried up the sparkle and the dew drops.[1]

Coleridge's language here is very close to that of his famous description, in chapter 14 of the *Biographia*, of the genesis of the *Lyrical Ballads*, in which he recalls discussing with Wordsworth "the two cardinal points of poetry, the power of exciting the sympathy of the reader by a faithful adherence to the truth of nature, and the power of giving the interest of novelty to the modifying colors of imagination."[2] But the language of both accounts is so general that it is difficult to tell, for instance, what particular passages most impressed Coleridge when he heard "Salisbury Plain" and what particular moments came to seem to him most exemplary of the "modifying" powers of the imaginative faculty.

My purpose here is not to provide the commentary or interpretation of Wordsworth's poem that Coleridge might have written or that he perhaps did write when he read a greatly revised draft of the poem a few weeks later.[3] Rather, I hope to substantiate something of the extensive effect of "Salisbury Plain" on Coleridge's own poems and, by so doing, not only to shed light on what he meant by the "imaginative faculty" but also to establish in fuller detail the nature of the literary relationship with Wordsworth. Taken together, the poems that Wordsworth and Coleridge wrote during the years of their closest association after 1795 are so extensively influenced by one another as to constitute, metaphorically speaking, a dialogue of considerable importance for appreciating the achievement of each poet. The dialogue is most explicit, of course, with Coleridge's "To William Wordsworth, Composed on the Night after his Recitiation of a Poem on the Growth of an Individual Mind," and it has been long recognized that three major poems of 1802, the "Intimations Ode" (the first four stanzas), "Dejection: An Ode," and "Resolution and Independence" gain in interest when read as part of a poetic conversation of crisis and resolve growing out of Coleridge's and Wordsworth's personal lives. Close relationships have also been noted between "Tintern Abbey" and "Frost at Midnight" and, to a lesser extent, between "Lines Left upon a Seat in a Yew-Tree" and "This Lime-Tree Bower My Prison." ("Dialogue" is a somewhat misleading term for the complex mutual influence of Wordsworth and Coleridge; in spite of the impression such pairings as the above might generate, it was by no means simply a back-and-forth "statement-counterstatement" situation.) My contention is that, although Coleridge knew of Wordsworth as a poet as early as

1793 (again the *Biographia* records his admiration of *Descriptive Sketches*) and echoed him in his own poems before the fall of 1795, the significant influence really begins with "Salisbury Plain." The playfulness of that influence, involving an intercourse of situation, incident, and imagery, can be heard in a number of subsequent poems. Tracing that influence sheds light on the processes of imagination in both poets.

2

To see the immediate impact "Salisbury Plain" had on Coleridge, we need to reconstruct his situation as a writer in 1795 and 1796. The months from the lectures of early 1795 to the collapse of *The Watchman* in May 1796 were a time of great political and journalistic activity for him, and we can assume fairly safely that it was not, therefore, the dissenting politics *per se* of "Salisbury Plain" that he found so novel and compelling. (In fact, judging from what is known of Coleridge's political activity at Cambridge and from Wordsworth's "Letter to the Bishop of Llandaff" [1793], they were already quite closely aligned on the major issues of the day.) Moreover, the same months were also a time of considerable poetic activity for Coleridge. Though recent studies have tended to emphasize the developing "conversational" mode in Coleridge's verse at this time, focusing on such poems as "The Eolian Harp" and "Reflections on Having Left a Place of Retirement," there can be no doubt that the major poetic undertakings for Coleridge in 1795 and 1796 were "Religious Musings" and what he called for a time "Visions of the Maid of Orleans," the latter a work that grew out of 255 lines contributed to Southey's *Joan of Arc* and ended in *Sibylline Leaves* as a fragment titled "The Destiny of Nations."

"Religious Musings" is a convenient "control" in assessing Wordsworth's influence on Coleridge. Begun, according to the subtitle of the first edition, on Christmas Eve 1794, it is both the most Miltonic (in part because it imitates aspects of the hymn "On the Morning of Christ's Nativity") and the least Wordsworthian of Coleridge's major poems. Its strained, elevated diction and resonant periodicity show Coleridge laboring under the inspiration of Milton's grandest style. In like style (with less "*mind*" but with a "diffused air of severe Dignity"), as the opening passage illustrates, is the epic slice Coleridge wrote sometime prior to November 1795 for the second book of the blank-verse *Joan of Arc:*

> No more of Usurpation's doom'd defeat,
> Ere we the deep preluding strain have pour'd
> To the Great Father, Only Rightful King,
> Eternal Father! King Omnipotent!
> Beneath whose shadowy banners wide unfurl'd
> Justice leads forth her tyrant-quelling Hosts.
> Such Symphony requires best Instrument.
> Seize then my Soul! from Freedom's trophied Dome
> The Harp which hanging high between the shields
> Of Brutus and Leonidas, oft gives
> A fitful music to the breezy touch
> Of patriot Spirits that demand their fame.

It was these lines, and others like them "majestic and high-sounding," that Charles Lamb praised when he told Coleridge in June 1796, in language that might have appeared in a publisher's puff, that the "poem is alone sufficient to redeem the character of the age we live in from the imputation of degenerating in poetry." Lamb was Coleridge's closest friend and most sympathetic critic during this period of his development; his undistinguished but not unimportant role with regard to these poems was primarily to reinforce Coleridge's Miltonic pretensions. He applauded the labored grandeur of "Religious Musings," on which Coleridge was at the time content "to rest for all [his] poetic credit."

But, as we have seen, despite all his quickness of mind and his admiring solicitude for Coleridge's genius, Lamb was not the critic Coleridge needed. The evidence of Lamb's correspondence indicates that the major poetic enterprise for Coleridge—in terms of the effort involved if not the success attained—in the latter part of 1796 and early 1797 when he was coming more and more under the influence of Wordsworth, was carried on virtually without Lamb's advice at all. This project was the extensive revision of the material contributed to *Joan of Arc*.[4] Coleridge's goal was to make that material into an independent poem with some such title as "The Progress of Liberty" or "Visions of the Maid of Orleans." When he finally sent a draft of the new poem to Lamb ("whose *taste* & *judgment*" he paired, perhaps surprisingly, with Wordsworth's as "more correct & philosophical than my own") in January 1797, very shortly before he hoped to include it in an expanded second edition of his own poems, Lamb's reaction was one of dismay and unironic disbelief:[5]

You cannot surely mean to degrade the Joan of Arc into a pot-girl. You are not going, I hope, to annex to that most splendid ornament of Southey's poem all this cock and a bull story of Joan, the publican's daughter of Neufchatel, with the lamentable episode of a waggoner, his wife, and six children. The texture will be most lamentably disproportionate. . . . And the lines, considered in themselves as an addition to what you had before written (strains of a far higher mood), are but such as Madame Fancy loves in some of her more familiar moods, at such times as she has met Noll Goldsmith, & walk'd and talk'd with him, calling him old acquaintance.[6]

Lamb's vigorous disapproval of the new version reflects perhaps his apprehension over the state of the close personal and literary relationship he had enjoyed with Coleridge since they had been together briefly in London in December 1794. He may have sensed that the style of the new material was symptomatic of how far Coleridge had moved beyond him. In any case, Coleridge responded, in the last letter he was to write to Lamb for almost three months, voicing his own dismay at Lamb's criticism. Lamb's reply repeated, in somewhat more moderate language, his sense of the new poem's stylistic inconsistency. Citing the solemnity and sublimity of the opening "deep preluding strains," he complained that "after all this cometh Joan, a *publican's* daughter, sitting on an ale-house *bench*, and marking the *swingings* of the *signboard*" (Lamb's emphasis).[7]

This attack on the uneven decorum of the new version had enough force, apparently, to dissuade Coleridge from including the poem in his 1797 collection, issued that October. (He had intended to print it as the opening selection.)[8] The decision to withhold the poem, which he came almost at once to "deeply regret," is indicative of the uncertainty Coleridge seems to have felt during a period of stylistic experimentation. He did, however, as David Erdman discovered, send the new part of the poem as a fragment (without mentioning its connection to the original *Joan of Arc* material) to the *Morning Post*, which published it on December 26, 1797. The *Morning Post* text is the closest version we have to the lines that nettled Lamb, for it contains passages that are closer than those in "The Destiny of Nations" to the ones he lamented as descents from epic loftiness to bathos. The first of these sketches Joan's humble origins, as a servant chosen "from such mean estates / As still the Epic song half fears to name":

> For lowly was her birth,
> And Heaven had doomed her early years to toil
> That pure from Tyranny's least deed, herself
> Unfeared by Fellow-natures, she might wait
> On the poor labouring man with kindly looks,
> And minister refreshment to the tired
> Way-wanderer, when along the rough-hewn bench
> The sultry man had stretched him, and aloft
> Watch'd the gay sign-board on the mulberry bough
> Swing to the pleasant breeze! Here too the Maid
> Learnt more than Schools could teach: Man's shifting
>   mind,
> His vices and his sorrows! And full oft
> At tales of cruel wrong and strange distress
> Had wept and shivered. To the tottering Eld
> Still as a daughter she would run: she placed

His cold limbs at the sunny door, and loved
To hear him story, in his garrulous sort,
Of his eventful years, all come and gone.   [143–161][9]

But what Lamb felt here as an egregious breach of decorum he might also have heard as a distinctly Wordsworthian mode, for in the early spring of 1796—about nine months before he read this passage—Coleridge had sent him the manuscript of "Adventures on Salisbury Plain" that Wordsworth had forwarded to him. (According to Azariah Pinney, Wordsworth's intermediary, Coleridge read the poem "with great attention" and interleaved it with blank pages for a detailed commentary.)[10] For the truth seems to be that the "degrading" of Joan into a pot-girl that so upset Lamb was not, as he chided, an imitation by Coleridge of one of the "more familiar moods" of Oliver Goldsmith, but an amalgam of various elements from the world of weary travelers, swinging pub signs, and humble family relationships that characterize the revised version of "Salisbury Plain" both he and Coleridge had so recently read. Joan's new background provided her with the sympathy, strength, and devotion that would foster the human (and divine) ministry to remedy the ills of the desolate world of "Adventures on Salisbury Plain," a world caught clearly in this stanza describing the wandering sailor's plight:

No swinging sign creak'd from its cottage elm
To bid his weary limbs new force assume;
'Twas dark and void as ocean's watry realm
Roaring with storms beneath night's starless gloom;
No gypsey cowr'd o'er fire of furze or broom;
No labourer watch'd his red kiln glaring bright,
Nor taper glimmer'd dim from sick man's room;
Along the heath no line of mournful light
From lamp of lonely toll-gate stream'd athwart the
    night.   [20][11]

"Adventures on Salisbury Plain" may well be the bleakest poem Wordsworth ever wrote. More than any other of his major poems, including the lyric drama *The Borderers*, it is a poem of social protest and moral despair. As Wordsworth said in late 1795, "its object is partly to expose the vices of the penal law and the calamities of war as they affect individuals." Partly also, as Stephen Gill has argued, it was to explore the ways in which the experience of suffering, injustice, and guilt deepen the humanity of the afflicted.[12] (Such readings are fully compatible with readings that, emphasizing autobiographical aspects of the poem, see in the poem a clear poetic expression of the compound distress Wordsworth felt over his abandonment of Annette Vallon and over his nation's role in bringing about the degeneration and defeat of France's hopes.) The main figures in the poem are studies in the bereft wretchedness of the exploited poor. They are driven to sin and crime; relief is temporary, fated to turn into further desolation and tragedy. Whereas at the end of the version Wordsworth finally published in 1842, *Guilt and Sorrow*, the sailor is granted a reprieve from the gallows, in this intermediate version, after having surrendered himself and acknowledged his guilt in the murder of another man, he is made the victim of a hypocritical system of social "justice." Even a character so benevolently disposed as the female vagrant seems designed primarily to cast into clearer perspective the tragic suffering endured by common citizens in a nation at war; as such she is an anticipation of the more profound figure of Margaret in "The Ruined Cottage," Wordsworth's next major narrative poem. Her agency in "Adventures on Salisbury Plain" is primarily to deepen the sailor's moral sensibility and his experience of guilt: she can console but not deliver him from suffering.

Coleridge had this poem in mind, then, when in the *Biographia* he described its

union of deep feeling with profound thought; the fine balance of truth in observing, with the imaginative faculty in modifying the objects observed; and above all the original gift of spreading the tone, the *atmosphere* and with it the depth and height of the

ideal world around forms, incidents, and situations, of which, for
the common view, custom had bedimmed all the lustre, had dried
up the sparkle and the dew drops.

Such was, in effect, his delayed response to Lamb, to whose
"common view" the incidents and situations added in the revised Joan of Arc poem seemed so ordinary. But what did
Coleridge mean by his phrase "the ideal world," and what is
its bearing on his attempt to infuse the deep preluding strain
of his *Joan of Arc* material with some of the powerful Wordsworthian music? One way to approach these difficult questions about Coleridge's *Biographia* passage would be to emphasize the essential difference between Coleridge's elevated
Miltonics in "Religious Musings" and the original *Joan of Arc*
and Wordsworth's earthier and lustier Spenserian effects. We
are inclined, I think, partly because of our shortcomings as
readers and our shortsightedness as literary historians, to assume too readily that Spenser constituted an archaic mode for
the romantic poets. Wordsworth's poem is the most powerful
and successful imitation of Spenser in the eighteenth century;
its excellence and power are inseparable from its assimilation
of Spenserian descriptive and narrative effects. Consider, for
example, the sense of bleakness generated by the alliterative
and largely monosyllabic description of the sailor's plight:

> No tree was there, no meadow's pleasant green,
> No brook to wet his lips or soothe his ear.
> Vast piles of corn-stack here and there were seen,
> But thence no smoke upwreathed his sight to cheer.
> He mark'd a homeward shepherd disappear
> Far off and sent a feeble shout, in vain;
> No sound replies but winds that whistling near
> Sweep the thin grass and passing wildly plain,
> Or desart lark that pours on high a wasted strain.   [7]

Or, again, the use of sudden transition, fantastic abrupt encounter, and extravagant detail, as in this stanza:

> The proud man might relent and weep to find
> That now, in this wild waste, so keen a pang

Could pierce a heart to life's best ends inclined.
For as he plodded on, with sudden clang
A sound of chains along the desart rang:
He looked, and saw on a bare gibbet nigh
A human body that in irons swang,
Uplifted by the tempest sweeping by,
And hovering round it often did a raven fly.   [13]

So pervasive and effective are the "tone" and "atmosphere" of this imaginative world and so inseparable are its qualities from the verse in which they are embodied that to speak of the poem primarily as a realistic indictment of the 1790's— what F. W. Bateson calls its "sober eye-on-the-object realism" —is to neglect its essential genius, and in so doing to reduce it to a versified political tract, a Godwinian exposition of the societal calamities caused by governmental abuse.[13] As argued in the last chapter, even in the earliest works of Wordsworth and Coleridge, poetry is not journalism or political argument. The "ideal" world Coleridge cites in his *Biographia* passage (in which he makes no mention of politics, Godwinian reform, or even social despair) is in part the result of that imaginative, and in this case notably Spenserian, coloration whereby the familiar phenomena of the world are felt to take on a heightened life and meaning, so that, for example, the "vast piles of corn-stack" or the "winds that whistling near / Sweep the thin grass" become manifestations in the landscape of the sailor's despair, for him and for the reader. (One thinks ahead, perhaps, to the deep sense of pathos evoked in both narrator and reader by the wanderer's description of the unsensational but moving details of the ruining of Margaret's cottage.)

This element in literary experience, the reader's quickening response on seeing the objects and appearances of his familiar world thrown into more intense liveliness by the power of an "ideal" (read "mental" or "fictive") world, is itself built into the narrative structure of "Adventures on Salisbury Plain,"

so that the experience of events in the poem in the sailor's imagination is recapitulated in the experience of the reader. One
of the chief narrative motifs in the poem is that of the guilt-
burdened sailor's trances: some object or action in the landscape or society or a chance expression in the female vagrant's
tale or in the abusive language of the battered child's irate
father weighs in upon the sailor with unusual devastation because he finds in it a mirror that rouses his ideal world of
guilty memory. The sailor's sudden encounter with the bare,
corpse-burdened gibbet (quoted above) is for our purposes
the salient instance of this motif. "It was," as the poet says, "a
spectacle which none might view / In spot so savage but with
shuddering pain," but for the sailor, burdened by the anxiety
of his secret crime, it not only at once renewed

> All he had feared from man, but rouzed a train
> Of the mind's phantoms, horrible as vain.
> The stones, as if to sweep him from the day,
> Roll'd at his back along the living plain;
> He fell and without sense or motion lay,
> And when the trance was gone, feebly pursued his way.
>
> [14]

In the *Biographia*, discussing the distinction between fancy
and imagination Wordsworth's poem led him to, Coleridge
cites Lear's remark on seeing Tom O' Bedlam ("What! have
his daughters brought him to this pass?") as an instance of imaginative mania, Lear projecting onto another wretch his sense
of the causes of his own calamity. (He points also to Lear's
apostrophe to the elements, and in a 1808 notebook entry describes how Lear's "deep anguish . . . *spreads* the feeling of
ingratitude and cruelty over the very elements of heaven").[14]
The sailor shows a similar mania, though in some ways more
extravagant, and the essence of Coleridge's argument about
the imagination is that both manic reactions, Lear's and the
sailor's, are analogous to the freshness of sensation brought to
the common phenomena of life by readers of great poetry.

"Who has not a thousand times seen snow fall on water?"
Coleridge asks.

Who has not watched it with a new feeling, from the time that
he has read Burns' comparison of sensual pleasure

> To snow that falls upon a river
> A moment white—then gone for ever!

What "Salisbury Plain" engendered in the reader Coleridge,
in other words, was an imaginative participation analogous to
the manic experience of its central character. This doubling in
the reader of the sailor's visionary experience is made almost
explicit at the end of the poem when the narrator extends
what is virtually an invitation for the sympathetic reader himself, perhaps burdened with his own guilt, to become a wretch
replicating the sailor's first fit:

> They left him hung on high in iron case,
> And dissolute men, unthinking and untaught,
> Planted their festive booths beneath his face;
> And to that spot, which idle thousands sought,
> Women and children were by fathers brought;
> And now some kindred sufferer driven, perchance,
> That way when into storm the sky is wrought,
> Upon his swinging corpse his eye may glance
> And drop, as he once dropp'd, in miserable trance.   [92]

With this perspective on Coleridge's reaction to the poem,
we can see that in rebegetting his Joan upon Wordsworth's
muse, he sought in effect to make her over into a step-sister of
the female vagrant. The violation of lofty epic decorum in
"Visions of the Maid of Orleans. A Fragment" (note how the
new title reflects an orientation toward the humble) was Coleridge's attempt to open up in Joan a nature that would permit the powerful narrative exploration of the familiar and
lowly he had been so attentive to in Wordsworth's "Adventures on Salisbury Plain." But equally important, it was at the
same time an effort to counter the provocative Wordsworthian
gloom with a story of visionary deliverance achieved through

commiseration with a suffering world. In this latter aspect, Coleridge's response to the Wordsworthian initiative strikes a keynote for his role in their ensuing literary dialogue. Whatever the relative merits of the two poems, the distinctions we can draw between "Adventures on Salisbury Plain" and "Visions of the Maid of Orleans" in this regard are instructive about the characteristic poetic stances adopted by the two poets during the years of their closest and most creative association.

3

In his letters criticizing Coleridge's reworking of *Joan of Arc*, Lamb protested not only the added lines about Joan's humble origins but also "the lamentable episode of a waggoner, his wife, and six children." He satirized the intrusion of contemporary politics into a poem about the historical French saint:

After all this cometh Joan . . . finding a poor man, his wife, and six children, starved to death with cold, and thence roused into a state of mind proper to receive visions emblematical of equality; which what the devil Joan had to do with, I don't know, or indeed with the French and American revolutions.[15]

The episode he referred to was the longest addition Coleridge had made, and it will be useful to us to have it entire as it appeared in the *Morning Post* version ten months later:

> She went forth alone
> Urged by the indwelling angel-guide, (that oft,
> With dim inexplicable sympathies
> Disquieting the heart, shapes out our course
> To some predoom'd adventure) and the ascent
> Now pass'd of that steep upland (on whose top
> Not seldom some poor nightly-roaming man
> Shouts to himself, there first the cottage lights
> Seen in Neufchatel's vale) she slop'd a-down
> The bleak hill's further side, till at the base,
> In the first entrance of the level road

A waggon stay'd her speed. Its foremost horse
Lay with stretched limbs; the others, yet alive
But stiff with cold, stood motionless, their manes
Hoar with the frozen night-dews. Dismally
The dark-red dawn now glimmered; but its gleams
Disclosed no face of man. The maiden paused,
And hailed who might be near. No voice replied.
At length she listen'd, from the vehicle
A voice so feeble that it almost seemed
Distant: and feebly, with slow effort pushed,
A miserable man crawl'd forth: his limbs
The silent frost had eat, scathing like fire.
Faint on the shafts he rested. She meanwhile,
Saw crowded close beneath the coverture
A mother and her children—lifeless all,
Yet lovely! not a lineament was marred—
Death had put on so slumber-like a form!
It was a piteous sight! and one, a babe,
Lay on the woman's arm, its little hand
Smooth on her bosom. Wildly pale the maid
Gaz'd at the living wretch, mute questioning.
He, his head feebly turning, on the group
Looked with a vacant stare, and his eye spoke
The drowsy calm that steals on worn-out anguish.
She shuddered; but, each vainer pang subdued,
Quick disentangling from the foremost horse
The rustic bands, with difficulty and toil
The stiff cramped team forced homewards. There arriv'd,
Anxious she tended him with healing herbs
And wept and pray'd; but green putridity
Spread o'er his limbs, and ere the noontide hour,
The hovering spirits of his Wife and Babes
Hailed him immortal! Yet amid his pangs,
With interruptions strange from ghastly throes,
His voice had faltered out this simple tale.   [185–232]

The chief source for this passage, as Lamb might have recalled, was a British officer's narrative of the domestic ravages
of the campaign of 1794–1795 in revolutionary France, a nar-

rative Coleridge had printed the previous spring in one of the last numbers of his ill-starred *Watchman*.[16] That journal's dissenting politics were Coleridge's response to the climate of increasing government hostility toward Jacobin sympathizers in England in 1795 and 1796, and the inclusion of the officer's narrative was part of his continuing effort to make available to a reading public in the west country around Bristol the kind of antiwar materials that the government-controlled London press censored. But it would be wrong to conclude, as Lamb seems to have, that the adaptation of the narrative anecdote as an incident instrumental in shaping Joan's political destiny was simply an attempt on Coleridge's part to make "Visions of the Maid of Orleans" more relevant to the turmoil of his own times.

As Emile Legouis first suggested, Joan's encounter with the dying waggoner and his frozen family was probably inspired also by the female vagrant's similar encounter in "Adventures on Salisbury Plain."[17] Immediately after she parts from the sailor, who has listened to her tale of wretchedness and decided out of guilt and sorrow to abandon human intercourse by withdrawing to the sea, the female vagrant unexpectedly meets his dying wife:

> He had resolved to turn toward the seas
> Since he that tale had heard, and while her heart
> Struggled with tears, nor could its sorrow ease,
> She left him there; for, clustering round his knees,
> With his oak staff the cottage children play'd;
> And soon she reach'd a spot o'erhung with trees
> And banks of ragged earth; beneath the shade
> Across the pebbly road a little runner stray'd.
>
> A cart and horse beside the rivulet stood;
> Chequering the canvass roof the sunbeams shone.
> She saw the carman bend to scoop the flood,
> And now approach'd the wain, wherein was one,
> A single woman, lying spent and gone;
> The carman wet her lips as well behoved;

Bed under her lean [?shadow] there was none;
Though even to die near one she most had loved
She could not of herself those wasted limbs have moved.

The Soldier's widow learn'd with honest pain
And homefelt force of sympathy sincere,
Why thus that worn-out wretch must there sustain
The jolting road and morning air severe.
And crying, "Would, my friend, thy aid were here,
Or yours, good cottagers," her steps retraced
To that same house, the wain still following.
She found her comrade there and cried in haste,
"Come, come, my friends, and see what object here is
    placed." [77–79]

But this effort of mercy is futile. In Legouis's words, "The good woman's cares are useless. The wretched creature's strength fails when her story is told, and she dies almost immediately."[18]

With this evidence, a plausible genesis of the episode Lamb faulted as indecorous and anachronistic is not hard to reconstruct. Impressed by the power of Wordsworth's Spenserian narrative when he heard and subsequently read it, Coleridge seems to have been prompted first to incorporate in *The Watchman* passages describing a similar domestic calamity and then to adapt the British officer's narrative to his own poem. To summarize the motivation for this imitative gesture, we may suppose that "Adventures on Salisbury Plain," with its scarcely relieved sense of wretchedness, betrayal, injustice, and despair, must have seemed to Coleridge in early 1796 a strong disputation of the very providence Coleridge had so confidently invoked, both in the original version of *Joan of Arc* and in the poem he told Lamb he was ready to rest his poetic claims upon, "Religious Musings." It seems likely that, in responding to the uncomfortable challenge Wordsworth's relentless despair presented, he was at pains to demonstrate that the same powerful sense of pathos he felt in "Adventures on Salisbury Plain" was equally possible in a contrary vision.

His vision argued that the universal distress of the world in 1796 was but a prelude to millennial tranquility virtually at hand. "Visions of the Maid of Orleans," then, was Coleridge's strenuous attempt to bend the bitter despair of Wordsworth's world to his own Christian theodicy.

Confronting the wretched survivor of social atrocity in "Adventures on Salisbury Plain," Wordsworth's heroine had recourse to social ministry. Having summoned the aid of the sailor (not knowing he is the dying woman's husband) and the cottagers, the female vagrant disappears from the poem, her human agency complete in that gesture:

> her steps retraced
> To that same house, the wain still following.
> She found her comrade there and cried in haste,
> "Come, come, my friends, and see what object here is
>   placed." [79]

For Coleridge's Joan, by contrast, the encounter with the victims of war's disasters proves more critical: it has the impact of epiphany. The "tales of cruel wrong and strange distress" over which she had wept and shivered as a child prepared her for a response of agitated sympathy exceeding anything depicted in Wordsworth's female vagrant, and that response provides the occasion for the supervening agency of divine vocation:

> Ah! suffering to the height of what was suffered,
> Stung with too keen a sympathy, the Maid
> Brooded with moving lips, mute, startful, dark!
> And now her flushed tumultuous features shot
> Such strange vivacity, as fires the eye
> Of Misery fancy-crazed! and now once more
> Naked, and void, and fixed, and all within
> The unquiet silence of confused thought
> And shapeless feelings. For a mighty hand
> Was strong upon her, till in th' heat of soul
> To the high hill-top tracing back her steps
> Aside the beacon, down whose mouldered stones

The tender ivy-trails crept thinly, there,
Unconscious of the driving element,
Yea, swallowed up in th' ominous dream, she sate
Ghastly as broad-eyed Slumber! a dim anguish
Breathed from her look! and still with pant and sob,
Inly she toiled to fly, and still subdued,
Felt an inevitable presence near.
   Thus as she toiled in troubled ecstasy,
A horror of great darkness wrapt her round,
And a voice uttered forth unearthly tones,
Calming her soul,—"O thou of the Most High
Chosen, whom all the perfected in Heaven
Behold expectant—"   [253–277]

The original *Joan of Arc* lines had argued, in a passage Coleridge retained in his revision, the uses of superstition in generating a capacity for feeling and faith:

                    For Fancy is the power
That first unsensualizes the dark mind,
Giving it new delights; and bids it swell
With wild activity; and peopling air,
By obscure fears of Beings invisible
Emancipates it from the grosser thrall
Of the present impulse, teaching self control
Till Superstition with unconscious hand
Seat Reason on her throne.   [80–88]

And by this argument, even the most trancelike states among such primitives as Greenland's Indian wizards, though productive of wild fantasies, are

                    yet wise,
Teaching reliance, and medicinal hope,
Till from Bethabra northward, heavenly Truth
With gradual steps, winning her difficult way,
Transfer their rude Faith perfected and pure.

Coleridge's (and Southey's) Joan had been originally also thus taught, and the new passage Lamb objected to replaced a long, lumbering, allegorical vision of the reign of Ambition, accompanied by Hypocrisy, Slaughter, Cruelty, and other minions, which served as an induction to Joan's subsequent vision of her triumphant martyrdom. In Coleridge's new poem, the refurbished Joan, under the weight of the suffering and confusion stirred in her by the wagon scene, struggles back up the hill to the mouldered tower. There, exposed to the wind, she toils within "in troubled ecstasy," a humble, peasant embodiment of the figure of "heavenly Truth / With gradual steps, winning her difficult way." The long passage detailing her stunned prelude to divine summons is an attempt to provide a fuller psychological grounding, in what Coleridge seems already to have thought of as a Wordsworthian experience, for Joan's calling, and thus to give her "voices" continuity with her daily being. Joan's response to the wagon atrocity exceeds anything we see in Wordsworth's female vagrant, because it is closely modeled instead on the sailor's terrific trance, with its peculiarly tranquil aftermath, at the gallows-encounter. Coleridge quarried much of the language for the description of Joan's approach to vision (quoted above) from the stanza in "Adventures on Salisbury Plain" that follows the account of that trance:

> As doth befall to them whom frenzy *fires*,
> His *soul*, which in such *anguish* had been toss'd,
> Sank into deepest *calm*; for now retires
> Fear; a terrific *dream* in *darkness* lost
> The dire phantasma which his sense had cross'd.
> His mind was still as a deep evening stream;
> Nor, if accosted now, in *thought* engross'd,
> Moody, or inly-*troubled*, would he seem
> To traveller who might talk of any casual theme.   [15]

(Italics indicate words Coleridge echoed exactly.) The sailor likewise has arrived at a ruined structure (Stonehenge), where the wind buffets a bustard. Coleridge's description of Joan by her tower seems also to have been influenced by Wordworth's account of that frightened bird's difficulty in escaping the stranger:

> Hurtle the clouds by deeper darkness piled,
> Gone is the raven timely rest to seek;
> He seem'd the only creature in the wild
> On whom the elements their rage might wreak;
> Save that the bustard, of those limits bleak
> Shy tenant, seeing by the uncertain light
> A man there wandring gave a mournful shriek,
> And half upon the ground, with strange affright
> Forc'd hard against the wind a thick unwieldly flight.
> [17]

But in shifting away from the heavy allegorical machinery of Southey's version to imitate Wordsworthian narrative, Coleridge still insisted on the supernatural dimension of Joan's experience: "a mighty hand was strong upon her." Though her experience has clear affinities with the trance undergone by Wordsworth's sailor as the hallucinatory affirmation of his guilt, she is still unequivocally under the influence of an "inevitable presence." A notebook entry dating from late September or early October 1796 (when Coleridge was in all likelihood in the midst of altering his poem) gives some indication of how interested he was in recovering a supernatural foundation for the kind of imaginative experience Wordsworth's poem had so powerfully depicted. From a volume of Jeremy Taylor's sermons, he copied out this paragraph, which may well have influenced his shaping of Joan's vision:

She had in her sickness some curious & well-becoming fears respecting the final state of the soul—but from thence she passed into a deliquium, or a kind of Trance, and as soon as she came forth of it, as if it had been a Vision or that she had conversed with an angel, & from his hand had received a Labell or Scroll of the *Book of Life* & there seen her name enrolled, she cried out aloud / "Glory be to God on high; now I am sure, I shall be

saved." Concerning which manner of discoursing we are wholly
ignorant what Judgment can be made; but certainly there are
strange things in the other World; and so there are in all the immediate Preparations to it; & a little *Glimpse* of Heaven, a min-
ute's conversing with an angel, any ray of God, any communication from the Spirit of Comfort which God gives to his
servants in strange & unknown manners, are infinitely far from
Illusions; & they shall then be understood by us, when we feel
them, & when our new & strange needs shall be refreshed by such
unusual Visitations.[19]

In "This Lime-Tree Bower My Prison," Coleridge reinforced the *imitatio Christi* motif that is the informing idea of
the poem by describing Lamb's journey through "evil and
pain and strange calamity" in language resonant with *Paradise
Regained*. But as we noted in discussing that poem, Milton's
account of Christ's struggle in the wilderness had already been
in Coleridge's mind in *Joan of Arc* when he described the
figure of Truth "from Bethabra northward . . . / With
gradual steps, winning her difficult way." In "Visions of the
Maid of Orleans," he extended this analogy by further correspondences with the language of Milton's brief epic. These
correspondences in the revision of Joan's "calling" along
otherwise markedly Wordsworthian lines in effect reinforce
Coleridge's opening argument that Joan's career exhibited an
inevitable progress from superstition to Christian faith.[20] In
Paradise Regained, Milton's Christ is led meditating to the
desert:

> the Son of God, who yet some days
> Lodged in Bethabara where John baptized,
> Musing and much revolving in his breast,
> How best the mighty work he might begin
> Of saviour to mankind, and which way first
> Publish his godlike office now mature,
> One day forth walked alone, the spirit leading
> And his deep thoughts, the better to converse
> With solitude. . . .   [I, 183–191]

Joan's visionary encounter is likewise the aftermath to a meditative journey into the Neufchatel wilderness:

> She went forth alone
> Urged by the indwelling angel-guide, (that oft
> With dim inexplicable sympathies
> Disquieting the heart, shapes out our course
> To some predoom'd adventure). . . . [185–189]

It is important, I think, to see that these aspects of eternity in Joan's career are no merely accidental embellishments. They indicate what became a continuing resistance to the implications of Wordsworth's poetry by a Coleridge persuaded of the essential need for belief in Christian theodicy as the resolution of human suffering. The comparison, in this context, of Joan's experience with that of the sailor or the female vagrant in "Adventures on Salisbury Plain" provides an illuminating perspective for the terms Coleridge used almost twenty years later in the *Biographia* to describe the division of labor agreed to for *Lyrical Ballads:*

During the first year that Mr. Wordsworth and I were neighbours, our conversations turned frequently on the two cardinal points of poetry, the power of exciting the sympathy of the reader by a faithful adherence to the truth of nature, and the power of giving the interest of novelty by the modifying colours of imagination. . . . The thought suggested itself (to which of us I do not recollect) that a series of poems might be composed of two sorts. In the one, the incidents and agents were to be, in part at least, supernatural; and the excellence aimed at was to consist in the interesting of the affections by the dramatic truth of such emotions, as would naturally accompany such situations, supposing them real. And real in *this* sense they have been to every human being who, from whatever source of delusion, has at any time believed himself under supernatural agency. For the second class, subjects were to be chosen from ordinary life; the characters and incidents were to be such, as will be found in every village and its vicinity, where there is a meditative and feeling mind to seek after them, or to notice them, when they present themselves.[21]

4

Coleridge sought by adapting the Wordsworthian mode to
resist the bleaker implications of that mode in "Adventures on
Salisbury Plain." He thus reasserted his commitment to a
meditative theodicy by means of which personal, social, and
political distress could be brought round to a saving visionary
resolution. But Wordsworth did not leave his friend's rejoinder unanswered, for Coleridge's account of Joan's calling
had eventually, in turn, a palpable influence on one of the
most remarkable narrative passages Wordsworth ever wrote.
That passage subsequently became the first of the experiences
Wordsworth explicitly called "spots of time" in Book XI of
the 1805 *Prelude*, the story of the lost boy's stumbling upon
the murderer's grave and, immediately after, encountering the
pitcher-bearing girl. Seen from the perspective of Coleridge's
"Visions of the Maid of Orleans," the Wordsworth spot is
likewise a summons; as such it is a highly artful response to
Coleridge, in which the narrative deftly shifts the entire context of imaginative experience. The text quoted here is that of
the 1799 draft recently published by Jonathan Wordsworth:

> I remember well,
> While yet an urchin, one who scarce
> Could hold a bridle, with ambitious hopes
> I mounted, and we rode towards the hills;
> We were a pair of horsemen: honest James
> Was with me, my encourager and guide.
> We had not travelled long ere some mischance
> Disjoined me from my comrade, and through fear
> Dismounting, down the rough and stony moor
> I led my horse, and stumbling on, at length
> Came to a bottom where in former times
> A man, the murderer of his wife, was hung
> In irons; mouldered was the gibbet mast,
> The bones were gone, the iron and the wood;
> Only a long green ridge of turf remained

Whose shape was like a grave. I left the spot,
And reascending the bare slope, I saw
A naked pool that lay beneath the hills,
The beacon on the summit, and more near
A girl who bore a pitcher on her head
And seemed with difficult steps to force her way
Against the blowing wind. It was in truth
An ordinary sight, but I should need
Colours and words that are unknown to man
To paint the visionary dreariness
Which, while I looked all round for my lost guide,
Did at that time invest the naked pool,
The beacon on the lonely eminence,
The woman and her garments vexed and tossed
By the strong wind.[22]

The cluster of resonances this passage strikes with the narrative of Joan's supernatural calling argues, I think, an unmistakable link between that passage and Wordsworth's more famous spot of time: the guide, the descent to a terrifying encounter with death and crime, the troubled reascent toward a beaconed summit, the woman struggling to make her way, the severely buffeting wind, the onset of visionary awareness.

And yet, at least at first glance, it is not easy to interpret what Wordsworth did in transforming the Coleridgean moment. Certainly the heart of the change is in these bare, central lines:

I saw
A naked pool that lay beneath the hills,
The beacon on the summit, and more near
A girl who bore a pitcher on her head
And seemed with difficult steps to force her way
Against the blowing wind. It was in truth
An ordinary sight. . . .

In the splendid matter-of-factness of this last half-sentence there is a quiet, but firm and deliberate, repudiation of Coleridge's more laborious, allegorical abstraction, "heavenly Truth." By such sleights of language entire worlds are changed. Wordsworth's woman, he avows, is nothing more than a woman, though to the agitated receptivity of the child's imagination she is part of an experience so *extra*ordinary as to be ineffable: "I should need / Colours and words that are unknown to man." A girl with a pitcher on her head is no saintly Joan, charged with the burden of imitating Christ's progress from Bethabara northward toward divinity, though she is, like the leech-gatherer, an emblem of patience, perseverance, and uncanny equanimity. In fact she is thoroughly one with a world whose ordinariness precludes the possibility of supernatural analogs.

Related to this but of greater consequence for defining the Wordsworthian shift is the fact that the visionary trance (if trance is still the right word four years after "Adventures on Salisbury Plain") possesses not the woman but the boy who witnesses her toiling progress through that entirely natural and elemental landscape. (In Coleridge's narrative, by contrast, the witness to Joan's struggle toward prophetic awareness is the "inevitable presence" of divine energy, the irresistible intervention of "a mighty hand.") The paradox is that Wordsworth's solitaries are *never* solitary: their solitude is charged with power by the imagination of those who come upon them. The hovering presence shaping the visionary nature of this scene is the child himself, prepared for his extraordinary encounter by no force more extraordinary than that of human circumstances and human accident. In the language of Coleridge's consolatory letter to Lamb, Joan is "a soul set apart and made peculiar to God!" but with Wordsworth her vocation to martyrdom is transferred to the irrecoverable "visionary dreariness" with which the child's mind invests the world. And that dreariness is also a calling. The clear implication of the powerful centrality of this "spot of time" in the two-part *Prelude* of 1799 is that out of such experiences the child is set apart and made peculiar to the resources of his own imagination, a calling that will nourish and fructify the later poet.

Jonathan Wordsworth has recently argued that Wordsworth's greatest verse, including the spots of time that are the essence of the earliest *Prelude*, was written in the wake of losing his belief in the One Life, a belief that was the major effect of Coleridge's influence on him in 1797 and 1798. Of the two-part *Prelude* he says that "the structure of Wordsworth's poem, and the structure of his thought seem to require a supernatural frame of reference. Yet it is the fact of being without one that spurs him to write his greatest poetry."[23] In lodging his challenge to that strenuous, exhilarating Coleridgean creed, Wordsworth made use of the very narrative in which Coleridge, himself artfully drawing on "Adventures on Salisbury Plain," had imagined it.

4

"Frost at Midnight": Coleridge's
Companionable Form

Excuse "A Father's Tale" if, with respect to the later collection, I cherish the belief, that the mood and the time will come when the Ode on the Departing Year, that entitled Dejection, the Hymn at Chamouny, and three or four of the meditative blank-verse Poems, will stand at a less distance from the Mariner, the Christabel, and the Love, in your good opinion, than they do at present.

COLERIDGE (1819)

Frost at Midnight

The Frost performs its secret ministry,
Unhelped by any wind. The owlet's cry
Came loud—and hark, again! loud as before.
The inmates of my cottage, all at rest,
Have left me to that solitude, which suits   5
Abstruser musings: save that at my side
My cradled infant slumbers peacefully.
'Tis calm indeed! so calm, that it disturbs
And vexes meditation with its strange
And extreme silentness. Sea, hill, and wood,   10
This populous village! Sea, and hill, and wood,
With all the numberless goings-on of life,
Inaudible as dreams! the thin blue flame
Lies on my low-burnt fire, and quivers not;
Only that film, which fluttered on the grate,   15
Still flutters there, the sole unquiet thing.
Methinks, its motion in this hush of nature
Gives it dim sympathies with me who live,
Making it a companionable form,
Whose puny flaps and freaks the idling Spirit   20
By its own moods interprets, every where
Echo or mirror seeking of itself,
And makes a toy of Thought.
                              But O! how oft,
How oft, at school, with most believing mind,
Presageful, have I gazed upon the bars,   25
To watch that fluttering *stranger!* and as oft
With unclosed lids, already had I dreamt

Of my sweet birth-place, and the old church-tower,
Whose bells, the poor man's only music, rang
From morn to evening, all the hot Fair-day,   30
So sweetly, that they stirred and haunted me
With a wild pleasure, falling on mine ear
Most like articulate sounds of things to come!
So gazed I, till the soothing things, I dreamt,
Lulled me to sleep, and sleep prolonged my dreams!   35
And so I brooded all the following morn,
Awed by the stern preceptor's face, mine eye
Fixed with mock study on my swimming book:
Save if the door half opened, and I snatched
A hasty glance, and still my heart leaped up,   40
For still I hope to see the *stranger's* face,
Townsman, or aunt, or sister more beloved,
My play-mate when we both were clothed alike!

    Dear Babe, that sleepest cradled by my side,
Whose gentle breathings, heard in this deep calm,   45
Fill up the interspersèd vacancies
And momentary pauses of the thought!
My babe so beautiful! it thrills my heart
With tender gladness, thus to look at thee,
And think that thou shalt learn far other lore,   50
And in far other scenes! For I was reared
In the great city, pent 'mid cloisters dim,
And saw nought lovely but the sky and stars.
But *thou*, my babe! shalt wander like a breeze
By lakes and sandy shores, beneath the crags   55
Of ancient mountain, and beneath the clouds,
Which image in their bulk both lakes and shores
And mountain crags: so shalt thou see and hear
The lovely shapes and sounds intelligible
Of that eternal language, which thy God   60
Utters, who from eternity doth teach
Himself in all, and all things in himself.
Great universal Teacher! he shall mould
Thy spirit, and by giving make it ask.

Therefore all seasons shall be sweet to thee,   65
Whether the summer clothe the general earth
With greenness, or the redbreast sit and sing
Betwixt the tufts of snow on the bare branch
Of mossy apple-tree, while the nigh thatch
Smokes in the sun-thaw; whether the eave-drops fall   70
Heard only in the trances of the blast,
Or if the secret ministry of frost
Shall hang them up in silent icicles,
Quietly shining to the quiet Moon.

We have seen that Coleridge's continuing interest in a Christian visionary resolution to human suffering led him to resist the bleakness of Wordsworth's powerful mode even as he imitated it, undertaking in 1796–1797 a radical revision of his most ambitious poem to date, "Visions of the Maid of Orleans." The following summer, as I have argued in the first chapter, he combined the modes of landscape meditation and visionary apocalypse, the latter deriving ultimately from Revelation, in the poem "This Lime-Tree Bower My Prison."

The autumn and winter of 1797 were by any estimate the most remarkable months in Coleridge's brief career as an intensely productive poet. In that time he composed "Kubla Khan" and "The Ancient Mariner," and in late winter he wrote the most universally admired of his meditative poems, "Frost at Midnight." Among those poems it is the quietest in tone; its relative softness and evenness accompany a muting of the specifically scriptural, apocalyptic analogies Coleridge experimented with in the poems so far examined. In this sense, "Frost at Midnight" may be seen as something of a turning point in Coleridge's poetry, a genuine concession to the Wordsworthian mode and a yielding of the ultimately apocalyptic definition of the spiritual theodicy we have been concerned with. In another sense, as we shall see, it announces his continuing resistance to his friend's dogged and unsettling vision of pathos.

126

1

M. H. Abrams speaks for most readers when he calls "Frost at Midnight" one of the "masterpieces of the greater [Romantic] lyric, perfectly modulated and proportioned"; Humphry House thought its ending was "one of the finest pieces of short descriptive writing in the language, intricate and yet at the same time so sparsely clear."[1] Such praise is obviously not faint, nor intended to be; yet it is difficult not to hear in these and other appreciations of the poem a sense that "Frost at Midnight" is Coleridge in his best minor key, not so daring and breath-taking as "Kubla Khan," not so rich and mythic as "The Ancient Mariner," and above all not so *strong* as the poem with which it is often compared, Wordsworth's "Tintern Abbey." My purpose here is not to challenge this consensus but to see further into the poem's art, which in intricacy and resourcefulness equals that of Coleridge's other great meditative poems. "Frost at Midnight" is the work of a poet who thinks, and its art is in the building of its beauty upon a deft and complicated structure.

That structure has been aptly described by Abrams and others as a "return-upon-itself." As a device for the diseases-into-pearls argument, it closely resembles the structure of "This Lime-Tree Bower My Prison." The return at the end (in the coda) is to the wintry situation of the opening, though now developed so the "secret ministry of frost" is informed with sacramental meaning.[2] The crucial image is "the stranger," the film of ash fluttering on the fire gate, which provides an associative link to the poet's recollection of childhood experience (and, through that, of infancy), and the central theme is the "companionable form." As in "This Lime-Tree Bower My Prison" and "Dejection: An Ode," the significant movement in the poem is from the willful and superstitious solipsism of a depressed sensibility, toying with a companionable form, to the apprehension of a regenerate companionship, based not on superstition but on substantial belief. So characteristic is this progress that no adequate study of Coleridge's poems of the 1790's and early 1800's can neglect the emphasis in them on the instrumentality of superstition in transcending its own errors.

The earliest extant version of the poem, published in a quarto pamphlet in 1798, emphasizes the elements of superstition and willfulness in the poet's melancholy. The "stranger" in the opening lines is the focus of the mind's idling fantasies, but as with the storm in "Dejection" four years later, the superstition invoked (according to Coleridge's note, "in all parts of the kingdom these films are called *strangers* and supposed to portend the arrival of some absent friend") also establishes the terms for a meditative resolution of the despair that in the opening can only dally with that superstition:

> Only that film, which fluttered on the grate,
> Still flutters there, the sole unquiet thing.
> Methinks, its motion in this hush of nature
> Gives it dim sympathies with me who live,
> Making it a companionable form,
> With which I can hold commune. Idle thought!
> But still the living spirit in our frame,
> That loves not to behold a lifeless thing,
> Transfuses into all its own delights,
> It own volition, sometimes with deep faith
> And sometimes with fantastic playfulness.[3]

In the logic of the poem, of course, Coleridge's *proper* companion in the evening setting is his sleeping infant Hartley, but in his vexed state of mind at the outset he cannot realize that. So out of sorts with himself and his surroundings is the poet that what soothes his child and should soothe him, the extreme stillness, "vexes" instead of fosters meditation.

This state of mind both resembles and differs from the recollection of an earlier gazing at another stranger that his idling mind offers up. His present brooding distress is similar to, though perhaps less overtly anguished than, the misery of the Christ's Hospital schoolboy. Early orphaned and packed off to London, he could at that time suspend his wretchedness and loneliness only by dreaming of the soothing pleasures of his "sweet birth-place" and yearning with most believing mind for the advent of a companionable form who might alleviate his present desolation by restoring the bonds of the past:

> Ah me! amus'd by no such curious toys
> Of the self-watching subtilizing mind,
> How often in my early school-boy days
> With most believing superstitious wish,
> Presageful, have I gazed upon the bars,
> To watch the *stranger* there! and oft belike
> With unclosed lids, already had I dreamt
> Of my sweet birth-place, and the old church-tower,
> Whose bells, the poor man's only music, rang
> From morn to evening, all the hot Fair-day,
> So sweetly, that they stirred and haunted me
> With a wild pleasure, falling on mine ear
> Most like articulate sounds of things to come!
> So gazed I, till the soothing things, I dreamt,
> Lulled me to sleep, and sleep prolonged my dreams!
> And so I brooded all the following morn,
> Awed by the stern preceptor's face, mine eye
> Fixed with mock study on my swimming book:
> Save if the door half opened, and I snatched
> A hasty glance, and still my heart leaped up,
> For still I hoped to see the *stranger's* face,
> Townsman, or aunt, or sister more beloved,
> My play-mate when we both were clothed alike![4]

The wistful progression of these last lines, from stranger through acquaintance and relative to sister-playmate recalled from infancy, "when we both were clothed alike," is integral to the structure of the poem, though it might seem at first glance a lapse into sentimentality. For at the end of the series, the companionable form to soothe most fully the schoolboy's desolation is also (like the fluttering film for the mind of the vexed poet) an "echo or mirror . . . of [him]self," the sister recalled as a narcissistic twin from the lost paradise when even sexual differentiation was unperceived. What the schoolboy dreamed of was that other whose affection would constitute a bond of security in an undifferentiated world. Similarly, in Coleridge's contemporary Gothic drama *Osorio*, Maria naively and yearningly protests her father's injunction to love another than Albert: "Were we not / Born on one day, like twins of the same parent? / Nursed in one cradle?[5] For Coleridge, Maria and the schoolchild of "Frost at Midnight" are types of a blameless but pathetic solipsism.

Whatever we may think about Coleridge's interest in such scenes of narcissistic pathos, they are offered in the poems as states of innocence. Such innocence, entailing the forlorn child's resort to superstition as a way of alleviating distress and domesticating the unknown, contrasts with the mood of fantastic playfulness in the adult's "idling Spirit." But the melancholy poet comes to participate in the pleasure of that "most believing superstitious wish" by imagining it through memory. What is absent in space in "This Lime-Tree Bower My Prison" is remote in time in "Frost at Midnight," "lost and gone," as Coleridge would later put it in his definition of elegiac poetry. But both losses are recoverable to the meditative imagination.

The theme of companionable forms shapes the poem throughout. The critical transition to the third movement, when Coleridge turns to address his sleeping son, replicates that moment in school when the dream-fueled expectations of the boy imagined the fulfillment of the stranger's promise in his sister, "my playmate when we both were clothed alike!" But it is a replica with a difference. What worked only momentarily, in dreams, to suspend the schoolboy's misery—we may assume his sister most beloved never materialized at the Christ's Hospital door—is fulfilled in imagined reality for the poet. In a sense, then, the schoolboy's superstitious wish finally comes true when the poet "discovers" his own sleeping infant.

No longer "inmates" in the cottage prison, the poet and his
son are now companionable forms:

> Dear Babe, that sleepest cradled by my side,
> Whose gentle breathings, heard in this deep calm,
> Fill up the interspersèd vacancies
> And momentary pauses of the thought!
> My babe so beautiful! it thrills my heart
> With tender gladness, thus to look at thee,
> And think that thou shalt learn far other lore,
> And in far other scenes! For I was reared
> In the great city, pent 'mid cloisters dim,
> And saw nought lovely but the sky and stars.
> But *thou*, my babe! shalt wander like a breeze
> By lakes and sandy shores, beneath the crags
> Of ancient mountain, and beneath the clouds,
> Which image in their bulk both lakes and shores
> And mountain crags: so shalt thou see and hear
> The lovely shapes and sounds intelligible
> Of that eternal language, which thy God
> Utters, who from eternity doth teach
> Himself in all, and all things in himself.
> Great universal Teacher! he shall mould
> Thy spirit, and by giving make it ask.

He imagines for his son the sort of visionary progress through
the divinely informed natural world that the prisoner-poet
imagines for Charles Lamb in the Quantock landscape in
"This Lime-Tree Bower My Prison." Noteworthy in this
imagined country is that the lakes and sandy shores and mountain crags find *their* companionable forms in the shapes of the
clouds, which in their bulk "image" the topography of the
land beneath. (Coleridge's word here pointedly invokes the
earlier phrase "Echo or mirror seeking of itself.") Moreover,
this world of reflective resonances is itself an image of the Divine, "who from eternity doth teach / Himself in all, and all
things in himself." God, in other words, teaching in nature an
image of himself, will thus shape ("mould") the child as He

has shaped Himself in the world of lakes and crags and clouds. The result is that the spirit so shaped will recapitulate, though in a regenerate way, the action of the poet's idling spirit, "every where / Echo or mirror *seeking* of itself":

> he shall mould
> Thy spirit, and by giving make it *ask*.   [my emphasis]

Such regenerate seeking and asking for companionable forms, which the poet imagines for his son's future, are a projection of Coleridge's own continuing effort at meditative apprehension of oneness with the divine shape of the natural world. Consider, for example, one of the most frequently cited of his notebook entries:

Saturday Night, April 14, 1805—In looking at objects of Nature while I am thinking, as at yonder moon dim-glimmering thro' the dewy window-pane, I seem rather to be seeking, as it were *asking*, a symbolical language for something within me that already and forever exists, than observing any thing new. Even when that latter is the case, yet still I have always an obscure feeling as if that new phaenomenon were the dim Awakening of a forgotten or hidden Truth of my inner Nature. It is still interesting as a Word, a Symbol! It is Logos, the Creator! (and the Evolver!)[6]

In a gesture characteristic of the meditative poems, this quest for an adequate symbology in the natural world, which was the focus of so much of Coleridge's religious and aesthetic philosophy, is displaced onto the poet's companion. In addition to "my gentle-hearted Charles" in "This Lime-Tree Bower My Prison," one thinks of the maiden in "The Nightingale," communing with the glittering eyes of the birds, and of the Lady in "Dejection: An Ode."

A further extension of the companionable-form motif was contained in the original ending of "Frost at Midnight," which readers generally agree is inferior to the revised, abbreviated version ending with the universally admired coda. (According to House, "the decision to stop at line 74 was one of the best decisions Coleridge ever made.")[7] But the original conclusion was not simply unshapely domestic detail, mere spilt Coleridgean emotion:

> Or whether the secret ministry of cold
> Shall hang them up in silent icicles,
> Quietly shining to the quiet moon,
> Like those, my babe! which ere tomorrow's warmth
> Have capp'd their sharp keen points with pendulous
>   drops,
> Will catch thine eye, and with their novelty
> Suspend thy little soul; then make thee shout,
> And stretch and flutter from thy mother's arms
> As thou wouldst fly for very eagerness.[8]

Such fledgling energy points up the difference between Hartley's eagerness and the lassitude of the vexed poet at the beginning. A new companionable form has replaced the stranger: the fluttering of the film in puny flaps and freaks gives way to the child's livelier stretch and flutter. What catches the child's eye is no "sole unquiet thing" flapping on the firegrate in a school-prison but the sharp, keen points of icicles that, themselves hanging, will suspend his soul in a gesture of companionable ecstasy and grace. No doubt Coleridge was right in deciding against these lines, for their intricate extension of the companionable-form theme muted the effect of the "return" to the secret ministry of frost. But the original version serves to remind us that for Coleridge the art of poetry was very much an art of structural ingenuity.

2

The other major motif in "Frost at Midnight," developed with corresponding intricacy, is that of sound and silence, with the metaphor of sound (or, more accurately, sound heard in silence) as a language hovering, in suspension, everywhere. The frost is the master agent of silent ministry. It operates throughout with an artistry that counterpoints the poet's verbal (and, in this conversation poem, oral) work and toward which that work moves and builds—hence the serenity of the coda. This paradox is compounded at the very beginning by the fact that the calm is unsettling,

> so calm, that it disturbs
> And vexes meditation with its strange
> And extreme silentness. Sea, hill, and wood,
> This populous village! Sea, and hill, and wood,
> With all the numberless goings-on of life,
> Inaudible as dreams!

What *should* punctuate for him this stillness, the peaceful breathing of the sleeping infant, does not, as we have seen: instead, what the poet notices as the sole unquiet thing is the stranger. His sympathies with its unquietness lead him to find in it an echo of himself. But an unexpected echo intervenes from his childhood at school. Awareness of disturbing silence, with all the numberless goings-on of life "inaudible as dreams," yields to his memory of other and different dreams, those

> Of my sweet birth-place, and the old church-tower,
> Whose bells, the poor man's only music, rang
> From morn to evening, all the hot Fair-day,
> So sweetly, that they stirred and haunted me
> With a wild pleasure, falling on mine ear
> Most like articulate sounds of things to come!

The stirring in the child of such pleasurable expectations is associated still with dreams, however soothing and inaudible, born of superstitious longing for release from imprisonment; but as Coleridge had already argued in his contribution to Southey's *Joan of Arc*, such most believing wishes play an instrumental role in unsensualizing the mind and are thus types for such release. The release is achieved finally in the poet's mature imagination when the expectation is transferred to his son:

> so shalt thou see and hear
> The lovely shapes and sounds intelligible
> Of that eternal language, which thy God

Utters, who from eternity doth teach
Himself in all, and all things in himself.
Great universal Teacher! he shall mould
Thy spirit, and by giving make it ask.

The extent to which Hartley's education in nature is seen not
as a bucolic vacation but as sacramental discipline parallels the
shift from superstition to meditative faith, which is the principal movement of the poem: the metaphor of the child's God
as the "Great universal Teacher" points to the redemption,
through the effect of the imagined future on the mood of the
present, of time past endured in misery under a "stern preceptor." Through such metaphors as these the language of the
poem is itself articulated into a coherent structure. The shapes
and sounds that proved so vexing in the opening lines are now
intelligible as God's utterance. Typically in Coleridge's meditative poems the release comes with a blessing of another, with
the optative prayer answered in language that achieves a sacramental return to the situation of the opening.

The coda thus emphasizes the currents of reciprocity in the
natural and human worlds that were so lacking at the beginning. As with the solitary bee in "This Lime-Tree Bower My
Prison," there is, in the singing redbreast, a counterpart of the
singing poet, each triumphing over the barrenness of his setting. "The nigh thatch / Smokes in the sun-thaw" as though
offering up incense in gratitude for the sun's warmth; the
eave-drops heard in the trances of the blast (like the infant's
breathing filling up the vacancies and pauses of the poet's
thought) are another instance of a "dear under-song in
clamor's hour," like "the stilly murmur of the distant Sea"
telling of silence, evidence of a continuing process underlying
nature's more immediate and obstreperous sounds. The return,
however, to the entire, though now not disquieting, quiet of
the opening, is probably Coleridge's most masterly stroke, the
stillness of the icicles permitting awareness of the interplay of
reflective energies of light between companionable forms,
each serving as the mirror which the other seeks.

3

Wordsworth's major effort in 1797–1798 was on the poem
known as "The Ruined Cottage" or "The Pedlar," and there
are indications, chiefly in "Frost at Midnight," that Coleridge's enthusiasm for the poem involved him in adaptations of
Wordsworthian expression and situation for his own serious
and playful ends. The third of the "Nehemiah Higginbottom"
sonnets, for example, phrases for which, he disingenuously
asserted, were "borrowed entirely from my own poems," can
also be considered as a genially ribald burlesque of Wordsworth's poem:

On a Ruined House in a Romantic Country

And this reft house is that the which he built,
Lamented Jack! And here his malt he pil'd,
Cautious in vain! These rats that squeak so wild,
Squeak, not unconscious of their father's guilt.
Did ye not see her gleaming thro' the glade?
Belike, 'twas she, the maiden all forlorn.
What though she milk no cow with crumpled horn,
Yet *aye* she haunts the dale where *erst* she stray'd;
And *aye* beside her stalks her amorous knight!
Still on his thighs their wonted brogues are worn,
And thro' those brogues, still tatter'd and betorn,
His hindward charms gleam an unearthly white;
As when thro' broken clouds at night's high noon
Peeps in fair fragments forth the full-orb'd harvest-moon![9]

These lines may be compared with the passage from the end
of "The Ruined Cottage" Coleridge sent to John Prior Estlin
in June 1797:

Yet, ever as there passed
A man, whose garments shewed the Soldier's red,
Or crippled mendicant in Sailor's garb,
The little child, who sat to turn the wheel,
Ceased from his toil, and she, with faultering voice,
Expecting still to learn her husband's fate,

Made many a fond inquiry; and when they,
Whose presence gave no comfort, were gone by,
Her heart was still more sad—And by yon gate
That bars the traveller's road, she often sat,
And if a stranger-horseman came, the latch
Would lift; & in his face look wistfully,
Most happy, if from aught discovered there
Of tender feeling, she might dare repeat
The same sad question—Meanwhile, her poor hut
Sank to decay: for he was gone, whose hand,
At the first nippings of October frost,
Closed up each chink, and with fresh bands of straw
Checquered the green-grown thatch; and so she sat
Through the long winter, reckless and alone,
Till this reft house by frost, and thaw, and rain
Was sapped; and, when she slept, the nightly damps
Did chill her breast, and in the stormy day
Her tattered clothes were ruffled by the wind,
Even by the side of her own fire. Yet still
She loved this wretched spot, nor would for worlds
Have parted hence: and still, that length of road,
And this rude bench one torturing hope endeared,
Fast rooted at her heart; and, Stranger, here
In sickness she remained, and here she died,
Last human tenant of these ruined walls—[10]

In addition to triggering the Higginbottom ribaldry, this same passage—certainly the most powerful and moving in Wordsworth's poem—had an extensive influence on "Frost at Midnight." Margaret's impulsive (and compulsive) questioning of each stranger-horseman passing her gate, in hope that some compassionate face would answer with news to restore her absent husband, has its analogy in the child's troubled yearning for the face of a "stranger" in Coleridge's poem:

And so I brooded all the following morn,
Awed by the stern preceptor's face, mine eyes
Fixed with mock study on my swimming book:
Save if the door half opened, and I snatched

A hasty glance, and still my heart leaped up,
For still I hoped to see the *stranger's* face,
Townsman, or aunt, or sister more beloved,
My play-mate when we both were clothed alike!

Both hopes for the recovery of lost worlds, Margaret's and the schoolboy's, were disappointed. Whereas Wordsworth's emphasis is on the bleak desolation of Margaret's obsessive brooding over irrecoverable loss, however, with Coleridge the expectation is the means, ultimately, through memory, to the alleviation of wretchedness.

We have seen that "Visions of the Maid of Orleans" was in part a response to the powerful pathos of "Adventures on Salisbury Plain"; in a notably similar way, "Frost at Midnight" makes a characteristically wishful adjustment to the unrelieved suffering of this moment in "The Ruined Cottage." The poet's fireside brooding in his midnight cottage is a Coleridgean replica of Margaret's fatal vigil, reckless and alone. In both poems the cottage mirrors the inmate's condition. Margaret's poor hut sinks to decay, its walls unchinked, its thatch neglected, "till this reft house by frost, and thaw, and rain / Was sapped." In Coleridge's superb coda, his cottage becomes the focus of a world alive with benevolent, sacramental energies that, in effect, substitute paradise for ruin. The "frost, and thaw, and rain" of Wordsworth's desolation are for Coleridge's son, as the meditating poet envisions them, the very emblems of imaginative release:

Therefore all seasons shall be sweet to thee,
Whether the summer clothe the general earth
With greenness, or the redbreast sit and sing
Betwixt the tufts of snow on the bare branch
Of mossy apple-tree, while the nigh thatch
Smokes in the sun-thaw; whether the eave-drops fall
Heard only in the trances of the blast,
Or if the secret ministry of frost
Shall hang them up in silent icicles,
Quietly shining to the quiet Moon.

5

Coleridge's "Hymn Before Sun-rise":
Mont Blanc, Mon Frère,
Mon Semblable

How little the Commentators of Milton have availed themselves of the writings of Plato / Milton's Darling! But alas! commentators only hunt out verbal Parallellisms—*numen abest.* I was much impressed with this in all the many Notes on that beautiful Passage in Comus from l. 629 to 641—all the puzzle is to find out what Plant Haemony is—which they discover to be the English Spleenwort—& decked out, as a mere play & licence of poetic Fancy, with all the strange properties suited to the purpose of the Drama—They thought little of Milton's platonizing Spirit—who wrote nothing without an interior meaning. 'Where more is meant, than meets the ear' is true of himself beyond all writers. He was so great a Man, that he seems to have considered Fiction as profane, unless where it is consecrated by being emblematic of some Truth / What an unthinking & ignorant man we must have supposed Milton to be, if without any hidden meaning, he had described [it] as growing in such abundance that the dull Swain treads on it daily—& yet as never *flowering*—Such blunders Milton, of all others, was least likely to commit—Do look at the passage—apply it as an Allegory of Christianity, or to speak more precisely of the Redemption by the Cross—every syllable is full of Light!

COLERIDGE TO WILLIAM SOTHEBY (10 September 1802)

Hymn Before Sun-rise, in the Vale of Chamouni

Hast thou a charm to stay the morning-star
In his steep course? So long he seems to pause
On they bald awful head, O sovran BLANC,
The Arve and Arveiron at thy base
Rave ceaselessly; but thou, most awful Form!   5
Risest from forth thy silent sea of pines,
How silently! Around thee and above
Deep is the air and dark, substantial, black,
An ebon mass: methinks thou piercest it,
As with a wedge! But when I look again,   10
It is thine own calm home, thy crystal shrine,
Thy habitation from eternity!
O dread and silent Mount! I gazed upon thee,
Till thou, still present to the bodily sense,
Didst vanish from my thought: entranced in prayer   15
I worshipped the Invisible alone.

   Yet, like some sweet beguiling melody,
So sweet, we know not we are listening to it,
Thou, the meanwhile, wast blending with my Thought,
Yea, with my Life and Life's own secret joy: 20
Till the dilating Soul, enrapt, transfused,
Into the mighty vision passing—there
As in her natural form, swelled vast to Heaven!

   Awake, my soul! not only passive praise
Thou owest! not alone these swelling tears,   25
Mute thanks and secret ecstasy! Awake,
Voice of sweet song! Awake, my heart, awake!
Green vales and icy cliffs, all join my Hymn.

Thou first and chief, sole sovereign of the Vale!
O struggling with the darkness all the night,   30
And visited all night by troops of stars,
Or when they climb the sky or when they sink:
Companion of the morning-star at dawn,
Thyself Earth's rosy star, and of the dawn
Co-herald: wake, O wake, and utter praise!   35
Who sank thy sunless pillars deep in Earth?
Who filled thy countenance with rosy light?
Who made thee parent of perpetual streams?

And you, ye five wild torrents fiercely glad!
Who called you forth from night and utter death,   40
From dark and icy caverns called you forth,
Down those precipitous, black, jagged rocks,
For ever shattered and the same for ever?
Who gave you your invulnerable life,
Your strength, your speed, your fury, and your joy,   45
Unceasing thunder and eternal foam?
And who commanded (and the silence came),
Here let the billows stiffen, and have rest?

Ye Ice-falls! ye that from the mountain's brow
Adown enormous ravines slope amain—   50
Torrents, methinks, that heard a mighty voice,
And stopped at once amid their maddest plunge!
Motionless torrents! silent cataracts!
Who made you glorious as the Gates of Heaven
Beneath the keen full moon? Who bade the sun   55
Clothe you with rainbows? Who, with living flowers
Of loveliest blue, spread garlands at your feet?—
God! let the torrents, like a shout of nations,
Answer! and let the ice-plains echo, God!
God! sing ye meadow-streams with gladsome voice!   60
Ye pine-groves, with your soft and soul-like sounds!
And they too have a voice, yon piles of snow,
And in their perilous fall shall thunder, God!

Ye living flowers that skirt the eternal frost!
Ye wild goats sporting round the eagle's nest!   65

Ye eagles, play-mates of the mountain-storm!
Ye lightnings, the dread arrows of the clouds!
Ye signs and wonders of the element!
Utter forth God, and fill the hills with praise!

  Thou too, hoar Mount! with thy sky-pointing peaks,   70
Oft from whose feet the avalanche, unheard,
Shoots downward, glittering through the pure serene
Into the depth of clouds, that veil thy breast—
Thou too again, stupendous Mountain! thou
That as I raise my head, awhile bowed low   75
In adoration, upward from thy base
Slow travelling with dim eyes suffused with tears,
Solemnly seemest, like a vapoury cloud,
To rise before me—Rise, O ever rise,
Rise like a cloud of incense from the Earth!   80
Thou kingly Spirit throned among the hills,
Thou dread ambassador from Earth to Heaven,
Great Hierarch! tell thou the silent sky,
And tell the stars, and tell yon rising sun
Earth, with her thousand voices, praises GOD.   85

The next three chapters deal with three poems that, in varying degrees of explicitness, derive from what by all odds was Coleridge's besetting preoccupation as a poet during the period of roughly ten years following his first major successes in a meditative style, "This Lime-Tree Bower My Prison" and "Frost at Midnight." That preoccupation was, to put it simply, Wordsworth. More and more in the years following 1798 an increasingly anxious Coleridge turned to him for support, friendship, and a precarious self-definition. Recent studies of Coleridge have offered a number of views of his relationship with Wordsworth; while these chapters do not propose an extensive analysis of that relationship, in discussing the art that informs the poems I draw on aspects of Coleridge's ideas and feelings about himself and Wordsworth that seem to me to bear on an adequately imaginative reading of them.

1

The most problematic of the three poems is the "Hymn Before Sun-rise in the Vale of Chamouni." I think it calls for the boldest departure from traditional readings. Coleridge's hope that it would eventually gain something of the high admiration readers in his own day accorded to "The Ancient Mariner" and "Christabel" has remained unfulfilled. It would be simplifying subsequent history to say that De Quincey's exposure, two months after Coleridge's death, of the "plagiarism" from Friederika Brun's ode "Chamouny Beim Sonnenaufgange" cast the poem in a shadow from which it has

never emerged, but the fact is that the poem has found few
enthusiastic readers even after much has been done to enhance
appreciation of Coleridge's meditative poetry.[1] Though some
readers today are inclined to make rather less of the plagiarism
charge or, with Adrian Bonjour, to insist on the essential originality of the poem's inspiration despite an indebtedness to
several sources, still it seems generally felt that Coleridge was
not at ease in what Southey might have called a Dutch attempt at Swiss sublimity.[2] Most readers find its stridency un-
interesting and its worshipful posturing uncongenial, if not
actually distasteful. The truth is we like our reverence laid on
less heavily.

In the most extensive and generous appreciation of the
hymn that has yet appeared, Harold Bloom—one of Coleridge's sympathetic readers—uses it as a minor term for comparison with the more exciting powers of Shelley's "Mont
Blanc." He comments that its notorious stridency undoubtedly
stems from the strength with which Coleridge sought to re-
vitalize the modes of Christian orthodoxy in his own poetry:
"To have challenged the poet of Job, as Coleridge comes very
close to doing, on his own prime ground is not an inconsider-
able achievement."[3] For others, the poem is rather less satis-
factory, a reversion, after Coleridge's success in the so-called
conversational mode, to the frenetic pseudo-sublimity of such
earlier efforts as "Religious Musings" and the "deep preluding
strains" of his contribution to *Joan of Arc*, evidence that Coleridge's was at best a minor talent when he strained after the
mode of sublime genius. This chapter is not intended as a
head-on refutation of that verdict, which is in any case partly
a matter of taste. What I hope to establish is that the poem
deserves to be judged in a rather more complicated biographical, psychological, and literary context than has so far been
supposed.

The poem, we can assume, was controversial from the very
start. Wordsworth may have reacted negatively as early as
September 1802, when the original version appeared in the

Morning Post, but it was apparently in reaction to the expanded version published in the 1812 *Friend* that he struck
what has been in effect the keynote for most later readers.
Wordsworth's critique was recalled by Coleridge in a letter
seven years later:

> In a Copy of Verses entitled, "a Hymn before Sunrise in the
> Vale of Chamouny," I described myself under the influence of
> strong devotional feelings gazing on the Mountain till as if it
> had been a Shape emanating from and sensibly representing her
> own essence, my Soul had become diffused thro' "the mighty
> Vision"; and there
>> As in her natural Form, swell'd vast to Heaven.
> Mr. Wordsworth, I remember, censured the passage as strained
> and unnatural, and condemned the Hymn in toto (which never-
> theless I ventured to publish in my "Sibylline Leaves") as a speci-
> men of the Mock Sublime.[4]

Then, in a characteristic way both deferring to and resisting
this censure, Coleridge went on:

> It may be so for others; but it is impossible that I should myself
> find it unnatural, being conscious that it was the image and ut-
> terance of Thoughts and Emotions in which there was no Mock-
> ery. Yet on the other hand I could readily believe that the mood
> and Habit of mind out of which the Hymn rose—that differs
> from Milton's and Thomson's and from the Psalms, the source
> of all three, in the Author's addressing himself to *individual*
> Objects actually present to his Senses, while his great Predeces-
> sors apostrophize *classes* of Things, presented by the Memory
> and generalized by the understanding—I can readily believe, I
> say, that in this there may be too much of what our learned
> Med'ciners call the *Idiosyncratic* for true Poetry.

This is a difficult passage to make sense of, and what follows
is offered as a conjecture. On the one hand Coleridge seems to
be acknowledging that, judged by criteria applicable to Milton, Thomson, and the Psalmists, his own poem was too
closely linked to the immediate and potentially accidental in
his own experience. But he cannot, at the same time, resist

suggesting (partly through his wry phrase "learned Med'-ciners") that such bloodless judgments about the nature of "true poetry" are the technical speciality of critics practicing their own remedial arts. Poems, he implies, are not written by doctors, whose criteria cannot always be easily reconciled with his own intimate experience. While he can formulate a critical indictment of his poem, his own instinct is to defend it against that change. Coleridge said rather similar things about "To William Wordsworth" in 1815 when Wordsworth opposed publication of that poem because of potential embarrassment. At that time, Coleridge had written quickly to reassure his friend: "I wanted no additional reason for it's not being published in my Life Time, than its *personality* respecting myself. . . . It is for the Biographer, not the Poet, to give the *accidents* of *individual* Life. Whatever is not representative, generic, may indeed be poetically exprest, but is not Poetry."[5] Struck there is a familiar Coleridgean note, the self-deprecating reassurance, in the face of criticism, that the poems are indeed more casual than classic, more personal than public. Such self-deprecation he formulated, in the late 1790's, as the equivocal tag, "sermoni propriora," accompanying such poems as "Reflections on Having Left a Place of Retirement" or "Fears in Solitude." The tag might have accompanied each of the poems we are here concerned with. But "sermoni propriora," functions less as a critical instrument than as a psychological hedge; properly seen, it is indicative of the nervous self-effacement W. J. Bate has described so persuasively.[6] Rather than risk flying in the face of public standards and thus incurring the imagined censure of the doctors, he will disavow any claim to innovative self-assertion as a poet.

If this interpretation is plausible in shifting attention from the critical aptness of Coleridge's remarks to their revelation of his own insecure personality, one must also hasten to add that for Coleridge, both "To William Wordsworth" and "Hymn Before Sun-rise," engaged the central issues about meditative verse with which we are properly involved as readers and literary historians. Successful poems are made out of memory and the generalizing understanding and entail a transcending of mere personality: we can recognize here (as M. H. Abrams has suggested) a structure of mental operation notably similar to that defined by traditional religious meditative verse.[7] Wordsworth, too, not accustomed to "make a present joy the matter of my song," characteristically dredged his memory for the alluvial soil of experience. The risk for Coleridge—as for all romantic and postromantic poets—is that in engaging material "actually present to his senses" he will become mired in solipsism and triviality. However spontaneous and natural (and therefore "sincere") such personal poetry is, if its life depends too extensively on accident rather than essence, in the eyes of other readers it can become simply a pathological curiosity (as some of Coleridge's better poems are to many readers), a specimen of idiosyncrasy without relation to the grounds of knowledge of "learned Med'ciners." For "true Poetry," the mere circumstances of personal experience are insufficient.

Coleridge recognized, then, that his mode of meditative poetry in the Hymn constituted a departure from the precedent of Thomson, Milton, and the Psalmists. Still, he could argue, and did, that it was a departure stemming from habits as deep seated as memory itself: "For from my very childhood I have been accustomed to *abstract* and as it were unrealize whatever of more than common interest my eyes dwelt on; and then by a sort of transfusion and transmission of my consciousness to identify myself with the Object." (This statement may remind us of "Frost at Midnight," where the poet's attention is arrested by the fluttering "stranger" on the grate, in which he finds a "companionable form," his spirit everywhere "echo or mirror seeking of itself." "Frost at Midnight" draws more evidently on memory and the generalizing understanding, faculties that take him back to his own childhood and infancy and then forward to the education of his son.)[8]

Coleridge's remarks in this 1819 letter about "addressing an object actually present to his Senses," along with a statement (see below) in 1802 to William Sotheby, lend authority to a good deal of cogent speculation by scholars who have sought to trace the inspiration of the "Hymn Before Sun-rise" to early August 1802, when during a walking trip Coleridge climbed Sca'Fell, one of the highest peaks in the region of the Lakes, or to the end of that month when, reflecting on the trip in conjunction with notebook entries and recollections of descriptions he had sent to Sara Hutchinson, he perhaps read Friederika Brun's Swiss ode. Writing to Sotheby about the poems of William Bowles the day before the hymn was published in *The Morning Post*, he cited the experience of pouring it forth as an illustration of how the "Poet's *Heart* & *Intellect* should be *combined, intimately* combined & *unified* with the great appearances in Nature—& not merely held in solution & loose mixture with them, in the shape of formal Similies":

Bowles has indeed the *sensibility* of a poet; but he has not the *Passion* of a great Poet. His latter Writings all want *native* Passion—Milton here & there supplies him with an appearance of it—but he has no native Passion, because he is not a Thinker—& has probably weakened his Intellect by the haunting Fear of becoming extravagant. . . .

> Poetic Feelings, like the flexuous Boughs
> Of mighty Oaks, yield homage to the Gale,
> Toss in the strong winds, drive before the Gust,
> Themselves one giddy storm of fluttering Leaves;
> Yet all the while, self-limited, remain
> Equally near the fix'd and parent Trunk
> Of Truth & Nature, in the howling Blast
> As in the Calm that stills the Aspen Grove.

That this is deep in our Nature, I felt when I was on Sca'fell—. I involuntarily poured forth a Hymn in the manner of the *Psalms*, tho' afterwards I thought the Ideas &c disproportionate to our humble mountains—& accidentally lighting on a short Note in some swiss Poems, concerning the Vale of Chamouny,

& its Mountain, I transferred myself thither, in the Spirit, & adapted my former feelings to these grander external objects.[9]

My suggestion is that the real purport of these remarks has not been understood. Because his language is so general, and because what I take to be its full significance is only latent in that language, readers have too readily accepted the poem for what, on its face, it appears to be, simply a landscape hymn, celebrating God through the book of *natura naturata*. But in distinguishing himself (implicitly) from Bowles as a *thinking* poet, Coleridge was claiming to be more complicated than a merely sensitive wind instrument "tossing in the strong winds" of influences from the natural world. Adopting his terms, I would propose that his "Hymn Before Sun-rise" is a product of "native Passion" and that, no matter what truth there is to his claim that the occasion of composition was an "involuntary" pouring forth on Sca'Fell, in substance the poem was a deeply thoughtful reflection of the "fixed and parent trunk / Of Truth & Nature." In other words, the poem was not a casual piece of mock-sublime extravagance *anyone* might have tossed off or poured forth, but an imagined experience grounded in Coleridge's own deeply personal concerns. Those concerns were, I think, essentially those of the so-called "Dejection" crisis of the spring and summer of that year, broadly conceived to include personal and literary problems which went back to at least 1800–1801: a combination of domestic discord and anguish involving contemplated separation from his wife and children and the futile attraction to Sara Hutchinson, of precarious health involving (though he could not perceive the connections clearly) increasing narcotic dependency, and of apprehensions about poetic decline. All these were brought to a dreadful focus by his sense of being denied the very grace of strong personal and poetic achievement his idolized rival Wordsworth was so manifestly entering upon in establishing his home at Grasmere. In "On Poesy or Art," Coleridge wrote of the artist's power as that "of humanizing nature, of infusing the thoughts and passions of man into every thing which is the object of his contemplation; color, form, motion, and sound are the elements which it combines, and it stamps them into unity in the mould of a moral idea," and I would argue that it is this very power, working with Coleridge's highly personal concerns, that we see operating in the "Hymn Before Sun-rise."[10]

That such moralized landscapes were not uncongenial to Coleridge's ways as a poet ought to be clear, first of all, simply on the evidence of a poem like "Dejection: An Ode," where, as I. A. Richards and others have argued, schemes of natural imagery and moral analysis are carefully intertwined. Kathleen Coburn, whose insight into the workings of Coleridge's poetic mind is as substantial and resourceful as that of anyone else now writing, has said: "The method of imagination as he sees it and practises it, is a process of self-ordering, of resolution of conflict in the self, of the reconciliation of personal and impersonal, of attachment and detachment, of sameness with difference, in fact of uniting polar opposites as he said. Is he not forging to the end of his life the subjective-objective conjunction or fusion of the forms of space and time in images which articulate experience in that thought-feeling enterprise which is poetry?"[11] Or one might cite the fragment of a letter to Sara Hutchinson, which E. L. Griggs says "must have been written shortly after 10 Aug. 1802," where Coleridge sketches this mental scene: "The black thick Cloud indeed is still over my head, and all the Landscape around me is dark & gloomy with its shadow—but the wind has risen, Darling! it blows this way a strong & steady gale, & I see already with the eye of confident anticipation the laughing blue sky, & no black thick Cloud!"[12]

But the major piece of evidence that points toward a strong personal element in the "Hymn Before Sun-rise" is the latter half of Coleridge's 1819 letter, which has been unaccountably disregarded in discussions of the poem. There, having acknowledged that his "great Predecessors apostrophize *classes* of Things, presented by the memory and generalized by the understanding," he noted he had often thought within the last five or six years

> that if ever I should feel once again the genial warmth and stir of the poetic impulse, and refer to my own experiences, I should venture on a yet stranger & wilder Allegory than of yore—that I would *allegorize* myself, as a Rock with its summit just raised above the surface of some Bay or Strait in the Arctic Sea,
>
> > While yet the stern and solitary Night
> > Brook'd no alternate Sway—
>
> all around me fixed and firm, methought as my own Substance, and near me lofty Masses, that might have seemed to "hold the Moon and Stars in fee" and often in such wild play with meteoric lights, or with the quiet Shine from above which they made rebound in sparkles or dispand in off-shoots and splinters and iridescent Needle-shafts of keenest Glitter, that it was a pride and a place of Healing to lie, as in an Apostle's Shadow, within the Eclipse and deep substance-seeming Gloom of "these dread Ambassadors from Earth to Heaven, Great Hierarchs"! and tho' obscured yet to think myself obscured by consubstantial Forms, based in the same Foundation as my own. I grieved not to serve them—yea, lovingly and with gladsomeness I abased myself in their presence: for they are my Brothers, I said, and the Mastery is theirs by right of elder birth and by right of the mightier strivings of the hidden Fire that uplifted them above me.[13]

As Lamb would have rightly said, this prospectus was only Coleridgizing: no such visionary allegory was ever written. But the plan has interest in its own right as a confession of his poetical situation that illuminates the context of the "Allegory . . . of yore" Coleridge did write. (There seems little reason to doubt that it is the "Hymn Before Sun-rise" this phrase refers to, given the subject of the first part of the letter.) Consider the plan as Coleridge sketches it: he would envision himself as a small eminence, barely higher than the frozen Arctic sea around him, with which he is equally benighted, partly because of the shadows cast by the loftier peaks surrounding. Those peaks themselves, however, partake of the brilliant play of star- and meteor-light and of the calmer moonlight; reflections on their surfaces of these lights are visible from the small eminence as sparkling displays of "off-shoots and splinters and iridescent Needle-shafts of keenest Glitter." Though eclipsed by their greater mass, instead of resentment he feels a kinship with them and a pride in being thus ministered to by them.

This "Allegory" is, I suggest, a landscape fantasy about what Keats, and W. J. Bate after him, call "the burden of the past." The resolution of the problem imposed upon him by the mighty achievements of his predecessors is one that students of Coleridge will recognize as characteristic self-deprecation, tinged with the pathos of assentatious self-fulfillment: "lovingly and with gladsomeness I abased myself in their presence." Bate has recently argued that such abasement—what he calls the "usher" tendency in Coleridge—was a salient trait of Coleridge's intellectual activity.[14] It is, moreover, typical of Coleridge to associate literary anxieties with the language of disease, to identify failed powers with sickness and restoration to health with generous acceptance of the burden of disability and inferiority. Here is a notebook entry from about 1808: "O there are some natures which under the most cheerless, all-threatening, nothing-promising circumstances can draw Hope from the invisible, as the tropical Trees that in the sandy desolation produce their own lidded vessels, full of the waters from Air & Dew! Alas! to my root not a drop trickles down but from the watering-pots of immediate Friends. —And even so it seems much more a sympathy with their feeling rather than Hope of my own."[15] Read in this light, Coleridge's projected allegory of 1819 is what we might expect: pathetically yet eloquently aware of his limitations, he will rejoice in the obscurity to which he is condemned by the brilliant achievement of his poetic betters, in this case no doubt the Psalmists, certainly Milton, perhaps even Thomson.

But even as amateur psychologists we might expect that

there would be a more immediate stimulus for this response, and I think it is impossible to read the "allegory" as a parable of literary relationships without also including the name of Wordsworth, the poet whose example of strength did more than anything else to lead Coleridge to doubt his own capacities. Indeed, the imagery of Coleridge's allegorical sketch reminds one of the conclusion of "To William Wordsworth," where the greater poet is lofted into stellar permanence over a Coleridge set adrift in tide-bound, ephemeral, imitative reflection:

> In silence listening, like a devout child,
> My soul lay passive, by thy various strain
> Driven as in surges now beneath the stars,
> With momentary stars of my own birth,
> Fair constellated foam, still darting off
> Into the darkness; now a tranquil sea,
> Outspread and bright, yet swelling to the moon.[16]

Part of the pathos of the "later" Coleridge, of course, is that such imagery of reflecting surfaces, used so desolatingly to distance himself even farther from the source of light and inspiration, was once, in more promising times, the language with which he envisioned his ability, albeit through an intermediary like his son Hartley, to participate in the One Life of the universe:

> Or if the secret ministry of frost
> Shall hang them up in silent icicles,
> Quietly shining to the quiet Moon.

But if by 1819 the sense of direct involvement in the conversations of love and natural energy in the Almighty's world had failed, the "deep, substance-seeming gloom" shed by his brothers is still a circumstance of solace. For the allegory is not only a parable of literary relationships; the mightier poets of sublimity are celebrated in their devotional activity as "dread Ambassadors from Earth to Heaven, Great Hierarchs!"

The genial warmth and stir of the poetic impulse would move him, he thought in 1819, to an allegory that, following the cue of his citation ("While yet the stern and solitary Night / Brooks no alternate sway"), would have in effect re-created and expanded a passage originally included in his contribution to Southey's *Joan of Arc* (1795) and eventually reprinted as part of *The Destiny of Nations* (1817). That passage was one of the earliest expressions of Coleridgean theodicy, an assertion that superstition and erring fantasy function to lead the "most believing mind" into an openness toward more substantial faith:

> And what if some rebellious, o'er dark realms
> Arrogate power? yet these train up to God,
> And on the rude eye, unconfirmed for day,
> Flash meteor-lights better than total gloom.
> As ere from Lieule-Oaive's vapoury head
> The Laplander beholds the far-off Sun
> Dart his slant beam on unobeying snows,
> While yet the stern and solitary Night
> Brooks no alternate sway, the Boreal Morn
> With mimic lustre substitutes its gleam,
> Guiding his course or by Niemi lake
> Or Balda Zhiok, or the mossy stone
> Of Solfar-kapper, while the snowy blast
> Drifts arrowy by, or eddies round his sledge,
> Making the poor babe at its mother's back
> Scream in its scanty cradle: he the while
> Wins gentle solace as with upward eye
> He marks the streamy banners of the North,
> Thinking himself those happy spirits shall join
> Who there in floating robes of rosy light
> Dance sportively.[17]

In the 1819 allegory, then, the self-abased poet is appropriately obscure because "unconfirmed for day," and the theodicy argued is that of the providential mediation, by mightier poetic spirits, of the "Eclipse and deep substance-seeming Gloom."

The apocalyptic "day" to come, by analogy, is that sublime dazzle evoked in "Religious Musings":

> Believe thou, O my soul,
> Life is a vision shadowy of Truth;
> And vice, and anguish, and the wormy grave,
> Shapes of a dream! The veiling clouds retire,
> And lo! the Throne of the redeeming God
> Forth flashing unimaginable day
> Wraps in one blaze earth, heaven, and deepest hell.[18]

These lines condense in a phrase ("vice, anguish, and the wormy grave") the association of sin, distress, and mortality that was for Coleridge the definitive but illusory disability with which he contended. And the struggle, begun in darkness but moving toward day as in the movement of the 1802 Hymn, was the characteristic solution he pursued, a process of meditative release, typically depending (also as in the Hymn) on the mediating influence of a greater, healing agency.

2

Among those who regard the "Hymn Before Sun-rise in the Vale of Chamouni" with substantial interest, only Adrian Bonjour has seen the poem as a significant document in the psychological and literary life of the poet. His contention, surely accurate, is that the writing and publication of the poem (on September 11, 1802, in the *Morning Post*) are best seen as gestures related to Coleridge's "Dejection crisis." Bonjour, however, invokes the crisis chiefly to explain Coleridge's embarrassing duplicity over the plagiarism from Friederika Brun's poem. Positing in the summer of 1802 a resurgence of interest in poetry and something of a recovery from the crippling despair of the spring, Bonjour argues that

this new atmosphere probably contributed to bring about the impulse which led him to the composition of a new poem. . . . We can suspect that the German poem seemed afterward somewhat obtrusive. If he could not really dismiss it in his own eyes, is it too adventurous to assume that he was tempted to ignore it when he came to publish the "Hymn," so that it should remain unknown to those friends whose opinion was of some weight to him, and whom he wished to feel confident again in his own power?[19]

The point is that Coleridge's use of Brun's ode was a triumph of meditative playfulness over anxiety. Distant Swiss sublimities were more appropriate than local English ones to the kind of poetic fiction Coleridge was intent upon, and Mont Blanc before sunrise made a richer and more oblique setting for the allegory, which, as I conceive it, is an imaginative meditation on his relationship with Wordsworth at a juncture in their personal lives Coleridge was compelled to acknowledge and define. If we bear in mind Coleridge's probable state of mind as he set out on the walking trip during which he allegedly composed the Hymn, we can make some tentative guesses at the nature of the "Thoughts and Emotions in which there was no Mockery" that were imaged and uttered in the Hymn.

In August and September 1802 the friendship of Wordsworth and Coleridge must have seemed to be approaching a crisis, about which Coleridge at least was no doubt apprehensive. It had been through many stages of growth and, for both of them, many trials, stemming largely, one guesses, from Coleridge's need, especially in his unhappy marriage and his deepening opium addiction, for steady evidence of love and esteem and from Wordsworth's own steady wish for independence from such encumbering claims. The months since early winter had seen the friendship sorely tested through Coleridge's mercurial pursuit of Sara Hutchinson's affections (partly no doubt as a way of establishing some safe nexus to the increasingly Edenic Wordsworth ménage at Grasmere) and through Wordsworth's enviable resolve in moving finally to settle the lingering claims of Annette and Caroline Vallon and thus clear the way for marriage to Mary Hutchinson. (Coleridge's Sca'Fell trip coincided, significantly, with the

visit of William and Dorothy to Calais to conclude arrange-
ments with the Vallons.) However dispassionately we may
be inclined, from the perspective of time and psychoanalytic
hypothesis, to regard that upcoming marriage as a move of
premeditated sexual politics undertaken to stabilize passion
(whether deflected from Dorothy or not), it was for Coleridge an act and occasion of consummate importance and one
he was inclined, as various pieces of notebook evidence indicate, to idealize. Since late 1799, Grasmere had been the goal
of his imaginary and actual pedestrian journeys. Dorothy's
journals and his own letters make that plain. He had watched,
with what ambivalent feelings one can guess, while Wordsworth not only made substantial headway on *The Recluse*
("Home at Grasmere" was drafted in 1800 and "The Pedlar"
perfected during the winter of 1801–1802) but also turned
out with impressive rapidity some thirty-odd shorter lyrics,
among them the first stanzas of the "Intimations Ode" and all
of "Resolution and Independence." The evidence indicated
that Wordsworth was emerging, like Mont Blanc, from the
dark night of doubts and personal anxieties that had, at least
to Coleridge's mind, beset him, and that he was entering on a
career of radiant and productive creativity, secure in the
undersong of domestic affections Coleridge likened to the
"still hive at quiet midnight humming."[20]

> The Arve and Arveiron at thy base
> Rave ceaselessly; but thou, most awful Form!
> Risest from forth thy silent sea of pines,
> How silently! Around thee and above
> Deep is the air and dark, substantial, black,
> An ebon mass: methinks thou piercest it,
> As with a wedge! But when I look again,
> It is thine own calm home, thy crystal shrine,
> Thy habitation from eternity!

(In "The Ancient Mariner" a similar moment of yearning
perception of the moon and stars in their heavenly progress
had occasioned for the mariner his release from the burden of

the slain albatross: as Coleridge's prose gloss subsequently put it, "In his loneliness and fixedness he yearneth towards the journeying Moon, and the stars that still sojourn, yet still move onward; and every where the blue sky belongs to them, and is their appointed rest and their native country and their own natural homes, which they enter unannounced, as lords that are certainly expected and yet there is a silent joy at their arrival." Coleridge, we know, was wont to live out the myth of the mariner, and the conjunction of Wordsworth's emerging day and his own darkness in dejection may have seemed one more occasion for such imaginative activity.) Though the idea may seem at first wholly improbable, I want to suggest that, on the analogy of the "still wilder" 1819 allegory, Mont Blanc is a figure for Wordsworth, a "bald awful head" that, in the opening lines of the poem, seems to exercise a mighty sway over the very heavens, to hold (in Coleridge's Miltonic phrase) "the moon and stars in fee":

> Hast thou a charm to stay the morning-star
> In his steep course? So long he seems to pause
> On thy bald awful head, O sovran BLANC.

Bloom has noted, tentatively, elements of anthropomorphism in the Hymn that give the mountain "almost the status of a Miltonic angel, contending against the dark forces of night."[21] But it would be an error, I think, to seek in all the topographical details of the scene vehicles for implicit human—in this case Wordsworthian—tenors. With Coleridge, allegory tends to be both less painstaking and more strenuously inventive than that. Consider, for example, this notebook entry a year and a half previous to the Hymn: "The soil is a deep, rich, dark Mould on a deep Stratum of tenacious Clay, and that on a foundation of Rocks, which often break through both Strata, lifting their back above the Surface. The Trees, which chiefly grow here, are the gigantic Black Oak, Magnolia, Fraxinus excelsior, Platane, & a few stately Tulip Trees.— Bart. p. 36. I applied this by a fantastic analogue & similitude to Wordsworth's Mind. March 26 1801. Fagus exaltata sylvatica."²² In the "Hymn Before Sun-rise," the massive strength and aloof, silent self-possession of the lofty mountain generate in the beholder language instinct with the awed reverence Coleridge, especially in his moments of anxious, generous self-abasement, was inclined to offer Wordsworth.

An implicit temporal structure informs Coleridge's Hymn. The chief narrative event is the emergence of the summit of Mont Blanc from the black of night to the light of day and, then, the progressive downward illumination of the mountain flanks by the sunlight, a light whose direct rays are still denied to the poet watching from the Vale of Chamouny. The Hymn is "before Sun-rise" but not "before dawn," and in fact constitutes a morning hymn in praise of God's works sung by one still himself in the shade of night.²³ Read as an allegorical celebration of Wordsworth's emergent being as poet and husband, two roles Coleridge cherished unavailingly for himself, the revelation, in the direct light of the rising sun, of the manifold energies and beauties of Mont Blanc represents Coleridge's perhaps envious but certainly yearning blessing of the marriage as the event to finally domesticate and humanize, in effect to realize, the sublime austerity of his Friend. (Or, as he addressed Wordsworth in a letter nearly two years after, "the man, for whom I must find another name than Friend, if I call any others but him by the name of Friend."²⁴ The poem is thus, I would suggest, along with the version of "Dejection" also published in the *Morning Post* (three weeks later, on October 4, Wordsworth's wedding day and his own anniversary) an epithalamic gesture.

3

As a morning hymn, the poem has a literary precedent, which Harold Bloom has noted, in the voice of Jehovah speaking out of the whirlwind to Job. Another is that of the Psalmist, especially the singer of Psalms 19 and 148, or that of the canticle Coleridge would have heard as a child hundreds of times at services in Ottery St. Mary and Christ's Hospital, *Benedicite omnia opera*, from the Book of Common Prayer. But in his 1819 letter Coleridge also cited "Milton's Hymn" as an analogy. The best guess, I think, is that he had in mind the morning song of Adam and Eve (*Paradise Lost*, V, 153–209), a "hymn" both Wordsworth and Coleridge would have known not only in the context of the poem they revered beyond all others but also as a famous anthology piece.[25] The presunrise hymn of praise by our first parents, rising from their nuptial bower in prelude to their daily labors in Eden, would have been for Coleridge a moving text by which to measure his sense of Wordsworth's emerging Grasmere paradise:

> Fairest of stars, last in the train of night,
> If better thou belong not to the dawn,
> Sure pledge of day, that crown'st the smiling morn
> With thy bright circlet, praise him in thy sphere
> While day arises, that sweet hour of prime.
> Thou sun, of this great world both eye and soul,
> Acknowledge him thy greater, sound his praise
> In thy eternal course, both when thou climb'st,
> And when high noon hast gained, and when thou
>   fall'st. . . .
> Ye mists and exhalations that now rise
> From hill or steaming lake, dusky or grey,
> Till the sun paint your fleecy skirts with gold,
> In honour to the world's great author rise,
> Whether to deck with clouds the uncoloured sky,
> Or wet the thirsty earth with falling showers,
> Rising or falling still advance his praise.
> His praise ye winds, that from four quarters blow,
> Breathe soft or loud; and wave your tops, ye pines,
> With every plant, in sign of worship wave.
> Fountains and ye, that warble, as ye flow,
> Melodious murmurs, warbling tune his praise.
> [V, 166–196]

Is it too implausible to suggest that Coleridge's lines may have

had a nearer terrain than the Vale of Chamouny for their allegorical locus? ("Now he never was at Chamouni, or near it,
in his life," said Wordsworth in 1844.)[26] And that the sublime
form, the summit of all Europe, should have been a playful
metaphor for his friend?

> Thou first and chief, sole sovereign of the Vale!
> O struggling with the darkness all the night,
> And visited all night by troops of stars,
> Or when they climb the sky or when they sink:
> Companion of the morning-star at dawn,
> Thyself Earth's rosy star, and of the dawn
> Co-herald: wake, O wake, and utter praise!
> Who sank thy sunless pillars deep in Earth?
> Who filled thy countenance with rosy light?
> Who made thee parent of perpetual streams?

The most striking (and most revised) passage in Coleridge's Hymn is the one he recalled, in the 1819 letter, as having particularly drawn Wordsworth's censure: "I described
myself under the influence of strong devotional feelings gazing on the Mountain till as if it had been a Shape emanating
from and sensibly representing her own essence, my Soul had
become diffus'd thro' 'the mighty Vision'; and there 'As in
her natural Form, swell'd vast to Heaven.'" Coleridge then
went on to offer this apology for the passage, which has, I
think, often been misunderstood: "For from my very childhood I have been accustomed to *abstract* and as it were unrealize whatever of more than common interest my eyes dwelt
on; and then by a sort of transfusion and transmission of my
consciousness to identify myself with the Object." In the
Morning Post version this passage ran thus:

> O dread and silent form! I gaz'd upon thee,
> Till thou, still present to my bodily eye,
> Did'st vanish from my thought. Entranc'd in pray'r
> I worshipped the INVISIBLE alone.
> Yet thou, meantime, wast working on my soul,

E'en like some sweet enchanting melody,
So sweet, we know not, we are list'ning to it.

And in revision the lines were expanded to this final version:

O dread and silent Mount! I gazed upon thee,
Till thou, still present to the bodily sense,
Didst vanish from my thought: entranced in prayer
I worshipped the Invisible alone.

Yet, like some sweet beguiling melody,
So sweet we know not we are listening to it,
Thou, the meanwhile, wast blending with my Thought,
Yea, with my Life and Life's own secret joy:
Till the dilating Soul, enrapt, transfused,
Into the mighty vision passing—there
As in her natural form, swelled vast to Heaven!

It is probably impossible to identify behind this language a single Ur-experience that took place on the slopes of Sca'Fell in August, 1802. It is true, according to a letter to Sara Hutchinson, that at one point in the descent from the summit, during a particularly harrowing passage when Coleridge felt himself foolishly and helplessly trapped on a series of ledges, he lapsed into a kind of visionary state:

My Limbs were all in a tremble—I lay upon my Back to rest myself, & was beginning according to my Custom to laugh at myself for a Madman, when the sight of the Crags above me on each side, & the impetuous Clouds just over them, posting so luridly & so rapidly northward, overawed me / I lay in a state of almost prophetic Trance & Delight—& blessed God aloud, for the powers of Reason & the Will, which remaining no Danger can overpower us![27]

But if the prayerful trance in the Hymn had its genesis in this triumph of "Reason & the Will" over the potential terror of Coleridge's Sca'Fell plight, it is a far different utterance in a substantially altered context. The Sca'Fell letter suggests no mediating presence of the mountain nor any striking process

of visionary "identification" with the mountain that prepares
the experience of exultation. In all versions of the Hymn that
experience of entranced self-projection and blending with
the mountain's huge shape serves as a transition leading the
poet from the blank, awed sense of darkness and silence associated with the dread of the sublime to the sense of a joyous,
mediated participation in the fully uttered worship of the
natural universe. We may compare the experience to Coleridge's description of the stranger in the *Sibylline Leaves*
(1828) version of "Frost at Midnight":

> Methinks, its motion in this hush of nature
> Gives it dim sympathies with me who live,
> Making it a companionable form,
> To which the living spirit in our frame,
> That loves not to behold a lifeless thing,
> Transfuses its own pleasures, its own will.

Paraphrasing a notebook passage, Kathleen Coburn argues
that with Coleridge "images must fuse, melt, dim, and unfix
themselves, fused by an energy that has more than the cerebral at stake, that is concerned with knowledge not merely as
percepts and concepts but knowledge as emotive, as animat-
ing, as power." Part of the long passage she then cites speaks
of "the worth & dignity of poetic Imagination, of the fusing
power, that fixing unfixes & while it melts & bedims the
Image, still leaves in the Soul its living meaning."[28] The similarity of this language to that of the identification passage in
its expanded version suggests that Coleridge shaped the moment in the poem as an experience of imaginative activity.

In the poem, that moment coincides, apparently (though
the scheme of verb tenses, shifting from narrative present to
past and back once more to present, is obscure at this point),
with the uncanny transition from the absolute blackness of
night to the first intimations, brought with the morning star,
of the rosy hue of dawn. The earnest of day and life in that
transition mediates for the poet—and for the mountain, "strug-

gling with the darkness all the night"—the dreadful isolation
and desolation of the night.

Coleridge's controversial "identification" passage presents
further evidence of his propensity for reimagining a Miltonic
situation so as to elicit from it subtle resonance and informing
significance for his own verse. The passage has its chief inspiration in Adam's account to Raphael of his creation, when
he recalls how, led into Eden and given dominion over the
beasts, he had pursued God boldly and presumptuously about
his need for a companion and mate. God, testing Adam's
faith and insight into his condition, counters with the example
of His own solitude; whereupon Adam, humbly but still with
the license of boldness, responds that Man is by nature deficient, as God is not, and therefore seeks "By conversation
with his like to help / Or solace his defects." God then praises
Adam's self-knowledge, declaring:

> I, ere thou spak'st
> Knew it not good for Man to be alone,
> And no such company as then thou sawest
> Intended thee, for trial only brought,
> To see how thou couldst judge of fit and meet:
> What next I bring thee shall please thee, be assur'd,
> Thy likeness, thy fit help, thy other self,
> Thy wish, exactly to thy heart's desire.   [VIII, 444–451]

Adam's narrative is one of those striking passages in *Paradise
Lost* when Milton, depicting man conversing with God, is
concerned to preserve, even if somewhat cumbersomely, human initiative and strength in the face of divine omnipotence
and omniscience. The strain of presenting his case takes its
toll of Adam, however, and what follows is the moment in
Adam's reminiscence when, exhausted by the effort of conversation with God, he collapses as in a trance:

> He ended, or I heard no more, for now
> My earthly by his heavenly overpowered,
> Which it had long stood under, strained to the highth

> In that celestial colloquy sublime,
> As with an object that excels the sense,
> Dazzled and spent, sunk down, and sought repair
> Of sleep, which instantly fell on me, called
> By nature as in aid, and closed mine eyes.
> Mine eyes he closed, but open left the cell
> Of fancy my internal sight, by which
> Abstract as in a trance methought I saw,
> Though sleeping, where I lay, and saw the shape
> Still glorious before whom awake I stood,
> Who stooping opened my left side, and took
> From thence a rib, with cordial spirits warm,
> And life-blood streaming fresh.   [VIII, 452–467][29]

Out of Adam's sublime trance is born, in Milton's words, "Thy likeness, thy fit help, thy other self, / Thy wish, exactly to thy heart's desire"; awaking to find his dream true, Adam finds the fit counterpart of himself, what his spirit had been yearning for, in Eve, a Creature

> so lovely fair,
> That what seemed fair in all the world, seemed now
> Mean, or in her summed up, in her contained
> And in her looks, which from that time infused
> Sweetness into my heart, unfelt before,
> And into all things from her air inspired
> The spirit of love and amorous delight.   [VIII, 471–477]

Out of the yearning struggle with the Almighty, Adam is vouchsafed an "other self," a double in the world, a counterpart to supply his sense of incompleteness and bring his situation into an approximation of God's.

Such moments of narcissistic fulfillment appealed to Coleridge. We have other evidence in the lines of "Frost at Midnight" where the poet recalls his loneliness at Christ's Hospital and his yearning for the visit of "Townsman, or aunt, or sister more beloved, / My playmate when we both were clothed alike!" and in *Osorio*, when Maria voices her fidelity to Albert, "Were we not born on one day / Nursed in one

cradle?" And that Coleridge had this part of Milton's Eden
story in mind at the time we may infer from a contemporary
poem, "To Matilda Betham" (which he quoted in the letter
to Sotheby cited above) where, playfully celebrating Matilda
Betham's poetic gifts, Coleridge proposes that

> The Almighty, having first composed a Man,
> Set him to music, framing Woman for him,
> And fitted each to each, and made them one!
> And 'tis my faith, that there's a natural bond
> Between the female mind and measured sounds.

The association here of a "sweet enchanting melody" and the
creation of a visionary counterpart is also part of the landscape experience of the "Hymn Before Sun-rise," where the
poet imagines that his soul has found *"her* natural form" (my
emphasis) in the mountain. But if Coleridge explores his situation, by analogy, as Adam's, moving through sublime colloquy and trance to visionary satisfaction, he may also be
using that analogy, as I have suggested, to address himself to
Wordsworth, and especially to the occasion of marrying
Mary Hutchinson. The appropriateness of Coleridge's adaptation of the "trance" passage from *Paradise Lost* is illuminated if we recall Adam's account to Raphael, just after the
narrative of his trance, of leading the woman to the nuptial
bower:

> I led her blushing like the morn: all heaven,
> And happy constellations on that hour
> Shed their selectest influence; the earth
> Gave sign of gratulation, and each hill;
> Joyous the birds; fresh gales and gentle airs
> Whispered it to the woods, and from their wings
> Flung rose, flung odours from the spicy shrub,
> Disporting, till the amorous bird of night
> Sung spousal, and bid haste the evening star
> On his hill top, to light the bridal lamp. [VIII, 511–520]

Seen in the allegorical light created out of these passages in

Milton, the "Hymn Before Sun-rise" is more obviously in keeping with the familiar pattern of Coleridge's meditative poems. To address Mont Blanc and to celebrate its living nature in an adaptation of Adam's experience of the spousal mediation of his sublime vacancy is to offer, simultaneously, a gesture of blessing toward his friend on the eve of his wedding. (That Wordsworth, in the section of *The Recluse* known as "Home at Grasmere," also likened himself to Adam and his poetic situation to that of a spousal consummation with nature may have provided Coleridge with the impetus his analogical mind wanted.) It is a gesture that permits him, again momentarily as in "Dejection: An Ode" (and as in "To William Wordsworth" four years later), to shed the burden of his own personal distress and to participate imaginatively in the bliss he wished for his friend.

The cost of that momentary easing of distress, though strictly speaking incalculable, was no doubt great. Geoffrey Hartman has recently emphasized, in connection with the "Hymn Before Sun-rise," how intimately connected in Coleridge are the impulse to the sublime and the process of sublimating anxiety through self-sacrifice.[30] The stridency in the poem, which resonates with momentary efforts at sublimity in "Dejection: An Ode" (the poem we turn to next), can be seen as an aspect of the exhausting effort involved in attempting over the years to transcend his own feelings of rivalry with his friend Wordsworth, just as the loving and gladsome self-abasement in the company of greater poetic brethren in the allegory he projected in 1819 can be seen as generosity achieved at the cost of his own need for self-assertion. We should not ignore the stridency, nor should we imagine that if he had written that parable of the rocks as a poem, it would have been any less strident than the "Hymn Before Sun-rise": too long a sacrifice makes a stone of the heart. What I wish to emphasize again, however, is the resourcefulness Coleridge was capable of in elaborating such meditative fantasies. If the 1802 Hymn remains a minor achievement, its context in Coleridge's personal history suggests again the importance, in interpreting his meditative poems, of seeing his analogical propensities at work as they inform his personal experience with a rich literary tradition.

4

Coleridge, the emerging Sage of Highgate, heard in June 1820 the devastating and mortifying news that his son Hartley was to be refused a permanent fellowship at Oriel College, Oxford, because of charges of "culpable intemperance" and inattention to college duties during his year as a probationary fellow. (The statements and correspondence relating to the controversy that ensued are assembled in the fifth volume of E. L. Griggs' edition of the *Collected Letters*.) Through the summer and fall Coleridge became a whirlwind of frenetic activity in support of Hartley's efforts to have the blow softened or to have himself reinstated. Two letters he wrote in October are of particular interest here. They provide a curious sidelight on his defense of the "Hymn Before Sun-rise," and, at least in the inferences one is tempted to draw from them, place both the writing and the defense of that poem in a revealing psychological light.

One letter was written by Coleridge to be presented to the fellows of Oriel as Hartley's own; the second was signed and sent by Coleridge himself as a father's intercession on behalf of his son's maligned character. Immediately striking about these letters, in the context of our discussion of the "Hymn Before Sun-rise," is the profile they offer of Hartley, virtually a facsimile of the self-portrait Coleridge had sketched in the 1819 letter, when, defending his poem against Wordsworth's censure, he declared: "From my very childhood I have been accustomed to *abstract* and as it were unrealize whatever of more than common interest my eyes dwelt on; and then by a sort of transfusion and transmission of my consciousness to identify myself with the Object." Here is the father's tale Coleridge wrote to the Oriel fellows:

You will not, I trust, regard it as an impertinent or useless interference, if I lay before you what I myself know of Hartley Coleridge's Habits and Dispositions, (I might say, of his Nature) previously to his last term at Oriel. . . . From his earliest he had an absence of any contra-distinguishing Self, any conscious "I," that struck every one, the most unobserving, & which I never saw in the same *degree* in any other instance. . . . There was in this case no semblance produced by accident of language, or the more than usually prolonged habit of speaking in the third person, of himself & others indifferently, but a seemingly constitutional insensibility to the immediate impressions on the senses, & the necessity of having them generalized into *thoughts*, before they had an interest, or even a distinct place, in his Consciousness. . . . [Coleridge then goes on to defend Hartley against imputations of "Pharisaic Pride."] The same measuring of act and deed by the abstract rule of Right, without adverting to the frequency of still wider deviations in others . . . [that] was the result of religious Discipline, & profound meditation in [the Protestant Divines], is in him *Nature*—for by what other word can I express a quality or character prominent from earliest childhood? the germ of which disclosed itself even in earliest Infancy. . . . The little fellow never shewed any excitement at the *thing*, whatever it was, but afterwards, often when it had been removed, smiled or capered on the arm as at the *thought* of it. . . . And to this habit of being absent to the present, often indeed from the reverse extreme, and still oftener from eagerness of reasoning, & exclusive attention to mental acts or impressions, but not seldom from a mere absorption of the active powers, a seeming entire suspension of all distinct Consciousness—I intreat your attention with peculiar anxiety—. . . . And even up to the present year no one can have been intimate with him without having occasionally seen him, sometimes in abstraction, but of late more frequently in eagerness of conversation, eating fruit, or bread, or whatever else was before [him], utterly unconscious of what he was doing, or repeatedly filling his glass from the Water-bottle—for his friends were so well aware of this, that they either recalled his attention to what he was doing, or putting the Water by him silently, counted the times, in order to impress him afterwards with the unbecomingness & even danger of these fits of absence—.[31]

In the context of such self-portraiture it is more than a little ironic that, with his unacknowledged authorship of the other letter he wrote to the Oriel fellows, Coleridge thus consigned Hartley to the role of plagiarist he himself had so often played. In the fervent rationality of that letter, moreover, one can hear, without I think straining for the analogy, instead of Hartley defending himself against charges of intemperance, his father defending himself against charges of indulgence in opium:

I here, secondly, protest against the charge of *frequent* acts of Intoxication, if by the word frequent more than two or at the utmost three single instances be meant; and declare that I am permitted by my conscience to admit the truth even of so many, only as far as by intoxication a culpable degree of Intemperance be understood, and not if by intoxication a temporary deprivation of my mental & bodily faculties, such as we commonly mean to express when we say that a man is thoroughly *drunk*.[32]

Indeed, such similitudes between father and son seem to spring up often in the letter he wrote for Hartley. A solemn protest, for example, against the inferences drawn from his nonattendance at Morning Chapel begins to sound like Coleridge's own exculpations of his failure to produce writings when promised. The crowning irony of the ghost-letter, however, is in the parting asseveration: "If in the pursuit of this end I have in any word or sentence transgressed the limits of mere self-defence, I disclaim the same—& subscribe [MS. breaks off thus]."

The Hartley Coleridge letters are not, of course, the only instance in his father's life when the defense of another becomes an *apologia pro vita sua*, though surely the directing of such good offices toward the companionable form of his son is a gesture readers of "Frost at Midnight" can appreciate for its particular poignance.[33] Coleridge was never more himself than when he was moved, as he said, to "*abstract* and as it were unrealize whatever of more than common interest my eyes dwelt on; and then by a sort of transfusion and transmission of my consciousness to identify myself with the Object." He keeps putting us in the situation of the fellows of Oriel, to whom he wrote, "I intreat your attention with peculiar anxiety."

6

"Dejection: An Ode":
The Old Moon's Effluence

I ought to say for my own sake that on the 4th of April last I wrote you a letter in verse; but I thought it dull & doleful—& did not send it—

CoLERIDGE TO THOMAS POOLE (7 May 1802)

Dejection: An Ode

> Late, late yestreen I saw the new Moon,
> With the old Moon in her arms;
> And I fear, I fear, my Master dear!
> We shall have a deadly storm.
> *Ballad of Sir Patrick Spence*

I

Well! If the Bard was weather-wise, who made
  The grand old ballad of Sir Patrick Spence,
  This night, so tranquil now, will not go hence
Unroused by winds, that ply a busier trade
Than those which mould yon cloud in lazy flakes,   5
Or the dull sobbing draft, that moans and rakes
Upon the strings of this Æolian lute,
    Which better far were mute.
  For lo! the New-moon winter-bright!
  And overspread with phantom light,   10
    (With swimming phantom light o'erspread
    But rimmed and circled by a silver thread)
I see the old Moon in her lap, foretelling
  The coming-on of rain and squally blast.
And oh! that even now the gust were swelling,   15
  And the slant night-shower driving loud and fast!
Those sounds which oft have raised me, whilst they awed,
    And sent my soul abroad,
Might now perhaps their wonted impulse give,
Might startle this dull pain, and make it move and live!   20

II

A grief without a pang, void, dark, and drear,

A stifled, drowsy, unimpassioned grief,
Which finds no natural outlet, no relief,
      In word, or sigh, or tear—
O Lady! in this wan and heartless mood,   25
To other thoughts by yonder throstle woo'd,
      All this long eve, so balmy and serene,
Have I been gazing on the western sky,
      And its peculiar tint of yellow green:
And still I gaze—and with how blank an eye!   30
And those thin clouds above, in flakes and bars,
That give away their motion to the stars;
Those stars, that glide behind them or between,
Now sparkling, now bedimmed, but always seen:
Yon crescent Moon, as fixed as if it grew   35
In its own cloudless, starless lake of blue;
I see them all so excellently fair,
I see, not feel, how beautiful they are!

                    III
      My genial spirits fail;
      And what can these avail   40
To lift the smothering weight from off my breast?
      It were a vain endeavour,
      Though I should gaze for ever
On that green light that lingers in the west:
I may not hope from outward forms to win   45
The passion and the life, whose fountains are within.

                    IV
O Lady! we receive but what we give,
And in our life alone does Nature live:
Ours is her wedding garment, ours her shroud!
      And would we aught behold, of higher worth,   50
Than that inanimate cold world allowed
To the poor loveless ever-anxious crowd,
      Ah! from the soul itself must issue forth
A light, a glory, a fair luminous cloud
      Enveloping the Earth—   55

And from the soul itself must there be sent
　A sweet and potent voice, of its own birth,
Of all sweet sounds the life and element!

v

O pure of heart! thou need'st not ask of me
What this strong music in the soul may be!　　　　　　60
What, and wherein it doth exist,
This light, this glory, this fair luminous mist,
This beautiful and beauty-making power.
　Joy, virtuous Lady! Joy that ne'er was given,
Save to the pure, and in their purest hour,　　　　　　65
Life, and Life's effluence, cloud at once and shower,
Joy, Lady! is the spirit and the power,
Which wedding Nature to us gives in dower
　A new Earth and new Heaven,
Undreamt of by the sensual and the proud—　　　　　　70
Joy is the sweet voice, Joy the luminous cloud—
　　We in ourselves rejoice!
And thence flows all that charms or ear or sight,
　All melodies the echoes of that voice,
All colours a suffusion from that light.　　　　　　75

vi

There was a time when, though my path was rough,
　This joy within me dallied with distress,
And all misfortunes were but as the stuff
　Whence Fancy made me dreams of happiness:
For hope grew round me, like the twining vine,　　　　80
And fruits, and foliage, not my own, seemed mine.
But now afflictions bow me down to earth:
Nor care I that they rob me of my mirth;
　　But oh! each visitation
Suspends what nature gave me at my birth,　　　　　　85
　My shaping spirit of Imagination.
For not to think of what I needs must feel,
　But to be still and patient, all I can;
And haply by abstruse research to steal
　From my own nature all the natural man—　　　　　90
　This was my sole resource, my only plan:

Till that which suits a part infects the whole,
And now is almost grown the habit of my soul.

VII

Hence, viper thoughts, that coil around my mind,
   Reality's dark dream!   95
I turn from you, and listen to the wind,
   Which long has raved unnoticed. What a scream
Of agony by torture lengthened out
That lute sent forth! Thou Wind, that rav'st without,
   Bare crag, or mountain-tairn, or blasted tree,   100
Or pine-grove wither woodman never clomb,
Or lonely house, long held the witches' home,
   Methinks were fitter instruments for thee,
Mad Lutanist! who in this month of showers,
Of dark-brown gardens, and of peeping flowers,   105
Mak'st Devils' yule, with worse than wintry song,
The blossoms, buds, and timorous leaves among.
   Thou Actor, perfect in all tragic sounds!
Thou mighty Poet, e'en to frenzy bold!
    What tell'st thou now about?   110
    'Tis of the rushing of an host in rout,
   With groans, of trampled men, with smarting wounds—
At once they groan with pain, and shudder with the cold!
But hush! there is a pause of deepest silence!
   And all that noise, as of a rushing crowd,   115
With groans, and tremulous shudderings—all is over—
   It tells another tale, with sounds less deep and loud!
    A tale of less affright,
    And tempered with delight,
As Otway's self had framed the tender lay,—   120
    'Tis of a little child
    Upon a lonesome wild,
Not far from home, but she hath lost her way:
And now moans low in bitter grief and fear,
And now screams loud, and hopes to make her mother hear.   125

VIII

'Tis midnight, but small thoughts have I of sleep:
Full seldom may my friend such vigils keep!

Visit her, gentle Sleep! with wings of healing,
  And may this storm be but a mountain-birth,
May all the stars hang bright above her dwelling,   130
    Silent as though they watched the sleeping Earth!
      With light heart may she rise,
      Gay fancy, cheerful eyes,
  Joy lift her spirit, joy attune her voice;
To her may all things live, from pole to pole,   135
Their life the eddying of her living soul!
  O simple spirit, guided from above,
Dear Lady! friend devoutest of my choice,
Thus mayest thou ever, evermore rejoice.

"Dejection," Coleridge's most famous meditative poem, raises once more the complex issues at the intersection of personality and art we have been tracing. The blank-verse version of April 1802, a letter addressed to Sara Hutchinson, has been called an incomparably greater poem than that published in the *Morning Post* six months later (on the day of Wordsworth's wedding) or than the somewhat further altered version included in *Sibylline Leaves*, chiefly on grounds of its being a less disguised personal lament over marital unhappiness, ill-health, and weakened poetic power. But there are also readers who prefer the final, shorter ode form for its greater lyric dignity and who find the sprawling earlier text embarrassing in its self-pity. One might characterize the disagreement since the publication of the letter version in 1927 as a conflict between those who like confessional sincerity in art and those whose inclination is for the orderliness of form. No one has carried the former view further than Beverly Fields, whose *Reality's Dark Dream* focuses on the letter as an instance not only of confessional honesty but also, and primarily, of subconscious expression accessible only to the instruments of psychoanalysis. And many readers on both sides of the issue have noted that the versions published in Coleridge's lifetime reflect the strain of suppressing potentially embarrassing personal elements: they emphasize the *lacunae* in logic that result when the sequence of the original poem is altered to produce the shapelier ode. (The chief instance of such a problem is the perplexing transition in the ode from the de-jected self-analysis of stanza six to the account of the wind in stanza seven.)[1]

The evidence points to the conclusion that Coleridge regarded the final version not primarily as a confession of lost poetic power or as a public farewell, for reasons partly concealed, to health, happiness, and creativity but as an epithalamic gesture, like the "Hymn Before Sun-rise," offered to reassure the Grasmere circle that he was capable of transcending the impulses toward despair and unseemliness that were so much responsible for the original letter and for the disturbing conduct, whatever it was, that precipitated that letter. In emphasizing the elements of personal distress discernible in and through the poem and in seeing it as a lament over suspended poetic imagination, readers in our time have done what they so frequently have in reading the major romantic writers: they have presumed a greater continuity than actually exists between the concerns of a poet like Coleridge, at the turn of the nineteenth century, and the characteristic preoccupation of many twentieth-century writers with alienation, self-doubt, and distrust of the artful imagination.

1

The goal of my reading in this chapter is to describe and interpret in the final version of "Dejection: An Ode" what Coleridge might have called the order of imitation—in other words to arrive at some description of the "general" and "universal" in the poem—and thus to argue that the poem was not merely the result of a purging of emotion in the interests of discretion. To deplore, for the sake of confessional sincerity, the imposition of form as a falsifying of actual behavior and experience is to misconstrue the processes of conscious (and unconscious) self-expression. In the preface to his 1796 *Poems* Coleridge argued for a salutary egotism in poetic composition, contending that "the communicativeness of our nature leads us to describe our sorrows" and that from this exerted intellectual activity "a pleasure results which is gradually associ-

ated and mingles as a corrective with the painful subject of the
description."[2] As we have seen, Coleridge thought that such
egotistic conversation could be heuristic, especially in the
heightened order of verse, and that the discovery toward
which the poet won his difficult way was not only intellectual
comprehension of the distress but also release of the mind's
processive energies, the life that opposed the death-in-life of
melancholy solipsism. About a year after publishing "Dejection: An Ode" in the *Morning Post*, Coleridge explored the
old ground of his 1796 preface in a notebook entry that has
the excitement of fresh recognition: "One excellent use of
communication of Sorrows to a Friend is this: that in relating
what ails us we ourselves first know exactly what the real
Grief is—& see it for itself, in its own form & limits. Unspoken
Grief is a misty medley, of which the real affliction only plays
the first fiddle—blows the horn, to a scattered mob of obscure
feelings." Though the remark emphasizes how communication leads one to articulate and focus what is otherwise scattered and dim, when it is read in conjunction with another
notebook entry almost immediately following, we can see that
Coleridge is also centrally concerned with the pleasurable activity resulting from such effort at meditative consciousness.
Analysis and creative release work hand in hand to alleviate
the initial wretchedness:

Some painful Feeling, bodily or of the mind / some form or
feeling has recalled a past misery to the Feeling, & not to the
conscious memory—I brood over what has befallen of evil /
what is the worst that could befall me? What is that Blessing
which is most present & perpetual to my Fancy & Yearnings?
Sara! Sara!—The Loss then of this first bodies itself out to me /
—& if I have not heard from you very recently, & if the last letter had not happened to be full of explicit Love & Feeling, then
I conjure up Shadows into Substances—& am miserable / Misery
conjures up other Forms, & binds them into Tales & Events—
activity is always Pleasure—the Tale grows pleasanter—& at length

you come to me / you are by my bed side, in some lonely Inn, where I lie deserted—there you have found me—there you are weeping over me!—Dear, dear, Woman![3]

This entry has affinities with the sequence of expression in the variously interpreted seventh stanza of the ode. Those affinities suggest the possibility that the entire poem ought to be read in much the same context of moral theodicy that informs others of Coleridge's meditative poems, a context governing progress from confusion and distress to willed resolution. In discussing "This Lime-Tree Bower My Prison," I argued for the relevance to that poem of two letters Coleridge wrote in 1821, in which he described meditation as an instrument for attaining "comforts and consolations," especially in situations of mental distress. These letters, published in *Blackwood's Magazine* as "Letters to a Junior Soph," contain a passage that, in the context of the notebook material just cited, illuminates the experience presented in "Dejection."

We imagine the presence of what we desire in the very act of regretting its absence, nay, *in order* to regret it the more livelily; but, while, with a strange wilfulness, we are thus engendering grief on grief, nature makes use of the product to cheat us into comfort and exertion. The positive shapings, though but of the fancy, will sooner or later displace the mere knowledge of the negative. All activity is in itself pleasure; and according to the nature, powers, and previous habits of the sufferer, the activity of the fancy will call the other faculties of the soul into action. The self-contemplative power becomes meditative, and the mind begins to play the geometrician with its own thoughts—abstracting from them the accidental and the individual, till a new and unfailing source of employment, the best and surest nepenthe of solitary pain, is opened out in the habit of seeking the principle and ultimate aim in the most imperfect productions of art, in the least attractive products of nature.[4]

As in "Frost at Midnight," in "Dejection: An Ode" the progress enacted is from voicing distress, by uneasy and fanciful toying with a superstitious belief, to discerning how the terms of that superstition and the imagery associated with them can sustain a different and more substantial creed. In no other meditative poem besides "Frost at Midnight" does imagery concerned with the eddying energies of the natural world work with more subtle or ingenious cogency. That imagery and what has, somewhat misleadingly, been called the controlling metaphor of the poem—the storm—warrant close attention.

The most remarkable image is, certainly, that of the moon in the opening stanza:

> Well! If the Bard was weather-wise, who made
>   The grand old ballad of Sir Patrick Spence,
>   This night, so tranquil now, will not go hence
> Unroused by winds, that ply a busier trade
> Than those which mould yon cloud in lazy flakes,
> Or the dull sobbing draft, that moans and rakes
> Upon the strings of this Æolian lute,
>   Which better far were mute.
>   For lo! the New-moon winter-bright!
> And overspread with phantom light,
>   (With swimming phantom light o'erspread
>   But rimmed and circled by a silver thread)
> I see the old Moon in her lap, foretelling
>   The coming-on of rain and squally blast.
> And oh! that even now the gust were swelling,
> And the slant night-shower driving loud and fast!
> Those sounds which oft have raised me, whilst they awed,
>   And sent my soul abroad,
> Might now perhaps their wonted impulse give,
> Might startle this dull pain, and make it move and live!

Coleridge's attention, both here and in the epigraph from the "Ballad of Sir Patrick Spence," to the lore of superstition introduces a mood of uneasy reflection (like that at the opening of "Frost at Midnight" or "This Lime-Tree Bower My Prison") in words that, as Donald Davie has observed, "slide down a long scale of emotion from something not far short of geniality to a desperate melancholy."[5] At the outset, then, the

state of dejection is associated with half-facetious receptivity
to bardic superstition and with a desire for a violent consummation to rouse the spirit from without. And yet, for all the
resemblances to the mood of "fantastic playfulness" besetting
the poet in "Frost at Midnight" as he settles down to meditate,
the poet's distress here seems more acute, more massive, more
extreme. Even more striking, therefore, than the attention to
the fluttering "stranger" on the grate in that earlier poem is
the description of the moon, which also goes far beyond the
ballad's brief "I saw the new Moon / With the old Moon in
her arms." In the elaborate *chiasmus* of lines 10–11, the "phantom light" spread over the "old" moon (that part of the moon
turned toward the earth but not illuminated by the sun's direct rays) is what I. A. Richards has called "earth-light," the
shining on the moon's surface of rays of sunlight reflected
from the earth. Richards several years ago suggested what is
surely the unstated thematic appropriateness of the image: in
our perception of the "phantom" earth-light swimming over
the moon's shadowy surface, we are in effect receiving what
we give.[6] Correspondingly, the bright crescent reflects onto
the surface of the earth what we call moonlight; both lights
are, of course, derived from the sun. In the context of the natural and cosmic imagery in "The Ancient Mariner" and the
other meditative poems we have considered these eddying
streams of moonlight and earthlight, each with its ultimate
source in the sun, announce at the outset, proleptically, the
values of a moralized Coleridgean Neoplatonism: a pervasive,
continuous flow of divine energy and solicitude.[7] Though the
poet's voice attends with nervous jocularity to a superstition,
his description of the emblem of that very superstition anticipates, as Richards suggested, the thematic core of the entire
poem.

> Ah! from the soul itself must issue forth
> A light, a glory, a fair luminous cloud
> Enveloping the Earth—

186 *Coleridge's Meditative Art*

And from the soul itself must there be sent
A sweet and potent voice, of its own birth,
Of all sweet sounds the life and element!

(The link between this passage and the initial moon-image is confirmed in line 10 of the April 4, 1802 manuscript, where Coleridge originally wrote "All-suffus'd" before cancelling it with "overspread"; in all versions of the poem the long passage elaborating "a light, a glory, a fair luminous cloud" includes the line "All colours a suffusion from that light.")[8]

In the first version of the poem the initial description of the moon (with the ballad phrase of the epigraph, "the old Moon in her arms," quietly altered to "the old Moon in her lap") also anticipates a vignette in the middle of the poem that the poet explicitly associates with the opening situation. In subsequent versions Coleridge dropped the vignette. A casual reading of the original version might find it merely a sentimental reminiscence, but, like the original ending of "Frost at Midnight," it had its imagistic appropriateness:

It was as calm as this, that happy night
When Mary, thou, & I together were,
The low decaying Fire our only Light,
And listen'd to the Stillness of the Air!
O that affectionate & blameless Maid,
Dear Mary! on her Lap my head she lay'd
    Her hand was on my Brow,
    Even as my own is now;
And on my Cheek I felt thy eye-lash play.
Such Joy I had, that I may truly say,
My Spirit was awe-stricken with the Excess
And trance-like Depth of its brief Happiness.   [99–110]

The congruence of detail between these lines and the opening of the poem—the calm night, the dim ("phantom") light cast on the face held in the womanly Lap, the experience of awe (cp. line 17)—is plainly more than coincidental. Apparently Coleridge intended this Grasmere idyl as an Edenic contrast to the melancholy apprehension, with its burden of superstition, figured in the opening lines. The image of the "old Moon" has here become a combination of lover, child, and patient, with the "affectionate and blameless Maid" (Mary Hutchinson) the crescent Moon (newly bright with the reflected light of Wordsworth's declared love?) able to shed its light on him and engender in him, at least momentarily, a trance-like suspension of grief.

But in the opening stanza the poet labors under such vexed melancholy that he can only wish for a storm to wrench him from his mood. In none of Coleridge's earlier (or later) poems does such a violent, sublime event operate to rouse the poet from depression, and it is indicative of his mind's disarray that the poet now invokes that stimulus from without as a *Sturm und Drang* release:

> And oh! that even now the gust were swelling,
>   And the slant night-shower driving loud and fast!
> Those sounds which oft have raised me, whilst they awed,
>   And sent my soul abroad,
> Might now perhaps their wonted impulse give,
> Might startle this dull pain, and make it move and live!

In "Frost at Midnight," for example, not the blast but the eavedrops, heard only in its trances, announce the poet's sense of sacramental joy; similarly, in "Recollections of Love" (1807) the "dear undersong in clamor's hour" becomes a metaphor for the ceaseless whisper of Love.

But precisely such subtler conversations in nature's language elude the poet's attention in the opening of "Dejection: An Ode" and, when he does turn to them in the second stanza, paradoxically intensify his sense of melancholy and isolation:

> A grief without a pang, void, dark, and drear,
>   A stifled, drowsy, unimpassioned grief,
>   Which finds no natural outlet, no relief,
>   In word, or sigh, or tear—
> O Lady! in this wan and heartless mood,
> To other thoughts by yonder throstle woo'd,
>   All this long eve, so balmy and serene,

188 Coleridge's Meditative Art

> Have I been gazing on the western sky,
>   And its peculiar tint of yellow green:
> And still I gaze—and with how blank an eye!
> And those thin clouds above, in flakes and bars,
> That give away their motion to the stars;
> Those stars, that glide behind them or between,
> Now sparkling, now bedimmed, but always seen:
> Yon crescent Moon, as fixed as if it grew
> In its own cloudless, starless lake of blue;
> I see them all so excellently fair,
> I see, not feel, how beautiful they are!

Unable to find joy in the tranquil eloquence of his natural surroundings, he is an exile from a universe of harmony.

The passage just quoted is like that deepening description
of the dell in "This Lime-Tree Bower My Prison," and the
details of the twilight sky are such as recall the gentle intercourse of natural phenomena in the bower when the noonday
dazzle is mitigated. The "peculiar tint of yellow green" that
lingers in the west, moreover, is the same light that in "Fears
in Solitude," an earlier meditative poem, lit the "spirit-healing
nook":

>   the dell,
> Bathed by the mist, is fresh and delicate
> As vernal corn-field, or the unripe flax,
> When, through its half-transparent stalks, at eve,
> The level sunshine glimmers with green light.

Such light manifests the shining of the divine through the
translucence of the natural, as in Coleridge's definition of a
symbol in *The Statesman's Manual* (1816). Or, as he wrote
in 1811, "The sun calls up the vapour—attenuates, lifts it—it
becomes a cloud—and now it is the Veil of the Divinity—the
Divinity transpiercing it at once hides & declares his presence
—We *see*, we are conscious of, *Light* alone; but it is Light embodied in the earthly nature, which that Light itself awoke
and sublimated."[9] The Coleridgean philanthropy whereby the

clouds in the second stanza of "Dejection" give away their motion to the stars, "Those stars, that glide behind them or between," is, to be sure, an optical illusion. But such motion was for Coleridge, in other contexts, a source of imaginative delight as an emblem of what he called continuousness. A couplet in *Venus and Adonis*, for example, prompted this account of poetic genius:

In its tranquil and purely pleasurable operation, it acts chiefly by producing out of many things, as they would have appeared in the description of an ordinary mind, described slowly and in unimpassioned succession, a oneness, even as nature, the greatest of poets, acts upon us when we open our eyes upon an extended prospect. Thus the flight of Adonis from the enamoured goddess in the dusk of evening—
> Look! how a bright star shooteth from the sky,
> So glides he in the night from Venus' eye.

How many images and feelings are here brought together without effort and without discord—the beauty of Adonis—the rapidity of his flight—the yearning yet hopelessness of the enamoured gazer—and a shadowy ideal character thrown over the whole.[10]

In "Dejection" the irresistible smoothness of gliding, combining with the slow, pulsing vitality of the stars, also resembles the magical continuousness celebrated in another meditative poem of the same year, the "Inscription for a Fountain on a Heath":

> Long may the Spring
> Quietly as a sleeping infant's breath
> Send up cold waters to the traveller
> With soft and even pulse!

But the poet's melancholy plight in "Dejection," so painfully evoked by his prolonged, futile gaze after the gliding stars, is that of the Ancient Mariner:

> I looked to heaven, and tried to pray;
> But or ever a prayer had gusht,

A wicked whisper came, and made
My heart as dry as dust.

I closed my lids, and kept them close,
And the balls like pulses beat;
For the sky and the sea, and the sea and the sky
Lay like a load on my weary eye,
And the dead were at my feet. . . .

The moving Moon went up the sky,
And no where did abide:
Softly she was going up,
And a star or two beside.

And Coleridge's prose gloss to this last stanza, in its rhythms as eloquently wistful as anything he wrote, tells us a great deal about the poet, the gliding stars, and the state of melancholy exile in "Dejection": "In his loneliness and fixedness he yearneth towards the journeying Moon, and the stars that still sojourn, yet still move onward; and every where the blue sky belongs to them, and is their appointed rest, and their native country and their own natural homes, which they enter unannounced, as lords that are certainly expected and yet there is a silent joy at their arrival." Indeed, it would be hard to imagine a more suitable gloss to all of Coleridge's meditative verse, or, for that matter, to all his most character-istic thought. "Still sojourn, yet still move onward" suggests the movement of the imagination described in the *Biographia* as that of a water-insect winning its way "up against the stream, by alternate pulses of active and passive motion, now resisting the current, and now yielding to it in order to gather strength and a momentary fulcrum for a further propulsion. This is no unapt emblem of the mind's self-experience in the act of thinking." Or one might cite his description of the pul-sing effects of meter in a poem, "effects . . . produce[d] by the continued excitement of surprise, and by the quick re-ciprocations of curiosity still gratified and still re-excited."[11]

In earlier versions of the second stanza, these emblematic

effects of gliding and pulsing continuousness in the clouds and
stars were reinforced by another image:

> In this heartless Mood,
> To other thoughts by yonder Throstle woo'd
> That pipes within the Larch tree, not unseen,
> (The Larch, which pushes out in tassels green
> Its bundled Leafits).

To this an 1803 notebook entry may be taken as a gloss:
"Continuousness a true foliation."[12]

The third and fourth stanzas define in more general, philosophic terms the crisis of being unable to *feel* the beauty of a
world so continuously alive:

> My genial spirits fail;
> And what can these avail
> To lift the smothering weight from off my breast?
> It were a vain endeavour,
> Though I should gaze for ever
> On that green light that lingers in the west:
> I may not hope from outward forms to win
> The passion and the life, whose fountains are within.
>
> O Lady! we receive but what we give,
> And in our life alone does Nature live:
> Ours is her wedding garment, ours her shroud!
> And would we aught behold, of higher worth,
> Than that inanimate cold world allowed
> To the poor loveless ever-anxious crowd,
> Ah! from the soul itself must issue forth
> A light, a glory, a fair luminous cloud
> Enveloping the Earth—
> And from the soul itself must there be sent
> A sweet and potent voice, of its own birth,
> Of all sweet sounds the life and element!

These lines present neither a deliberate manifesto in verse of a
newly espoused Berkeleyan psychology, nor a gesture to reject

some conversely conceived Hartleyan attitude proposed in earlier poems. "Dejection" *dramatizes* an emotional crisis; it does not simply record, from Coleridge's life, an about-face in psychological speculation. At no point in his meditative poetry does Coleridge suggest that "outward forms" can supply the imagination with passion and life. The "Joy" proclaimed in the fourth and fifth stanzas as the *sine qua non* of imaginative play, the "sweet and potent voice" of the soul's "own birth, / Of all sweet sounds the life and element!" is the same spontaneity that releases the prisoner from the lime-tree bower or from the curse of the albatross about his neck. That he can apprehend the phenomena of Nature's dower without Joy only testifies to the depth of his crisis.

The progress of the poem so far is illuminated by Coleridge's discussion, at the end of the second *Blackwood's* letter, of the way meditation turns "diseases into pearls" and provides consolation and support in times of illness. The first part of this discussion, directed to situations "where the suffering is not extreme," has some suggestive affinities with the language of Coleridge's more acute distress in the opening two stanzas of "Dejection":

We, too, may turn diseases into pearls. The means and materials are within ourselves: and the process is easily understood. By a law common to all animal life, we are incapable of attending for any continuance to an object, the parts of which are indistinguishable from each other, or to a series, where the successive links are only numerically different. Nay, the more broken and irritating (as, for instance, the *fractious* noise of the dashing of a lake on its border, comparing with the swell of the sea on a calm evening), the more quickly does it exhaust our power of noticing it. The tooth-ache, where the suffering is not extreme, often finds its speediest cure in the silent pillow; and gradually destroys our attention to itself by preventing us from attending to any thing else. From the same cause, many a lonely patient listens to his moans, till he forgets the pain that occasioned them. The attention attenuates, as its sphere contracts.

This is an apt account of the poet's response to the

> dull sobbing draft, that moans and rakes
> Upon the strings of this Æolian lute,
> Which better far were mute.

In the poem, however, oblivion does not follow. Rather, the poet's situation resembles what the *Blackwood's* letter goes on to describe:

So it is in the slighter cases of suffering, where suspension is extinction, or followed by long intervals of ease. But where the unsubdued causes are ever on the watch to renew the pain, that thus forces our attention in upon ourselves, the same barrenness and monotony of the object that in minor grievances lulled the mind into oblivion, now goads it into action by the restlessness and natural impatience of vacancy. We cannot perhaps divert the attention; our feelings will still form the main subject of our thoughts. But something is already gained, if, instead of attending to our sensations, we begin to *think* of them. But in order to this, we must reflect on these thoughts—or the same *sameness* will soon sink them down into mere feeling. And in order to sustain the act of reflection on our thoughts, we are obliged more and more to compare and generalize them, a process that to a certain extent implies, and in a still greater degree excites and introduces the act and power of abstracting the thoughts and images from their original cause.[13]

Such is the process "Dejection" traces in the movement from the poet's painful articulation of "stifled, drowsy, unimpassioned grief, / Which finds no natural outlet, no relief, / In word, or sigh, or tear" to his more energetic and exuberant advocacy of Joy in stanzas four and five. But though his voice recovers a living timbre during the process of generalizing, the crisis is not yet resolved. If the ode explores the fiction that at this point the original causes of his melancholy suffering have receded from the poet's attention (a fiction even more strongly urged in the letter version, which ends with that passage of jubilant generalization), they reassert themselves in the shift to his retrospective lament of the sixth stanza.

2

Those causes of the crisis defined in the sixth stanza as the suspension of his "shaping spirit of Imagination" are largely unspecified in the ode, though by ferrying to that poem the censored "personal" complaints about domestic unhappiness from the letter to Sara, we can supply the missing context for an autobiographical reading. But the apparently confessional voice of the poem is *not* necessarily the voice of Samuel Taylor Coleridge in 1802 providing an unmediated, definitive account of his personal plight.

> But oh! each visitation
> Suspends what nature gave me at my birth,
> My shaping spirit of Imagination.
> For not to think of what I needs must feel,
> But to be still and patient, all I can;
> And haply by abstruse research to steal
> From my own nature all the natural man—
> This was my sole resource, my only plan:
> Till that which suits a part infects the whole,
> And now is almost grown the habit of my soul.

The voice, here as elsewhere in the poem (one thinks of the opening lines), has a dramatic appropriateness, and the drama at this point, as in the opening lines of "This Lime-Tree Bower My Prison" and "Frost at Midnight," is that of a voice filled with solipsistic and self-indulgent desperation from which Coleridge the author stands at some distance. Read dramatically rather than autobiographically, the lines that Humphry House praised for their "firm, sad honesty of self-analysis" can be heard instead as an outburst of excessive self-pity.

That, at least, is the reading to be inferred from the opening of the seventh stanza, if one can identify the despair that infuses the end of the sixth with the "viper thoughts" the poet abjures as he turns to the wind:

> Hence, viper thoughts, that coil around my mind,
> Reality's dark dream!

I turn from you and listen to the wind,
    Which long has raved unnoticed. What a scream
Of agony by torture lengthened out
    That lute sent forth!

What seems here a sudden wrench in the poet's monologue
has been a serious obstacle to accepting the final version of
"Dejection" as a coherent poem. Virtually the same turn
comes at a wholly different juncture in the letter version,
where it signals a plausible, if somewhat hysterical, reversion
from the poet's "dark, distressful Dream" of helpless absence
from the side of a sick and wretched Sara. Certainly, deleting
that fantasy and shifting the turn to a later point in the poem
are the most drastic gestures at reshaping the poem Coleridge
made. But we do Coleridge an injustice if we assume that the
only motive for that reshaping was to conceal the elements
of bathetic autobiography. We underestimate his enterprise as
an artist if we assume out of hand that the turn does not take
on a new and psychologically coherent function in the published poem. The "dark distressful Dream" that had produced
such a crisis in the original draft has shifted in the first published version to an experience like that recorded on his Sca'-
Fell walking trip in early August when, after an exhausting
series of precarious, descending leaps he found himself trapped
("lounded" in his vernacular phrase) on a ledge, trembling
with fatigue and emotion, no way up or down:

The sight of the Crags above me on each side, & the impetuous
Clouds just over them, posting so luridly & so rapidly northward, overawed me / I lay in a state of almost prophetic Trance
& Delight—& blessed God aloud, for the powers of Reason &
the Will, which remaining no Danger can overpower us! O God,
I exclaimed aloud—how calm, how blessed am I now / I know
not how to proceed, how to return / but I am calm & fearless &
confident / if this *Reality* were a *Dream*, if I were asleep, what
agonies had I suffered! what *screams!*[14]

"Reality's dark dream!": the Sca'Fell passage suggests that the phrase in "Dejection" describes the sleep of "Reason & the Will" in the poet's voice during the previous stanza. As an emblem for what happens in the absence of safeguarding reason and will, the poet invokes the sound of the raving wind that *throughout* the previous stanza *has been* torturing a long "scream of agony" from the lute. (The past tense of "long has raved unnoticed" is as essential to the meaning as the metaphor of madness.) Put another way, the subsequent description of the turbulent wind is a deliberate deranging of the correspondent breeze motif: the wind "that rav'st without" is correlative to the melancholic access of viper thought in stanza six. To read the account of the wind as correlative to the mind that has the presence to turn from that melancholy is to confound the poem.[15]

It is the state of dejection itself, then, that he forswears in the opening of stanza seven, rather than the afflictions he is tempted, in his dejection, to blame it upon or the abstruse research undertaken in the past to alleviate the anguish of it.[16] If we project retroactively upon the poem at this point our sense of Coleridge's worsening state in 1803 and 1804 and see the poem as a cry of despair and a deliberate swan song of creative power, we not only misread the subtle logic of the argument within the poem but also become involved, in a way Coleridge would have found meretricious, in a crude biographical fallacy. Stanza seven should be read instead as the poet's reassertion of "Reason and the Will" in the face of tendencies in his mind and voice to give in to the indulgence of despair.

In thus apostrophizing the wind, the poet speaks in stanza seven from the vantage of one whose reasserted control enables him to hear it (and, by implication, his own recent voice) as something to set himself apart from:

> Thou Wind, that rav'st without,
> Bare crag, or mountain-tairn, or blasted tree,
> Or pine-grove whither woodman never clomb,
> Or lonely house, long held the witches' home,
> Methinks were fitter instruments for thee,

Mad Lutanist! who in this month of showers,
Of dark-brown gardens, and of peeping flowers,
Mak'st Devils' yule, with worse than wintry song,
The blossoms, buds, and timorous leaves among,
    Thou Actor, perfect in all tragic sounds!
Thou mighty Poet, e'en to frenzy bold!
    What tell'st thou now about?
'Tis of the rushing of an host in rout,
With groans, of trampled men, with smarting wounds—
At once they groan with pain, and shudder with the cold!
But hush! there is a pause of deepest silence!
And all that noise, as of a rushing crowd,
With groans, and tremulous shudderings—all is over—
It tells another tale, with sounds less deep and loud!
    A tale of less affright,
    And tempered with delight,
As Otway's self had framed the tender lay,—
    'Tis of a little child
    Upon a lonesome wild,
Not far from home, but she hath lost her way:
And now moans low in bitter grief and fear,
And now screams loud, and hopes to make her mother hear.

This passage has been variously interpreted as a resurgence of creative imagination and as an outburst of a still diseased sensibility; for the most part the commentary has been vague and puzzled. The controversy over the passage can best be resolved, I suggest, by reading it in an expanded literary context, derived from passages in Milton's *Paradise Lost* and the hymn "On the Morning of Christ's Nativity," and from Wordsworth's "Adventures on Salisbury Plain" and "Lucy Gray," passages that have to do with the fall of the angels and the expulsion of pagan deities, with the ravages of war and the triumph of a child. Consider, for example, the following two passages from Book Two of *Paradise Lost*. The first is from the mouth of Chaos, who recognizes Satan:

    I know thee, stranger, who thou art,
That mighty leading angel, who of late

> Made head against heaven's king, though overthrown.
> I saw and heard, for such a numerous host
> Fled not in silence through the frighted deep
> With ruin upon ruin, rout on rout,
> Confusion worse confounded.   [990ff]

The second is from Belial's speech in Pandemonium:

> what if all
> Her stores were opened, and this firmament
> Of hell should spout her cataracts of fire,
> Impendent horrors, threatening hideous fall
> One day upon our heads; while we perhaps
> Designing or exhorting glorious war,
> Caught in a fiery tempest shall be hurled
> Each on his rock transfixed, the sport and prey
> Of racking whirlwinds, or for ever sunk
> Under yon boiling ocean, wrapped in chains;
> There to converse with everlasting groans,
> Unrespited, unpitied, unreprieved,
> Ages of hopeless end; this would be worse. . . .
> Shall we then live thus vile, the race of heaven
> Thus trampled, thus expelled to suffer here
> Chains and these torments?   [174ff]

And in this context we should consider also the description of Lodore Falls that Coleridge sent to Sara Hutchinson on August 26, 1802, during the Sca'Fell trip: "Lodore is the Precipitation of the fallen Angels from Heaven, Flight & Confusion, & Distraction, but all harmonized into one majestic Thing by the genius of Milton, who describes it."[17]

The more immediate influence of Wordsworth's "Adventures on Salisbury Plain" may also be heard in the seventh stanza. A passage from the female vagrant's tale (which Coleridge may have imitated in 1796—see note 15 above) was among those Wordsworth, dissatisfied with aspects of the tale as it had appeared in *Lyrical Ballads* in 1798 and 1800, revised by early 1801 in anticipation of the third edition of that collection.[18] Coleridge, living at Keswick much of 1801, would

undoubtedly have seen the revisions in manuscript. In the
passage the woman recalls the calm on shipboard that followed her distressful sojourn in revolutionary America, where
she had lost "all, in one remorseless year, / Husband and children." Originally, and as late as 1800, the stanzas ran thus:

> Ah! how unlike those late terrific sleeps!
> And groans, that rage of racking famine spoke,
> Where looks inhuman dwelt on festering heaps!
> The breathing pestilence that rose like smoke!
> The shriek that from the distant battle broke!
> The mine's dire earthquake, and the pallid host
> Driven by the bomb's incessant thunder-stroke
> To loathsome vaults, where heart-sick anguish toss'd
> Hope died, and fear itself in agony was lost!
>
> Yet does that burst of woe congeal my frame,
> When the dark streets appeared to heave and gape,
> While like a sea the storming army came,
> And Fire from Hell reared his gigantic shape,
> And Murder, by the ghastly gleam, and Rape,
> Seized their joint prey, the mother and the child!
> But from these crazing thoughts my brain, escape!
> —For weeks the balmy air breathed soft and mild,
> And on the gliding vessel Heaven and Ocean smiled.

By 1801, this second stanza was somewhat less frenetic, and it
included the "midnight" setting of the vision that brings the
passage that much closer to the stanza Coleridge wrote in
1802:

> At midnight once the storming army came:
> Yet do I see the miserable sight,
> The bayonet, the Soldier, and the flame
> That follow'd us, and fac'd us, in our flight:
> When Rape and Murder by the ghastly light
> Seiz'd their joint prey, the Mother and the child!
> But I must leave these thoughts—From night to night
> From day to day the air breath'd soft and mild
> And on the gliding vessel heaven and ocean smil'd.[19]

The storm atmosphere, the groans, the host in rout, the mother
and child, the turn from crazing thoughts, the ensuing silence
at midnight—all can be said to anticipate Coleridge's stanza.

In composing the original draft of "Dejection," then,
Coleridge may have had these passages from Milton and
Wordsworth in mind as analogues for the "rushing of an host
in rout." Certainly there are interesting affinities of language
among all three passages (suggesting also that Milton had influenced Wordsworth). Perhaps we can say that, as with the
Lodore description, the Miltonic and Wordsworthian analogues were available as metaphors for sublime disarray and
that the thematic implications of those metaphors are worth
considering when we try to interpret Coleridge's seventh
stanza. The madness of the raving wind's song in the immediate past, when (as I have suggested) the poet's own voice gave
way to despair, is associated, as the poet turns to listen to it in
the present, with what we can hear as Miltonic and Wordsworthian narratives of the disasters of war: defeat, agony,
confusion, despair. The ability to hear this noisy "music" as
such corresponds to the shift from "Reality's dark dream!" to
the reawakening of the reason and the will in the poet's mind,
and it is punctuated in his voice by rhetorical apostrophes
that suggest fearlessness and confidence bordering on mockery instead of awe:

> Thou Wind, that rav'st without,
>
> . . . . .
> Thou Actor, perfect in all tragic sounds!
> Thou mighty Poet, e'en to frenzy bold!
> What tell'st thou now about?

This language accomplishes an absolute distancing of wind
and poet, a recognition that the correspondences in the poet's
frame of mind to the raving of the wind came at the price of
his submission to its impulses (as urged in stanza one) and that
such submission was, in the Miltonic context, a yielding to
satanic despair. Far from exalting *Sturm und Drang* roman-

ticism in the manner, say, of Byron, Coleridge puts it in its place as an abdication of moral imagination, a yielding to the demonic sublime.

From the context of "The Female Vagrant's Tale" and "Adventures on Salisbury Plain" a similar perspective can be gained on Coleridge's last stanza (the blessing of Sara) as another occasion, like that of "Visions of the Maid of Orleans," when Coleridge was concerned with responding to Wordsworthian bleakness. In "The Female Vagrant's Tale" the calm of "heavenly silence" on the ocean is merely an interlude in her life of unending hardship; it soon gives way to further experiences of fear and suffering. But in "Dejection: An Ode" the "pause of deepest silence!" that succeeds the chaotic music of the host in rout itself yields to a different tale. The nature of that tale has also been the subject of much dispute among Coleridge's readers. Essentially the issue is whether the intervening song is to be heard as evidence of a recovery of creative joy in the world of the poet's imagination or as evidence of persisting distress and melancholy:

> It tells another tale, with sounds less deep and loud!
> A tale of less affright
> And tempered with delight,
> As Otway's self had framed the tender lay,—
> 'Tis of a little child
> Upon a lonesome wild,
> Not far from home, but she hath lost her way:
> And now moans low in bitter grief and fear,
> And now screams loud, and hopes to make her mother
> hear.

The moans and bitter grief in the child's song are plainly meant to recall to our minds the "dull sobbing draft, that moans and rakes" on the Æolian lute in the opening stanza. They might therefore be construed as a structural device to reinforce the second interpretation of the tale, that the poet, for all his self-analysis, is back at ground zero in hopeless melancholy. Several things, however, point toward the first possibility, that in spite of the emphasis on desolation and suffering in the child's song the tale is emblematic of a recovery of strength and imagination in the poet. Again, passages from the letters and notebooks come in aid of interpretation. The first is from a letter of February 1801. Though its bearing would seem obvious, it is often neglected in discussions of the poem. Coleridge is writing to Thomas Poole in the wake of a bout of "Pain & Infirmity" during which (as he said the week before to John Thelwall) "my own moans grew stupid to my ears":

It mingles with the pleasures of convalescence, with the breeze that trembles on my nerves, the thought how glad you will be to hear that I am striding back to my former health with such manful paces. . . . I have begun to take Bark, and I hope, that shortly I shall look back on my long & painful Illness only as a Storehouse of wild Dreams for Poems. . . . I feel, that I have power within me: and I humbly pray to the Great Being, the God & Father who has bidden me "rise & walk" that he will grant me a steady mind to employ the health of my youth and manhood in the manifestation of that power. . . . O my dear dear Friend! that you were with me by the fireside of my Study here, that I might talk it over with you to the Tune of this Night Wind that pipes its thin doleful climbing sinking Notes like a child that has lost its way and is crying aloud, half in grief and half in the hope to be heard by its Mother.[20]

No doubt this is the "same" child heard in the seventh stanza's "tale of less affright." But the creation of the succession of tales ending with that child in "Dejection" has interesting affinities with a larger pattern of imaginative activity as Coleridge defined it in the notebook entry already cited:

What is that Blessing which is most present & perpetual to my Fancy & Yearnings? Sara! Sara!—the Loss then of this first bodies itself out to me—& if I have not heard from you very recently, & if the last letter had not happened to be full of explicit Love & Feeling, then I conjure up Shadows into Substances—& am miserable / Misery conjures up other Forms, & binds them into Tales & Events—activity is always Pleasure—the Tale grows pleasanter—& at length you come to me / you are by my bed side, in some lonely Inn, where I lie deserted—there you have found me—there you are weeping over me!—Dear, dear Woman!

Pursuing a psychoanalytic inquiry, one might point to an apparent similarity between this "tale" of wretchedness and rescue by a female who has the ambiguous sexual and maternal power to turn a desert into a home and that of the child moaning and screaming for its mother in stanza seven. (Beverly Fields, for instance, finds in such figures the elements of what, harking back to a childhood experience Coleridge wrote about in 1796, she calls the "runaway child" syndrome, entailing feelings of latent hostility and love for the threatening mother figure.)[21] In "Dejection," the fact that the tale leads into the prayerful wish for Sara (stanza eight) might be seen as an effort to sublimate his guilt over that hostility, the mother of the child and the all-powerful lover of the man being interchangeable in the unconscious. In the context of such unconscious discourse, Coleridge's 1821 *Blackwood's* analysis fits well:

The best and surest nepenthe of solitary pain is opened out in the habit of seeking the principle and ultimate aim in the most imperfect productions of art, in the least attractive products of nature; of beholding the possible in the real; of detecting the essential form in the intentional; above all, in the collation and constructive imagining of the outward shapes and material forces that shall best express the essential form, in its coincidence with the idea, or realize most adequately that power, which is one with its correspondent knowledge, as the revealing body with its indwelling soul.[22]

The essential form one would see emerging from Coleridge's habit of meditation in this instance, then, would be that of the enduring child in Coleridge's adult unconscious trying to bring a threatening and unmanageable world back into the

dream of the lost home. Even the sound of the wind is found
to have coincidence with that idea.

But the risk is that such analysis sees the poem only as a
manifestation of the forces in the unconscious that led to its
composition, that it neglects the range of conscious art. As
most readings of the seventh stanza point out, the child there
is derived as well from Wordsworth's "Lucy Gray," where
the voice of a child also figures in the aftermath of a storm:

> —Yet some maintain that to this day
> She is a living child;
> That you may see sweet Lucy Gray
> Upon the lonesome wild.
>
> O'er rough and smooth she trips along
> And never looks behind;
> And sings a solitary song
> That whistles in the wind.

One might argue that the choice of a poem by Wordsworth,
the member of the Grasmere household Coleridge saw as such
an inaccessible reincarnation of his own childhood idyl and
possessed of the strength Coleridge so ambivalently coveted,
should be seen primarily as validating a psychoanalytic approach to this moment in "Dejection" and authorizing a natural extension of its findings into the oedipal sphere: in this
time of stress Coleridge falls back on his friend's strong art.

But I think more craft is entailed here than such an analysis would suggest. A thoughtful reading of "Lucy Gray" is
implicit in Coleridge's invocation of the words and music of
that poem, a reading crucial to an understanding of the poet's
projected state of mind at this juncture in the ode. If Wordsworth's poem is heard only as a "tragic sound" in the sense
that the reader's reaction on hearing it is identical to that
which the parents display in experiencing the loss of their
daughter, then plainly, there is no release for the poet from
desolation and despair. (Such a reading would be, of course,
congruent with the implicit assumptions of Freudian interpre-

tation, that the infantile problems endure unresolved, no matter what the energy of sublimation involved.) But what then is to be made of the poet's assertion that the "tale" is "tempered with delight / As [William's] self had framed the tender lay"?[23] In recalling his poem to Isabella Fenwick, Wordsworth said that it was based on an actual story of a drowned girl and that the "way in which the incident was treated and the spiritualizing of character might furnish hints for contrasting the imaginative influences which I have endeavoured to throw over common life with Crabbe's matter-of-fact style of writing of subjects of the same kind." The implication of this remark for the moment in "Dejection" is that the poet's imagination casts over the *otherwise merely melancholy* wail of the wind a delight similar to that heard by the traveler in "Lucy Gray," who can take delight in imagining that the sound of the wind is Lucy Gray's voice upon the lonesome wild. To ignore the crucial structural element of the traveler or to diminish the significance of his delight in listening to the wind is to refuse to acknowledge the special province of art in mediating—perhaps even transcending—through a distancing aesthetic response, the realities of suffering; it is to substitute Crabbe's documentary verse-journalism for poetry. As Coleridge put it, "Misery conjures up other Forms, & binds them into Tales & Events—activity is always Pleasure—the Tale grows pleasanter."

In this instance Coleridge's art, while embracing such a reading of "Lucy Gray," may also go beyond it to invoke another literary context, this one provided by Milton's "On the Morning of Christ's Nativity." Coleridge's recasting of Wordsworth's stanza to " 'Tis of a little child / Upon a lonesome wild" brings the tale of less affright closer in sound to the opening lines of Milton's hymn:

> It was the winter wild
> While the heaven-born-child
> All meanly wrapped in the rude manger lies,

and it will be recalled that in Milton's poem also the child's advent is associated with a sacramental stillness in the wake of a raving storm:

> But peaceful was the night
> Wherein the Prince of Light
>   His reign of peace upon the earth began:
> The winds with wonder whist,
> Smoothly the waters kissed,
>   Whispering new joys to the mild ocean,
> Who now hath quite forgot to rave,
> While birds of calm sit brooding on the charmed wave.

This is a moment Coleridge was to echo four years later in another poem involving a storm situation, "To William Wordsworth":

> The tumult rose and ceased: for Peace is nigh
> Where Wisdom's voice has found a listening heart.
> Amid the howl of more than wintry storms
> The Halcyon hears the voice of vernal hours
> Already on the wing.

These affinities, if one grants that they are such and that they constitute a part of Coleridge's deliberate art in "Dejection," not only indicate his continuing interest in the Nativity Hymn (which he had openly invoked as a poetic inspiration as early as "Religious Musings" in 1796); they suggest that in "Dejection" Coleridge may have been exploring an analogy between the perpetual peace introduced by the Christmas Child, who "can in his swaddling bands control the damned crew" of pagan gods that "troop to the infernal jail," and the pause of deepest silence which announces the "tale of less affright," the undersong that puts an end to the "worse than wintry" clamor of the Devils' yule. That analogy would argue strongly for hearing the "sounds less deep and loud" at the end of the penultimate stanza of "Dejection" as correlative to a mind that, having gone through the process of deliberately exploring the melancholy grief with which the poem opens, is winning its way to a substantial calm. That this reading assumes a drastic reshaping of the experience sketched in the letter version of the previous April is not evidence, I think, of the insincerity of the final poem (or, for that matter, of the "sincerity" of the earlier version) so much as an indication that, in preparing the poem for publication on Wordsworth's wedding day, Coleridge was engaged in a significantly different poetic enterprise.

In a sense then, as with "Frost at Midnight," the superstition of the outset is fulfilled unexpectedly at the end. "Dejection" repeats the circular movement of the earlier poem, with the moaning that at the start was the correlative of the poet's melancholy now the occasion for imaginative delight. (We recall the original version of "Frost at Midnight," where the babe's fluttering arms, stretched toward the shining moon, were a sacramental recapitulation of the fitful fluttering of the ash on the grate.) Having heard the child upon a lonesome wild, the poet is able to "send his soul abroad" in the blessing that constitutes the final stanza:

> 'Tis midnight, but small thoughts have I of sleep:
> Full seldom may my friend such vigils keep!
> Visit her, gentle Sleep! with wings of healing,
>   And may this storm be but a mountain-birth,
> May all the stars hang bright above her dwelling,
>   Silent as though they watched the sleeping Earth!
>   With light heart may she rise
>   Gay fancy, cheerful eyes,
>   Joy lift her spirit, joy attune her voice;
> To her may all things live, from pole to pole,
> Their life the eddying of her living soul!
>   O simple spirit, guided from above,
> Dear Lady! friend devoutest of my choice,
> Thus mayest thou ever, evermore rejoice.

To wish for his friend the joy that endows all things with a life eddying back to its source in her living soul is to wish for her the situation of the reciprocal flow of earth- and moon-light in the opening superstition, defined later as "we receive but what we give." And the tone of the stanza argues that the same eddying process involves the poet, whose blessing upon Sara, in the manner of that upon his infant son in "Frost at Midnight," is the means for release from his own acute distress. The distinctive sacramental note is struck with "O simple spirit, guided from above"; as the friend devoutest, the Lady is another version of Coleridge's other Sara, in "The Eolian Harp," of the "meek Daughter in the family of Christ," and of Joan in "Visions of the Maid of Orleans."

More commentary has been offered on the line "And may this storm be but a mountain-birth" than it perhaps warrants, but given the state of disagreement, one further observation may be useful. Humphry House's suggestion that the appeal of the line is to the Horatian aphorism about the mountain laboring to bring forth a mouse seems to me improbable: aside from the comic note it would introduce in an otherwise prayerful ending, we should note that Coleridge hardly ever operates by such familiar aphoristic allusion.[24] But House was, I think, correct in emphasizing the obstetrical nature of Coleridge's metaphor. Those commentators who translate the figure into "may this be but a local storm" (that is, one whose effects are felt only on Coleridge's side of the mountainous divide between Keswick and Grasmere) are correct insofar as they offer a topographical focus for the poet's wish that Sara not be disturbed.[25] But figures of birth occur earlier in the poem and prepare a context for the phrase "mountain-birth," a context that involves the other expressions of "issuing forth" and "effluence" that are the master images of the poem, governing its theme throughout:

> Ah! from the soul itself must issue forth
> A light, a glory, a fair luminous cloud
>   Enveloping the Earth—
> And from the soul itself must there be sent
>   A sweet and potent voice, of its own birth,
> Of all sweet sounds the life and element!

The wish that "this storm be but a mountain-birth," is then, in addition to a prayer for clear skies over Sara, a wish that it be only a meteorological phenomenon, brought forth by the sky and earth, not by a mind in distress and not invoked by such a mind for its "wonted impulse" to send his soul abroad. Having achieved for himself in the seventh stanza an independence from the madness of the storm, the poet wishes the same autonomy of spirit for his friend.

7

Wordsworth's Whelming Tide:
Coleridge and the Art of Analogy

This alone be my Object, as this alone can be my Defence, the desire to kindle young men's minds, & to guard them against the temptation of the Scorners, by shewing that the Scheme of Christianity tho' not discoverable by reason, is yet accordant thereto—that Link follows Link by necessary consequence; that Religion passes out of the ken of Reason only where the Eye of Reason has reached its own Horizon; and that Faith is then but its Continuation, even as the Day softens away into the sweet Twilight, and Twilight hushed & breathless steals into the Darkness. It is Night, sacred Night! The upraised Eye views only the starry Heaven, which manifests only itself—and the outward Look gazes on the sparks twinkling in the awful Depth, only to preserve the Soul steady and concentrated in its Trance of inward Adoration.

COLERIDGE (1818)

To William Wordsworth
Composed on the Night after His Recitation of a Poem on the Growth of an Individual Mind

Friend of the wise! and Teacher of the Good!
Into my heart have I received that Lay
More than historic, that prophetic Lay
Wherein (high theme by thee first sung aright)
Of the foundations and the building up   5
Of a Human Spirit thou has dared to tell
What may be told, to the understanding mind
Revealable; and what within the mind
By vital breathings secret as the soul
Of vernal growth, oft quickens in the heart   10
Thoughts all too deep for words!—

                      Theme hard as high!
Of smiles spontaneous, and mysterious fears
(The first-born they of Reason and twin-birth),
Of tides obedient to external force,
And currents self-determined, as might seem,   15
Or by some inner Power; of moments awful,
Now in thy inner life, and now abroad,
When power streamed from thee, and thy soul received
The light reflected, as a light bestowed—
Of fancies fair, and milder hours of youth,   20
Hyblean murmurs of poetic thought
Industrious in its joy, in vales and glens
Native or outland, lakes and famous hills!
Or on the lonely high-road, when the stars
Were rising; or by secret mountain-streams,   25
The guides and the companions of thy way!

Of more than Fancy, of the Social Sense
Distending wide, and man beloved as man,

Where France in all her towns lay vibrating
Like some becalméd bark beneath the burst   30
Of Heaven's immediate thunder, when no cloud
Is visible, or shadow on the main.
For thou wert there, thine own brows garlanded,
Amid the tremor of a realm aglow,
Amid a mighty nation jubilant,   35
When from the general heart of human kind
Hope sprang forth like a full-born Deity!

—Of that dear Hope afflicted and struck down,
So summoned homeward, thenceforth calm and sure
From the dread watch-tower of man's absolute self,   40
With light unwaning on her eyes, to look
Far on—herself a glory to behold,
The Angel of the vision! Then (last strain)
Of Duty, chosen Laws controlling choice,
Action and joy!—An Orphic song indeed,   45
A song divine of high and passionate thoughts
To their own music chaunted!

                    O great Bard!
Ere yet that last strain dying awed the air,
With stedfast eye I viewed thee in the choir
Of ever-enduring men. The truly great   50
Have all one age, and from one visible space
Shed influence! They, both in power and act,
Are permanent, and Time is not with them,
Save as it worketh for them, they in it.
Nor less a sacred Roll, than those of old,   55
And to be placed, as they, with gradual fame
Among the archives of mankind, thy work
Makes audible a linkéd lay of Truth,
Of Truth profound a sweet continuous lay,
Not learnt, but native, her own natural notes!   60
Ah! as I listened with a heart forlorn,
The pulses of my being beat anew:
And even as Life returns upon the drowned,
Life's joy rekindling roused a throng of pains—
Keen pangs of Love, awakening as a babe   65

Turbulent, with an outcry in the heart;
And fears self-willed, that shunned the eye of Hope;
And Hope that scarce would know itself from Fear;
Sense of past Youth, and Manhood come in vain,
And Genius given, and Knowledge won in vain;   70
And all which I had culled in wood-walks wild,
And all which patient toil had reared, and all,
Commune with thee had opened out—but flowers
Strewed on my corse, and borne upon my bier,
In the same coffin, for the self-same grave!   75

  That way no more! and ill beseems it me,
Who came a welcomer in herald's guise,
Singing of Glory, and Futurity,
To wander back on such unhealthful road,
Plucking the poisons of self-harm! And ill   80
Such intertwine beseems triumphal wreaths
Strew'd before thy advancing!
                        Nor do thou,
Sage Bard! impair the memory of that hour
Of thy communion with my nobler mind
By pity or grief, already felt too long!   85
Nor let my words import more blame than needs.
The tumult rose and ceased: for Peace is nigh
Where Wisdom's voice has found a listening heart.
Amid the howl of more than wintry storms,
The Halcyon hears the voice of vernal hours   90
Already on the wing.
                     Eve following eve,
Dear tranquil time, when the sweet sense of Home
Is sweetest! moments for their own sake hailed
And more desired, more precious, for thy song,
In silence listening, like a devout child,   95
My soul lay passive, by thy various strain
Driven as in surges now beneath the stars,
With momentary stars of my own birth,
Fair constellated foam, still darting off
Into the darkness; now a tranquil sea,   100
Outspread and bright, yet swelling to the moon.

And when—O Friend! my comforter and guide!
Strong in thyself, and powerful to give strength!—
Thy long sustainéd Song finally closed,
And thy deep voice had ceased—yet thou thyself   105
Wert still before my eyes, and round us both
That happy vision of belovéd faces—
Scarce conscious, and yet conscious of its close
I sate, my being blended in one thought
(Thought was it? or aspiration? or resolve?)   110
Absorbed, yet hanging still upon the sound—
And when I rose, I found myself in prayer.

Of Coleridge's later meditative poems, the most notable is "To William Wordsworth," written at Coleorton in January 1807, after Wordsworth had recited his poem "on the growth of an individual Mind." Traditionally, readers have found it a window on Coleridge's personality and heard in its "confession voice" an uneven but moving *cri de coeur*.[1]

> Ah! as I listened with a heart forlorn,
> The pulses of my being beat anew:
> And even as Life returns upon the drowned,
> Life's joy rekindling roused a throng of pains—
> Keen pangs of Love, awakening as a babe
> Turbulent, with an outcry in the heart;
> And fears self-willed, that shunned the eye of Hope;
> And Hope that scarce would know itself from Fear;
> Sense of past Youth, and Manhood come in vain,
> And Genius given, and Knowledge won in vain;
> And all which I had culled in wood-walks wild,
> And all which patient toil had reared, and all,
> Commune with thee had opened out—but flowers
> Strewed on my corse, and borne upon my bier,
> In the same coffin, for the self-same grave!

Hearing Wordsworth read what Dorothy called "the poem to Coleridge" might well have overwhelmed the artist in him. *The Prelude* was, after all, the masterly product of years when Coleridge's own poetic creativity was most painfully in abeyance, his mind most subject to despair. The sojourn in Malta had failed to cure his troubles. He arrived at Coleorton

217

in precarious health, still using opium, and without money or prospects. The continuing distress of working out a separation from his wife and children was intensified by the apparent harmony of the Wordsworth household, for him the embodiment of everything he so desperately idealized in human relations. For years, from 1797 when Coleridge heard "The Ruined Cottage" at Racedown to the evenings in 1807 when he again listened, this time to a poem he had helped conceive, the intimacy of William's world, which now included Wordsworth's sister-in-law, Sara Hutchinson, charmed and excluded him. The stimulating friendship with Wordsworth himself cost Coleridge dearly, for he invested Wordsworth with a power destructive of his own self-assurance. The older poet had become to him little less than a father-figure, focus of the ambivalent affection and rivalry such oedipal transferences entail. Shortly after his arrival at Coleorton, for example, Coleridge's neurotic fantasy coupled William and Sara in an unthinkable adultery that for Coleridge had all the taboo of incest.

Such biographical considerations pertain to an adequate reading of "To William Wordsworth." But they do not in themselves comprehend the nature of the poem, which is more than a transparent expression of distress. Beyond question, the "personality" is there: in 1815, as we have seen, Coleridge himself reassured Wordsworth, who feared embarrassment if the poem was published, that he

wanted no additional reason for its not being published in my Life Time, than its *personality* respecting myself—After the opinions, I had given publicly, for the preference of the Lycidas (moral no less than poetical) to Cowley's Monody, I could not have printed it consistently—. It is for the Biographer, not the Poet, to give the *accidents* of *individual* Life.[2]

This appeal to aesthetic principle may have been a pretext to allay Wordsworth's fears, for if Coleridge had not already done so, in a few months he made the decision to publish the poem in *Sibylline Leaves*, with his friend's identity only thinly veiled.[3] But he also did what he could to rid the poem of purely personal and accidental elements, since for him the poem was never merely an egregiously autobiographical lament. However, readers have neglected its "representative" and "generic" nature. And the mention of "Lycidas" in his letter was no casual gesture, as Wordsworth knew. An important artistic design informs "To William Wordsworth," but it cannot be discerned by criticism focusing primarily on tone and diction and operating on the premise that structure and style in romantic poetry are chiefly unmediated expressions of psychological forces in the poet's personality.

1

Coleridge's inclination as a poet (or critic), however, was not toward objectivist formalism. He was the most purposefully egotistic writer of his day, and the subtlety of that egotism can be seen clearly in the artfulness of his poem to Wordsworth. As early as 1797 he defended egotism in his poems: "If I could judge of others by myself, I should not hesitate to affirm, that the most interesting passages in our most interesting poems are those in which the Author develops his own feelings." But there was a difference between "personality," dealing with the "*accidents* of *individual* Life," and its development into egotism. True egotism was not idiosyncratic, he had argued when acknowledging the weakness of the "Hymn Before Sun-rise," which failed to "apostrophize *classes* of Things, presented by the Memory and generalized by the understanding."[4] At the end of his life, he was still elaborating the same insight: "In the Paradise Lost—indeed, in every one of his poems—it is Milton himself whom you see; his Satan, his Adam, his Raphael, almost his Eve—all are John Milton; and it is a sense of this intense egotism that gives me the greatest pleasure in reading Milton's works. The egotism of such a man is a revelation of spirit."[5]

Like Wordsworth, Milton was a figure of awesome authority whose genius inspired Coleridge. "What joy to meet a

Milton in a future state, &, with that reverence due to a superior, pour forth our deep thanks for the noble feelings, he had aroused in us." But such reverence was also problematic for an imagination bent on competing and able to discern in the mirror of Milton's career an accusing reflection of his own plight:

No one can rise from the perusal of this immortal poem [*Paradise Lost*] without a deep sense of the grandeur and the purity of Milton's soul, or without feeling how susceptible of domestic enjoyments he really was, notwithstanding the discomforts which actually resulted from an apparently unhappy choice in marriage. He was, as every truly great poet has ever been, a good man; but finding it impossible to realize his own aspirations, either in religion or politics, or society, he gave up his heart to the living spirit and light within him, and avenged himself on the world by enriching it with this record of his own transcendent ideal.[6]

Coleridge knew that in interpreting Hamlet he drew an acute self-portrait. The same may be said of his response to both Milton and Wordsworth: each lived in his mind as an ideal representation of the figure within himself struggling for being. But the strength with which his mind endowed them fettered his own potential. In Milton, and increasingly in Wordsworth as his own prospects dimmed after the Nether Stowey years, he saw the figure he might have been, an ideal phantom of himself hovering in merciless rebuke of his own inadequacies. His most salutary influence on Wordsworth was to encourage him in a very Coleridgean undertaking, the use of his powers to scrutinize his own feelings and, especially in *The Prelude*, his own mental development. And in so encouraging him, he helped make Wordsworth into a successful version of his own failed self. The poem he listened to at Coleorton was addressed to himself, but in a sense it was also a poem whose authorship he could share. But most important, in the reawakened distress of his relationship to Wordsworth, who more and more seemed to possess the power of Milton,

Coleridge heard *The Prelude* as an elegy for himself, an elegy he had helped shape.

"To William Wordsworth" is Coleridge's counter-elegy. It is antiphonal to what he heard in Wordsworth's poem, conceived as though the whelmed poet was answering the verses sung over him by his sorrowing friend. From an objective viewpoint, his "hearing" of *The Prelude* was extravagant. Wordsworth's intent was not, of course, to bury Coleridge. Yet aspects of the poem drew from Coleridge's troubled but deliberate egotism a responsive funeral hymn, itself shaped in unique ways by the greatest English funeral hymn, "Lycidas."

Not that his response was purely neurotic. Wordsworth's address to his friend occasionally does sound aloof and condescending. But the immediate impetus in *The Prelude* for Coleridge's adaptation of the pastoral mode came from a major apostrophe to him at the end of Book Ten, the longest of a handful of passages when "the poem to Coleridge" addresses him in more than casual salutation.[7] The passage comes as a landing place in *The Prelude*, just after Wordsworth's account of his moral despair and the healing ministry at Racedown of Coleridge and Dorothy. In late 1804, however, when Wordsworth wrote the passage, it was Coleridge who, in his own crisis of despair, had undertaken the Malta exile in search of health. Though at Grasmere there was not much news of him—they knew he was in Sicily briefly as a government emissary from Malta—the Wordsworths had every reason to hope he had found conditions for coping with addiction and recovering health. It was much to Wordsworth's purpose to contemplate Coleridge in Sicily, for just as his own earlier despair had come over the degeneration of the political experiment in France, he could imagine the similar effect of Sicily's wretched decline on his friend,

> who now,
> Among the basest and the lowest fallen
> Of all the race of men, dost make abode
> Where Etna looketh down on Syracuse,

> The City of Timoleon! Living God!
> How are the Mighty prostrated! they first,
> They first of all that breathe should have awaked
> When the great voice was heard from out the tombs
> Of ancient Heroes. If for France I have griev'd
> Who, in the judgment of no few, hath been
> A trifler only, in her proudest day,
> Have been distress'd to think of what she once
> Promised, now is, a far more sober cause
> Thine eyes must see of sorrow, in a Land
> Strew'd with the wreck of loftiest years, a Land
> Glorious indeed, substantially renown'd
> Of simple virtue once, and manly praise,
> Now without one memorial hope, not even
> A hope to be deferr'd; for that would serve
> To chear the heart in such entire decay.   [947–966]

But the land of Theocritus was also a setting appropriate to the elegiac resolution Wordsworth wished to invoke, on the model of "Lycidas":

> But indignation works where hope is not,
> And thou, O Friend! wilt be refresh'd. There is
> One great Society alone on earth,
> The noble Living and the noble Dead:
> Thy consolation shall be there, and Time
> And Nature shall before thee spread in store
> Imperishable thoughts, and the Place itself
> Be conscious of thy presence, and the dull
> Sirocco air of its degeneracy
> Turn as thou mov'st into a healthful breeze
> To cherish and invigorate thy frame.
> Thine be those motions strong and sanative,
> A ladder for thy Spirit to reascend
> To health and joy and pure contentedness.   [967–980]

Just as, in Milton's poem, the shepherd's grief modulates to a heady vision of ultimate salvation for Lycidas, so here the poet's lament for a Sicily weltering to the parching wind ("the dull / Sirocco air of its degeneracy") shifts to a pleasing vision of Coleridge's restoration to health through the familiar motif of the correspondent breeze. The immortality of Lycidas, entertained by "all the Saints above, / In solemn troops, and sweet societies / That sing," has a closely conceived analogue in "Imperishable thoughts" that will console Coleridge in "the one great society on earth," thoughts prompted by the salutary intercourse of wretched landscape and indignant poetic consciousness.

The next lines, in which Wordsworth draws most openly on the language of "Lycidas," turn from this putative Coleridgean lament over Sicily to his own grief at his friend's absence from England in troubled times. Here Milton's Angel Michael, "the great vision of the guarded Mount," provides the model for Wordsworth's allegorical figure of Freedom, in her English refuge after the French debacle:

> To me the grief confined that Thou art gone
> From this last spot of earth where Freedom now
> Stands single in her only sanctuary,
> A lonely wanderer, art gone, by pain
> Compell'd and sickness, at this latter day,
> This heavy time of change for all mankind.   [981–986]

In what follows, Wordsworth invokes Coleridge's own meditative poems, "This Lime-Tree Bower My Prison" and "Frost at Midnight," quietly superimposing their shape and gestures on his adaptation of Miltonic elegy. Imitating the situation of "This Lime-Tree Bower," he addresses his absent, wandering friend, just as Coleridge in that poem addressed Charles Lamb and the Wordsworths. Sadly alone and abandoned to his melancholy, Wordsworth finds even the *locus amoenus* of his memory, like Coleridge's Bower, without its wonted power to cheer:

> My own delights do scarcely seem to me
> My own delights; the lordly Alps themselves,
> Those rosy Peaks, from which the Morning looks
> Abroad on many Nations, are not now

Since thy migration and departure, Friend,
The gladsome image in my memory
Which they were used to be. [990–996]

In Coleridge's earlier poem, as we have seen, the release from
the prison of dejection comes through imagined sharing of
Lamb's joy in the landscape Coleridge and the Wordsworths
knew from their walks in the Quantock Hills. That sharing
culminates in an act of blessing:

Yes! they wander on
In gladness all; but thou, methinks, most glad,
My gentle-hearted Charles! for thou hast pined
And hunger'd after Nature, many a year,
In the great City pent, winning thy way
With sad yet patient soul, through evil and pain
And strange calamity! Ah! slowly sink
Behind the western ridge, thou glorious Sun!
Shine in the slant beams of the sinking orb,
Ye purple heath-flowers! richlier burn, ye clouds!
Live in the yellow light, ye distant groves!
And kindle, thou blue Ocean!

Wordsworth's adaptation of this locates Coleridge in a Sicil-
ean landscape:

To kindred scenes,
On errand, at a time how different!
Thou tak'st thy way, carrying a heart more ripe
For all divine enjoyment, with the soul
Which Nature gives to Poets, now by thought
Matur'd, and in the summer of its strength.
Oh! wrap him in your Shades, ye Giant Woods,
On Etna's side, and thou, O flowery Vale
Of Enna! is there not some nook of thine,
From the first playtime of the infant earth
Kept sacred to restorative delight? [996–1006]

Then, compounding his art, he imitates the turn backward
through memory to schoolboy dreams that serves as a regen-
erative gesture for Coleridge's vexed mind in "Frost at Mid-

night." The turn also involves a pointed echo of "Lycidas" ("And, O ye dolphins, waft the hapless youth") and of the moment of resurgence in "This Lime-Tree Bower" ("A delight / Comes sudden on my heart"):

> Child of the mountains, among Shepherds rear'd,
> Even from my earliest school-day time, I lov'd
> To dream of Sicily; and now a strong
> And vital promise wafted from that Land
> Comes o'er my heart; there's not a single name
> Of note belonging to that honor'd isle,
> Philosopher or Bard, Empedocles,
> Or Archimedes, deep and tranquil Soul!
> That is not like a comfort to my grief. [1007–1015]

The solace Wordsworth derives from this roster of ancient Sicilian worthies resembles what the lime-tree bower afforded its liberated prisoner:

> Henceforth I shall know
> That Nature ne'er deserts the wise and pure;
> No plot so narrow, be but Nature there,
> No waste so vacant, but may well employ
> Each faculty of sense, and keep the heart
> Awake to Love and Beauty!

Still another Sicilian analogy Wordsworth finds in the Theocritean tale of King Comates. Coleridge, imprisoned in ill health and grief (again the parallel with "This Lime-Tree Bower"), nevertheless, like Comates, will bring to the pastoral landscape the poetic imagination to prevail over the circumstances of his plight, by that grace of spirit achieving the miracle of release.

> yea, not unmov'd
> When thinking of my own beloved Friend
> I hear thee tell how bees with honey fed
> Divine Comates, by his tyrant lord
> Within a chest imprison'd impiously
> How with their honey from the fields they came

> And fed him there, alive, from month to month,
> Because the Goatherd, blessed Man! had lips
> Wet with the Muse's Nectar.   [1020–1028]

Finally, in reminiscence of the conclusion to "Frost at Midnight," the benevolent imagining of his friend's resurgent joy in the Sicilian beauties brightens his own spirit and culminates in a vision of Coleridge on Etna:

> Thus I soothe
> The pensive moments by this calm fire side,
> And find a thousand fancied images
> That chear the thoughts of those I love, and mine.
> Our prayers have been accepted; Thou wilt stand
> Not as an Exile but a Visitant
> On Etna's top; by pastoral Arethuse
> Or, if that fountain be in truth no more,
> Then near some other Spring, which by the name
> Thou gratulatest, willingly deceived,
> Shalt linger as a gladsome Votary,
> And not a Captive, pining for his home.   [1028–1039]

Released, like Lamb, from pining captivity, this Coleridge is also the theorist of the imagination Wordsworth knew, "willingly deceived" with its fictions. But Wordsworth's boldest, most unlooked-for analogy is from *Paradise Lost*. In the eleventh book, Milton describes the dazzling descent of the Archangel Michael, the "great visitant" who, in answer to Adam's prayers after the fall, with

> the heav'nly bands
> Down from a sky of jasper lighted now
> In Paradise, and on a hill made alt,
> A glorious apparition.   [208–211]

This final analogy, between a fully regenerate Coleridge and Milton's sublime archangel, seems an extravagant triumph of generous and amused affection. It is true that Coleridge's speculative intelligence dazzled William and Dorothy, but they were hardly inclined to allow him the total moral authority that invests Michael when he brings the vision of human history to the fallen Adam and Eve. A similar judgment can be made about the *Prelude* passage as a whole, which is "un-Wordsworthian" in style and digressive from the poem's central concerns. Agile as imitation and resourceful in analogy, it nevertheless does not go beyond deft literary pastiche, and in its failure of coalescence between playful tribute and the investment of moral power it falls short of Wordsworth's great poetic achievements in *The Prelude*. In one sense, however, Wordsworth's subtle, complex appeal to the art of Coleridge's most successful meditative poems is more than a private, friendly salute: it indicates his recognition of the essential compatibility of that meditative mode and the emotional structure of elegy. It was a similar fusion Coleridge sought in "To William Wordsworth."

2

Book Ten must have stunned Coleridge. Not only had he betrayed Wordsworth's hopes, which came now simply to remind him of his continued degeneracy, but their expression in his own meditative mode gave painful emphasis to his poetic decline.

> For we were nursed upon the self-same hill,
> Fed the same flock; by fountain, shade, and rill.

Given the ambivalence of his emotional involvement with Wordsworth, it is not surprising that Coleridge felt moved to answer him in kind. What is surprising, under the circumstances, is that he could carry the elegiac motif further in a meditative poem of more daring structural unity, in its resourcefulness Coleridgean to the core. But "To William Wordsworth" is more than a feat of literary rivalry, a casual blending of "Lycidas" and his own meditative style. It is a poet's attempt to move beyond the accidental personality of his Coleorton situation to a more adequate idea of self, an assertion of spiritual being. Prompted by Wordsworth's own

inventive echoes of "Lycidas," he found in the analogue of
the drowned poet a congenial challenge to the play of his
imagination. A year later, lecturing on drama at the Surrey
Institute, he defined such imaginative play in terms which
help explain the achievement of his poem:

One great principle is common to all [the fine arts], a principle
which probably is the condition of all consciousness, without
which we should feel and imagine only by discontinuous moments, and be plants or animals instead of men. I mean that ever-
varying balance, or balancing, of images, notions, or feelings
(for I avoid the vague word, idea) conceived as in opposition to
each other; in short, the perception of identity and contrariety,
the least degree of which constitutes *likeness*, the greatest absolute difference; but the infinite gradations between these two
form all the play and all the interest of our intellectual and moral
being, till it lead us to a feeling and an object more awful than
it seems to me compatible with even the present subject to utter
aloud, tho' [I am] most desirous to suggest it.[8]

With Coleridge then, in "To William Wordsworth," the play
and interest of his intellectual and moral being is in balancing
his relationship to Wordsworth with that of the two shep-
herd-poets in "Lycidas." Through the mediating effect of
that analogy, Coleridge transformed his sense of personal
plight into an assertion of triumphant release in an access of
reflexive awareness.

Perhaps the chief reason why readers have treated the pastoral elegiac element in Coleridge's poem so casually is the
competing prominence of his remarkable recapitulation of *The
Prelude*. Lines eleven to forty-seven constitute an astonish-
ingly deft critical précis of Wordsworth's poem, elaborating
its themes in a linked series of thickly allusive clauses. At the
same time, however, Coleridge announced the analogical context of his own undertaking with a baldly Miltonic opening:

Theme hard as high!
Of smiles spontaneous, and mysterious fears

(The first-born they of Reason and twin-birth),
Of tides obedient to external force,
And currents self-determined, as might seem,
Or by some inner Power; of moments awful,
Now in thy inner life, and now abroad,
When power streamed from thee, and thy soul received
The light reflected, as a light bestowed—
Of fancies fair, and milder hours of youth,
Hyblean murmurs of poetic thought
Industrious in its joy, in vales and glens
Native or outland, lakes and famous hills!
Or on the lonely high-road, when the stars
Were rising; or by secret mountain-streams,
The guides and the companions of thy way!

Of more than Fancy, of the Social Sense
Distending wide, and man beloved as man,
Where France in all her towns lay vibrating
Like some becalméd bark beneath the burst
Of heaven's immediate thunder, when no cloud
Is visible, or shadow on the main.
For thou wert there, thine own brows garlanded,
Amid the tremor of a realm aglow,
Amid a mighty nation jubilant,
When from the general heart of human kind
Hope sprang forth like a full-born Deity!

—Of that dear Hope afflicted and struck down,
So summoned homeward, thenceforth calm and sure
From the dread watch-tower of man's absolute self,
With light unwaning on her eyes, to look
Far on—herself a glory to behold,
The Angel of the vision! Then (last strain)
Of Duty, chosen Laws controlling choice,
Action and joy!—An Orphic song indeed,
A song divine of high and passionate thoughts
To their own music chaunted!

Coleridge does more here than merely summarize the argument of *The Prelude*. In focusing on the crisis of despair sustained by Wordsworth in the aftermath of the French Revolution, he draws an unmistakable analogy between the calm strength achieved by Wordsworth at Racedown upon his return to England and the strength imaginatively vested by Milton in Michael, "the great vision of the guarded Mount." Put another way, Coleridge—responding to Wordsworth's figure, in the passage from Book Ten, of Freedom standing "single in her only sanctuary"—found in the language of "Lycidas" a powerful metaphor for the central theme of Wordsworth's poem: his development, out of affliction and despair and drawing on that experience, of an assured sense of self. For Coleridge, such strong egotism—what he so admired and envied in Milton and Wordsworth—was a fortress, a "dread watch-tower." The balance of identity and contrariety Coleridge created between the *Prelude* poet and Milton's angel is complex. Michael, gazing south "toward Namancos and Bayona's hold," is urged by the shepherd to "Look homeward . . . now"; with Coleridge, Wordsworth's sublime egotism in the latter part of his autobiography becomes a parabolic version of this: "summoned homeward," he is destined thenceforth "to look / Far on," to see (and here Coleridge is fully in touch with Wordsworth's argument) his own self as a projected vision, a "glory." He probably had in mind here the image of Wordsworth on Snowdon in Book Thirteen, gazing at the type of his own intellect in the moon shining on the rifted cloudscape, with the rising noise of waters. The careful echoes of the language of "Lycidas" (especially the "Look homeward, Angel" strewn over five lines) constitute more than a slyly punning code. They declare the essential link perhaps only Coleridge among contemporary poets would have cared to declare, the link between the sense of self and the sense of the divine, self-knowledge being the one certain means to knowledge of God. It is significant that Coleridge found in the language of "Lycidas" an adequate idiom for his response to Wordsworth's achieved self-assurance. Central to his analogical purpose is his own sense of awe before that language. No other tribute to Wordsworth could have cost more. Here the language of his 1808 Surrey Institute lecture is again helpful. To ponder the analogy between Wordsworth and Michael, he might have said,

> leads us to a feeling and an object more awful than it seems to me compatible with even the present subject to utter aloud, tho' I am most desirous to suggest it. For there alone are all things at once different and the same; there alone, as the principle of all things, does distinction exist unaided by division—will and reason, succession of time and unmoving eternity, infinite change and ineffable rest.

It is toward such a self-sufficient harmony that Coleridge heard *The Prelude* moving:

> Then (last strain)
> Of Duty, chosen Laws controlling choice,
> Action and joy!—An Orphic song indeed,
> A song divine of high and passionate thoughts
> To their own music chaunted!

The abject "confession" quoted earlier is part, then, of the larger elegiac structure, corresponding to the forlorn lament in "Lycidas." In an early draft of his answering poem, he acknowledged the turmoil of feeling Wordsworth's pity and hope engendered:

> Comfort from Thee and utterance of thy Love
> Came with such heights and depths of Harmony
> Such sense of Wings uplifting, that the Storm
> Scatter'd and whirl'd me, till my Thoughts became
> A bodily Tumult! and thy faithful Hopes,
> Thy Hopes of me, dear Friend! by me unfelt
> Were troublous to me. . . .[9]

Coleridge thus depicts himself as another Lycidas, scattered and whirled, in the aftermath of his own wrecked career, by a tempest of despair. Wordsworth's glorious self-sufficiency evokes despair, his Orphic song agitating the frantic imagination of a drowning man. Under the strong sway of that music,

Coleridge becomes Lycidas, overwhelmed by a contrasting sense of his own failure and wasted gifts. But immediate and "genuine" as the confessional seems, its pathos is mediated through the larger design of the poem, just as the larger comic movement of "Lycidas" leads anguish to resolution. With glances at Milton's language pointing up the chosen, controlling context, Coleridge's abrupt turn is more immediately cogent than the similar repudiation of "viper thoughts" in "Dejection":

> That way no more! and ill beseems it me
> Who came a welcomer in herald's guise
> Singing of Glory and Futurity,
> To wander back on such unhealthful road,
> Plucking the poisons of self-harm! And ill
> Such intertwine beseems triumphal wreaths
> Strew'd before thy advancing!

The impulses of rueful anxiety, leaves shattered before the mellowing year, are rejected as self-destructive and unseemly. Simultaneously, as with Milton's poem, counter-elegy moves toward orthodoxy: Coleridge assumes a heraldic role for Wordsworth's entry into a poetic Jerusalem. To retreat into despair at his own unfulfilled promise is to refuse this higher decorum. In Coleridge's poem, as in "Lycidas," elegiac and Christian structures are one—the paradigm toward which the unsettled psyche wills itself.

If one hears the isolated "confession" as the true voice feeling, as do readers for whom the final version of "Dejection" is at best an ambiguous triumph of art over passion, the movement beginning at line 76 will seem strained falsification on Coleridge's part, a disavowal, in shame and defensiveness, of the selfish jealousy of an insecure mind. Such readers will tend to identify pathetic intensity with poetic power, and to them there is no adequate reply beyond what Coleridge himself might have said, that the use of a wretched despair is precisely in providing the imagination with an occasion for release into an ecstasy of self-awareness unavailable to a mind in steadier equanimity. Or, as he put it to Thomas Clarkson four months before writing the poem:

> With a certain degree of satisfaction to my own mind I can define the human Soul to be that class of Being, as far as we are permitted to know, the first and lowest of that Class, which is endued with a reflex consciousness of its own continuousness, and the great end and purpose of all its energies & sufferings is the growth of that reflex consciousness.[10]

Put still another way, he discovers intellectual and moral being through pursuit of abstracted analogy. In the poem, release comes through the likeness, discerned by the play of imagination in mediating the identity and contrariety, between his reception of *The Prelude* and the fate of Lycidas.

The drowning poet's repudiation of solipsistic grief leads him to admonish his mourning friend against unseemly pity "already felt too long!" But he will not be held vindictive. "Nor let my words impart more blame than needs." As "personality" this is pusillanimous suppression of hostility for a crowned rival. But in a poem that moves beyond personality, the imputation of blame is checked less by insecure dependency on his mourner than by the willed pattern of counter-elegy, already proleptic of release. For a figure to announce that salvation Coleridge turned to the "birds of calm" in Milton's "On the Morning of Christ's Nativity": for them, in the midst of "winter wild," the tumult (like the storm in "Dejection") rose and ceased. In Coleridge's recasting,

> Peace is nigh
> Where Wisdom's voice has found a listening heart.
> Amid the howl of more than wintry storms,
> The Halcyon hears the voice of vernal hours
> Already on the wing.

Coleridge was ready enough to discern an echo of divine creative music in authentic acts of the poetic imagination such as he heard in *The Prelude*. And the likeness implied by extend-

ing the analogy, between a Miltonic nature's sacramental response to that music and his own reaction to Wordsworth's
voice, is fully consonant with the argument carefully elabo-
rated to Clarkson. God's action on the soul of man "awakes in
it a conscience of actions within itself analogous to the divine
action." The ultimate, definitive divine act, that of creative
self-comprehension ("I AM"), could be grasped by the human mind only through the analogy of growth in awareness
of one's own "continuousness." Growth in the power of such
reflection was "the first approach to, & shadow of, the divine
Permanency; the first effort of divine working in us to bind
the Past and Future with the Present, and thereby to let in
upon us some faint glimmering of that State in which Past,
Present, and Future are co-adunated in the adorable I AM."[11]
Wordsworth, like Milton's dancing Pleiades "shedding sweet
influence," lets in upon Coleridge such glimmering:

> O great Bard!
> Ere yet that last strain dying awed the air,
> With stedfast eye I viewed thee in the choir
> Of ever-enduring men. The truly great
> Have all one age, and from one visible space
> Shed influence! They, both in power and act,
> Are permanent, and Time is not with them,
> Save as it worketh for them, they in it.

A sense of one's continuousness—literally, sense of past and
future bound to an ontological present—is for Coleridge in-
conceivable "without the action of kindred souls on each
other." This is the hinge of his hypothesis. It accounts for the
crucial role of the Friend in Coleridge's meditative poems.
"Man is truly altered by the coexistence of other men; his
faculties cannot be developed in himself alone, & only by himself." So it takes Wordsworth to bring Coleridge to a sense of
his own past and future, "in which the Individual is capable of
being itself contemplated as a Species of itself, namely, by its
conscious continuousness moving on in an unbroken Line."[12]
    But that is not all. The mediation of another fosters partici-

pation in what Coleridge called "One Life," through which "the whole Species is capable of being regarded as one Individual." The limitations of the separately conceived self, lost in querulousness and melancholy, are not transcended by a release from the burden of self-demand that entails a diminishing of self. The paradox is that "every Thing has a Life of its own, & that we are all *one Life*."[13] If we read "To William Wordsworth" without understanding the analogies by which Coleridge projects his commitment to such a larger "Life," the poem will seem only an inventive and pathetic gesture commemorating an emotional experience. The poem argues for a mode of being that assumes a more radically Christian analysis of human life than most readers, even in Coleridge's time, would recognize. But because that analysis permits also the celebration of self (though at the point where self is part of a larger life), this meditative poem, like so many others Coleridge wrote, seems to anticipate the meditative verse of our own day.

The last section of the poem is a lingering narrative of his pleasure in the intimate household at Coleorton, with the pleasure of the recitation superadded:

> Eve following eve,
> Dear tranquil time, when the sweet sense of Home
> Is sweetest! moments for their own sake hailed
> And more desired, more precious, for thy song.

But such simplicity is deceptive. The poem has not reverted to an unmediated, merely personal narrative. In a very Coleridgean touch, the ensuing imagery reasserts the governing pastoral analogy, with the fate of Lycidas in view, if not fully prominent view. Eight years before, on the packet boat to Germany, he had noted the appearance of the phosphorescent sea, and, casting about in 1807 for imagery adequate to his meditation on spiritual death and rebirth, he turned back to that voyage with William and Dorothy (which had inaugurated an earlier release to a prosperous exile), when he "lay in the Boat, and looked at the water, the foam of which, that beat against the Ship & coursed along by its sides, & darted off over the Sea, was full of stars of flame."[14] Recalling that phenomenon at Coleorton, Coleridge found a metaphor to suggest the likeness between the motion of the drowned body of Lycidas in Milton's changing seas and his own response to the "various strain" of Wordsworth's poem:

> In silence listening, like a devout child,
> My soul lay passive, by thy various strain
> Driven as in surges now beneath the stars,
> With momentary stars of my own birth,
> Fair constellated foam, still darting off
> Into the darkness; now a tranquil sea,
> Outspread and bright, yet swelling to the moon.

A longer adaptation of his original description appeared in *The Friend* in 1809: "A beautiful white cloud of Foam at momently intervals coursed by the side of the Vessel with a roar, and little Stars of Flame danced and sparkled and went out in it: and every now and then light detachments of this white cloud-like foam darted off from the Vessel's side, each with its own small constellation, over the sea, and scoured out of sight like a Tartar Troop over a Wilderness."[15]

Behind this language and that of the poem is Milton's account in *Paradise Lost* of the excursions of Satan, Sin, and Death through Chaos after the fall, a passage too long to give here.[16] These echoes in Coleridge reinforce the suggestion of the Lycidas analogy that the drowning poet's momentary, despairing plunge is into a hellish confusion,

> Where thou perhaps under the whelming tide
> Visit'st the bottom of the monstrous world.

His figure is a rich emblem. Perhaps the darting marine constellations miming the steady Wordsworthian heavens are an allusion to his own ephemeral lines in imitative response to Wordsworth's apostrophe. There are also strong Platonic overtones. And it is useful to recall that he occasionally brooded over alphabetical shapes in the night skies, especially the brilliant W of Cassiopoeia. In notebook verses from 1807, the extremity of despair is the false starless night of a solar eclipse:

> What never is but only is to be
> This is not Life—
> O Hopeless Hope, and Death's Hypocrisy!
> And with perpetual Promise, breaks its Promises—
> The Stars that wont to start, as on a chase,
> And twinkling insult on Heaven's darkened Face,
> Like a conven'd Conspiracy of Spies
> Wink at each other with confiding eyes,
> Turn from the portent, all is blank on high,
> No constellations alphabet the Sky—
> The Heavens one large black Letter only shew,
> And as a Child beneath its master's Blow
> Shrills out at once its Task and its Affright,
> The groaning world now learns to read aright,
> And with its Voice of Voices cries out, O![17]

But intervening in this chaos is a mystic tranquility, "outspread and bright, yet swelling to the moon." The image recalls the honeydew words of the second voice in the Ancient Mariner's vision:

> "Still as a slave before his lord,
> The ocean hath no blast;
> His great bright eye most silently
> Up to the Moon is cast—
>
> If he may know which way to go;
> For she guides him smooth or grim.
> See, brother, see! how graciously
> She looketh down on him."

Such powerful, calming grace is symbolic of the ultimate "divine action" Coleridge heard in Wordsworth's voice, the redemptive efficacy of "The dear might of him that walk'd the waves":

> And when—O Friend! my comforter and guide!
> Strong in thyself, and powerful to give strength!—

> Thy long sustained Song finally closed,
> And thy deep voice had ceased—yet thou thyself
> Wert still before my eyes, and round us both
> That happy vision of belovéd faces—
> Scarce conscious, and yet conscious of its close
> I sate, my being blended in one thought
> (Thought was it? or aspiration? or resolve?)
> Absorbed, yet hanging still upon the sound—
> And when I rose, I found myself in prayer.

In this conclusion, what at the level of personality would be blasphemy, fraught with Coleridge's problematic, self-abnegating reverence for Wordsworth, is offered instead at the level of egotism as the validation of the "One Life." Under the sway of analogy, Coleorton is Kingdom Come, where "entertain him all the Saints above, / In solemn troops, and sweet societies / That sing."

Wordsworth's genial apostrophe ended by investing his friend with an archangelic mantle. Coleridge's description of an ineffable intercourse following Wordsworth's recitation may return the compliment by echoing the pause after Raphael's account of creation:

> The angel ended, and in Adam's Ear
> So charming left his voice, that he awhile
> Thought him still speaking, still stood fixt to hear.
>
> [VIII, 1–3]

The celestial condition of mind has its analogue for Coleridge in a meditative climax, where understanding, hope, and will fuse in a resurgence of spirit tantamount to resurrection. The analogue thus recalls the gesture of Milton's uncouth swain:

> At last he rose, and twitched his mantle blue:
> Tomorrow to fresh woods, and pastures new.

One last speculation on the part of the poet who told his nephew that "Elegy is the form of poetry natural to the reflective mind" will help put in perspective the state toward which his poem moves as more than an occasional neurotic whim.[18] In the *Blackwood's* selection "from Mr. Coleridge's Literary Correspondence" I have cited before, he urged the deliberate exertion of a meditative habit

as a source of support and consolation in circumstances under which we might otherwise sink back on ourselves, and for want of colloquy with our thoughts, with the objects and presentations of the inner sense, lie listening to the fretful *ticking* of our sensations. . . . something is already gained, if, instead of attend to our sensations, we begin to *think* of them. But in order to this, we must reflect on these thoughts—or the same *sameness* will soon sink them down into mere feeling. And in order to sustain the act of reflection on our thoughts, we are obliged more and more to compare and generalize them, a process that to a certain extent implies, and in a still greater degree excites and introduces the act and power of abstracting the thoughts and images from their original cause, and of reflecting on them with less and less reference to the individual suffering that had been their first subject. The *vis mediatrix* of Nature is at work for us in all our faculties and habits, the associate, reproductive, comparative, and combinatory.[19]

The inclination, unsurprising in an age that has seen the development of psychoanalysis, to find confessions of anxiety more interesting than professions of faith has probably contributed to the emphasis placed on "To William Wordsworth" as the mirror of a forlorn mind. The balance in the poem between the order of art and the unshapely energy of emotion may be precarious, but there seems no legitimate basis for misconceiving the nature of Coleridge's undertaking or for seeing in his analogical meditation only an elaborate strategy to conceal frustration and guilt. Not disavowing but recognizing the nature of his own ambivalent aspirations after Wordsworth's power, he turned "personal" anguish into strenuous charity, and avenged himself on his friend by enriching their relationship with a poem that recorded his own egotistic and transcendent ideal. Kathleen Coburn has said that the pathos of Coleridge is that he is haunted by his inability to fix an image of himself.[20] The complex analogical argument of "To William Wordsworth" posits one image of a "self" toward which he aspired most consciously and consistently. It is a thoughtful image, if an ephemeral one, and at least for the life of the poem it modifies the figure we are otherwise likely to project from dispassionate scrutiny of his personal proclivities and circumstances.

3

"My illustrations swallow up my thesis," Coleridge confessed, in a moment of exuberant self-deprecation, and it is impossible to miss, when reading the epigraph to this chapter, a marginal note from his copy of Jacob Behmen's *Aurora*, the way in which during its course his "Object" becomes the poetic elaboration of that extraordinary landscape nocturne.[21] But it is striking how cerebral Coleridge's illustrations in fact are, how little they obliterate his thesis even as they consume it. What begins here as an assertion barely tinged with figurative possibilities leads to a momentary conceit about the eye's horizon; the subsequent extension to an explicit simile brings also the first touch of narrative ("softens"), which with "hushed and breathless steals" blossoms into a full landscape myth, humanizing night by what Wordsworth called "the conferring, the abstracting, and the modifying powers of the Imagination, mediately and immediately acting." Then comes the familiarly strident surge of feeling ("It is Night, sacred Night!"), which subsides to a more polarized awareness: eye and heaven, mind and nature. But what follows is that surprising—yet utterly Coleridgean—detail of the starry heaven "which manifests only itself": a phrase that at the same time confirms the mythic vitality of the landscape and reasserts the informing religious theme, so that the note concludes in the familiar gesture of submissive ecstasy.

Given its frequent recurrence, I am tempted to say that the

trance of the upraised eye is the definitive image of stasis toward which Coleridge's meditative poems typically move. We
have the poet and his gentle-hearted Charles watching the
blessed rook, the poet holding his infant Hartley up to the
moonlight (in "The Nightingale"), the poet lifting his worshipful eyes to the summit of Mont Blanc, the poet and Sara
gazing at the moon (in the letter that became "Dejection: An
Ode"), and, most inventively, the passive soul of the poet
driven as in surges beneath the stars and gazing in reflection
on the lofty, constellated brilliance of Wordsworth's elegiac
art. In "Frost at Midnight" there is the analogous image of the
icicles, quietly shining to the quiet moon.

The image occurs elsewhere, too: for example, in the 1819
allegorical sketch, almost contemporary to the Behmen note,
of the poet "lovingly and with gladsomeness" abasing himself before loftier consubstantial Masses, rejoicing in the
"mightier strivings of the hidden fire that uplifted them above
me." Typically the upraised eye is both acquiescent in the
sway of some more exalted power and recipient of that
power's grace, which has ultimately a heavenly origin, as in
the allegory in "Religious Musings":

> God's altar grasping with an eager hand
> Fear, the wild-visag'd, pale, eye-starting wretch,
> Sure-refug'd hears his hot pursuing fiends
> Yell at vain distance. Soon refresh'd from Heaven
> He calms the throb and tempest of his heart.
> His countenance settles; a soft solemn bliss
> Swims in his eye—his swimming eye uprais'd:
> And Faith's whole armour glitters on his limbs!

Or in the virtually Shelleyan myth of the sea in "The Ancient
Mariner":

> "Still as a slave before his lord,
> The ocean hath no blast;
> His great bright eye most silently
> Up to the Moon is cast—

> If he may know which way to go;
> For she guides him smooth or grim.
> See, brother, see! how graciously
> She looketh down on him."

Or, finally, there is the figure of the Old Man in "Limbo,"
who

> is blind—a Statue hath such eyes;—
> Yet having moonward turn'd his face by chance,
> Gazes the orb with moon-like countenance,
> With scant white hairs, with foretop bald and high,
> He gazes still,—his eyeless face all eye;—
> As 'twere an organ full of silent sight,
> His whole face seemeth to rejoice in light!
> Lip touching lip, all moveless, bust and limb—
> He seems to gaze at that which seems to gaze on him!

This is one of Coleridge's boldest moments, when a momentary relenting of the vision of limbo becomes a triumphant
encounter, the moon in the old man and the old man in the
moon finding in each other a companionable form.

As I have argued in earlier chapters, Coleridge's meditative
poems are too often read as mirrors of his distressed psyche,
his postures of abasement and passivity seen as indicative of
lifelong emotional dependencies. To be sure, it is hard to find
anywhere in his poems the manly strength he admired and
envied in Wordsworth, and such clusters—to return to Kenneth Burke's term—as the recurrent images of the upraised-
eye invite us to dwell on their "personal" overtones. But
inherent in such psychoanalytic criticism is the risk of a self-
blinding tendentiousness that neglects in the poems the possibility of a subtler art than psychoanalysis prepares us to
imagine. The danger in reading the art so much in terms of
the life is that we may settle for too easy a version of the life
and then let the outlines of that version shape our expectations
of the art. I have tried in this book to balance the natural in-

clination to confessional readings by presenting evidence for interpretations of the poems that emphasize in Coleridge the capacity to shape the materials of distress into an unobtrusive but highly wrought poetic art. The point is that Coleridge's craft and subtlety as a meditative poet have been underestimated. Readers are entitled to find in his poems evidence of the self-pity and weakness that undoubtedly were major aspects of his personality, but the success or failure of his art ought not to be judged exclusively or even primarily on such a basis. Implicit in the readings offered here is my sense that the elaborate analogies informing the poems are a source of significant aesthetic pleasure. The remarkable play of his analogical imagination, drawing as it frequently does on a rich literary context, generates in the reader those combinations of expectation, gratification, and further surprise that are essential elements in the success of any art. There can be no doubt that Coleridge sought in his poems to transcend the merely personal and "idiosyncratic" or "accidental": the evidence indicates, I think, that in such poems as "This Lime-Tree Bower My Prison," "Frost at Midnight," "Hymn Before Sun-rise in the Vale of Chamouni," "Dejection: An Ode," and "To William Wordsworth" the elements of distress and anxiety are presented in a vision of theodicy achieved by the exertion of will and the play of imagination.

No doubt there are basic issues here about how one reads any poem. For Coleridge the discovery of what he called "intellectual and moral being" came through the pursuit of abstracted analogy, the mind coming to be and to know itself through the process of discerning its identity and contrariety with beings and experiences outside itself. If poetry was for Coleridge the occasion and instrument for the imaginative pursuit of self, then as readers we ought to approach his poems with the expectation that they will be more than mirrors of experience, that they will be essentially metaphorical, and that a process of essential definition rather than one of expression of mere unshapely emotion is underway. In this Coleridge sustains and extends what is surely the central tradition of English poetics. As Shelley contended, in marking the before unapprehended relations of things, poetry "awakens and enlarges the mind itself by rendering it the receptacle of a thousand unapprehended combinations of thought."

In Coleridge's meditative poems, as these individual readings have proposed, the materials of analogy through which the mind invents itself are often provided from other literature, with texts like Revelation and writers like Milton and Wordsworth supplying indispensable shapes. Coleridge might have agreed with Oscar Wilde's mischievous aphorism that life imitates art; without art we would not know how to know ourselves. "To think of a thing is different from to perceive it," Coleridge wrote, dismissing Lockean psychology. It is the process of *thinking*, of analogical imagining, that led to intellectual and moral self-discovery and at the same time to the making of an art where more is meant than meets the eye—unless the eye is upraised—where the reader's vision must be armed with the expectation that the poet's language will operate playfully. Coleridge persisted in believing that there was no opposition of head and heart, that thought came in aid of feeling and not to destroy it. In the motto for the meditative poems in *Sibylline Leaves*, he said: "He deserves to find himself deceived / Who seeks a heart in the unthinking man," and we should take the motto to heart in thinking about his poems. The processes of self-discovery and self-expression were for him identical, or nearly so, and therefore to read his poems as effusions of an unstructured heart—an unstated and perhaps unrecognized premise of many discussions of the "conversation" poems—is to risk misconstruing the self expressed in them.

Abbreviations

This list employs forms adopted by the editors of *The Collected Works of Samuel Taylor Coleridge*.

BL (1907)   S. T. Coleridge *Biographia Literaria* ed John Shawcross 2 vols (Oxford: The Clarendon Press, 1907).

CC   *The Collected Works of Samuel Taylor Coleridge* gen ed Kathleen Coburn (London: Routledge & Kegan Paul and Princeton, N.J.: Princeton Univ. Press, 1969–   ).

CL   *Collected Letters of Samuel Taylor Coleridge* ed Earl Leslie Griggs 6 vols (Oxford: The Clarendon Press, 1956–1971).

CN   *The Notebooks of Samuel Taylor Coleridge* ed Kathleen Coburn (New York: Bollingen Foundation and London: Routledge & Kegan Paul, 1957–   ).

C 17th C   *Coleridge on the Seventeenth Century* ed R. F. Brinkley (Durham, N.C.: Duke Univ. Press, 1955).

Complete Works   *Complete Works of Samuel Taylor Coleridge* ed W. G. T. Shedd 7 vols (New York: Harper, 1853).

Friend (*CC*)   S. T. Coleridge *The Friend* ed Barbara E. Rooke 2 vols (1969) *The Collected Works of Samuel Taylor Coleridge* IV.

Lay Sermons (*CC*)   S. T. Coleridge *Lay Sermons* ed R. J. White (1972) *The Collected Works of Samuel Taylor Coleridge* VI.

Lects 1795 (*CC*)   S. T. Coleridge *Lectures 1795: On Politics and Religion* ed Lewis Patton and Peter Mann (1971). *The Collected Works of Samuel Taylor Coleridge* I.

245

LL   The Letters of Charles Lamb to Which Are Added Those of His Sister Mary Lamb ed E. V. Lucas 3 vols (London: J. M. Dent, 1935).

PW (EHC)   *The Complete Poetical Works of Samuel Taylor Coleridge* ed E. H. Coleridge 2 vols (Oxford: The Clarendon Press, 1912).

Sh C   Coleridge's Shakespearean Criticism ed T. M. Raysor 2 vols (London: J. M. Dent, 1960).

SL   S. T. Coleridge *Sibylline Leaves* (1817).

Watchman (CC)   S. T. Coleridge *The Watchman* ed Lewis Patton (1970). *The Collected Works of Samuel Taylor Coleridge* II.

WL (E)   Letters of William and Dorothy Wordsworth: The Early Years ed Ernest de Selincourt, rev ed Chester L. Shaver (Oxford: The Clarendon Press, 1967).

WL (M)   Letters of William and Dorothy Wordsworth: The Middle Years ed Ernest de Selincourt, rev ed Mary Moorman and A. G. Hill 2 vols (Oxford: The Clarendon Press, 1969–1971).

WPW   The Poetical Works of William Wordsworth ed Ernest de Selincourt and Helen Darbishire 5 vols (Oxford: The Clarendon Press, 1940–1949).

Notes

Preface

1. In *SL* (1817), the following poems appeared after the half title *Meditative Poems in Blank Verse:*

Motto from Schiller
Hymn before Sunrise, in the vale of Chamouny
Lines Written in the Album at Elbingerode, in the Hartz Forest
On Observing a Blossom, on the 1st February, 1796
The Eolian Harp, Composed at Clevedon, Somersetshire
Reflections on having left a Place of Retirement
To the Rev. George Coleridge, Of Ottery St. Mary, Devon
Inscription For a Fountain on a Heath
A tombless Epitaph
This Lime-Tree Bower My Prison
To a Friend Who had Declared his Intention of Writing No More Poetry
To a Gentleman. Composed on the night after his recitation of a Poem on the Growth of an Individual Mind
The Nightingale; a Conversation Poem
Frost at Midnight

Many of these poems belong to a loosely conceived genre now widely known as the "conversation" poem, after the subtitle of "The Nightingale," which George MacLean Harper applied to the group in an influential essay in 1925, "Coleridge's Conversation Poems," *Quarterly Review* CCXLIV 284–298, reprinted in *English Romantic Poets* ed M. H. Abrams (New York: Oxford Univ. Press, 1960) 144–157. See also R. H. Fogle, "Coleridge's Conversation Poems," *Tulane Studies in English* V (1955) 103–110. Coleridge's original use of the phrase was, however, probably simply an allusion to examples of Dutch and Eng-

lish genre painting in the seventeenth and eighteenth centuries relevant
to the fictive situation of "The Nightingale" alone: two or three figures rendered in a moment of informal discourse against the backdrop
of a quiet landscape. Moreover, the relaxed colloquialism and domestic
joy that have been associated with the poems since Harper's essay (in
which he also called them "poems of friendship"—a phrase Coleridge
might have used for the genre but with more purposeful subtlety) do
not foster in readers the expectation that the poems are anywhere near
as intricate as I wish to argue. On balance, therefore, it seems prefer-
able to return to Coleridge's own designation, "meditative poems."

   2. The term "organic" is used most commonly today as an honorific
metaphor (in contrast, say, to "mechanic") either to describe the full
interdependence of the parts of a work of art and their integration
into the whole (a usage descending from Aristotle and in keeping with
Coleridge's definition of a poem in the *Biographia*) or to describe the
process of development "from within" by which the work ripens to
an inseparability of form and content. Though he did in 1805 describe
the "permanent and organic" form of blood seen under a microscope
(*CN* II 2444), he seems not to have used the word as an aesthetic term
in the second sense until sometime after 1811 when he borrowed it
from A. W. Schlegel. (On this plagiarism, see G. N. G. Orsini, "Coleridge and Schlegel Reconsidered," *Comparative Literature* XVI [1964]
100. For a discussion of the limited usefulness of the term, see W. K.
Wimsatt, "Organic Form: Some Questions about a Metaphor," in
Romanticism: Vistas, Instances, Continuities ed David Thorburn and
Geoffrey Hartman [Ithaca: Cornell Univ. Press, 1973] 13–37.) Before,
it is worth noting, he generally used the term to denote bodily or
physiological activity exclusive of anything that could be called voluntary. In 1801, for example, writing to William Godwin, he asked
"whether there be reason to hold, that an action bearing all the semblance of predesigning Consciousness may yet be simply Organic, and
whether a *series* of such actions are possible." In 1804, describing a
recent siege of illness, he affirmed that his "inner Being" had remained
serene and self-sufficing, "but the exceeding Pain, of which I suffered
every now and then, and the fearful Distresses of my sleep, had taken
away from me the connecting link of voluntary power, which contin-
ually combines that Part of us by which we hold communion with
our Like—between the Vital and the Organic—or what Berkeley, I
suppose, would call—Mind and it's sensuous Language" (*CL* I 625; II
1032; cf. *CN* II 2444). Or consider the context of his best known use
of the word, in "The Eolian Harp":

And what if all of animated nature
Be but organic Harps diversely framed,
That tremble into thought, as o'er them sweeps
Plastic and vast, one intellectual breeze,
At once the Soul of each, and God of all?

Here the sense, indicating simply the physiological substance upon which inspiration operates, excludes honorific connotations.

3. "The Systolic Rhythm: The Structure of Coleridge's Conversation Poems," *Essays in Criticism* n.s. X (1960) 307–319. A revised version of the essay appears in Gérard's *English Romantic Poetry* (Berkeley: Univ. of California Press, 1968).

4. House, *Coleridge* (London: Rupert Hart-Davis, 1953) *passim;* Abrams, "Structure and Style in the Greater Romantic Lyric," in *From Sensibility to Romanticism* ed F. W. Hilles and Harold Bloom (New York: Oxford Univ. Press, 1965).

5. "Wordsworth and Coleridge on Diction and Figures," in *English Institute Essays 1952* ed Alan S. Downer (New York: Columbia Univ. Press, 1954) 187.

6. *Harriet Martineau's Autobiography* ed Maria W. Chapman (Boston, 1870) 299.

1. Diseases into Pearls: "This Lime-Tree Bower My Prison" as Coleridgean Meditation

1. *LL* I 1–97.
2. "Coleridge's Debt to Charles Lamb," *Essays and Studies* n.s. XI (1958) 72. Whalley's is the most extensive—in fact the only sustained —commentary on this correspondence. He comes to somewhat different conclusions from mine about the importance of Lamb's criticism, in the nine months from May 1796 to February 1797, in shaping Coleridge's achievement, both in "The Ancient Mariner" and "Kubla Khan" and in the conversation poems. At best, it seems to me, Lamb encouraged Coleridge in strengths already established; at worst, in efforts at sublimity that might well have been discouraged; and in urging Coleridge to cultivate simplicity he greatly misconceived the subtle craft of Coleridge's developing meditative art.
3. *LL* I 13–22 (8–10 June 1796).
4. *CL* I 297.
5. *LL* I 53–56 (8 Nov 1796).
6. Ibid 39 (27 Sept 1796).
7. *CL* I 238-239.

8. *LL* I 178–179 (17 Mar 1800) and 245–248 (15 Feb 1801).

9. Ibid 112 (19 or 26 July 1797).

10. Ibid 198 (6 Aug 1800).

11. R. A. Durr, " 'This Lime-Tree Bower My Prison' and a Repeated Action in Coleridge," *ELH* XXVI (1959) 514–530. Davie, *Articulate Energy: An Enquiry into the Syntax of English Poetry* (London: Routledge & Kegan Paul, 1955) 68. See also Gérard, "The Systolic Rhythm," and A. W. Rudrun, "Coleridge's 'This Lime-Tree Bower My Prison,' " *Southern Review* (Adelaide) I (1964) 30–42. Rudrun's is in many ways the most imaginative reading.

12. Durr 519; 521–522.

13. *C 17th C* 334. He did read it at some point; the annotations to Baxter's *Reliquiae Baxterianae*, which probably date from later in his life, contain a familiar allusion to *Saints' Rest.*

14. *CL* I 245. A hand-list of editions of *The Saints' Everlasting Rest* is included as an appendix in the abridgment of the treatise edited by John T. Wilkinson (London: Epworth Press, 1962) 185–188. Twelve editions appeared in Baxter's lifetime; the most frequently reprinted abridgment in the eighteenth century was first published by Benjamin Fawcett in 1759.

15. It seems worth remarking at this point, however, that in general no other figure of comparable stature and popularity in the seventeenth century in England displays an orientation of mind and a temperament so close to Coleridge's own as we see it in his meditative interests. (Jeremy Taylor resembles Coleridge in his eloquence and inventiveness, as does Robert Leighton, the Anglican archbishop who inspired much of *Aids to Reflection* (1825), in his abstruse theological speculation, but neither of these seems so close to Coleridge as Baxter is in his combination of acute philosophical argument and openly affective temperament.) The tone of the annotations to *Reliquiae Baxterianae*—the main source for evidence of Coleridge's attitude to Baxter—suggests that he was one of the rare thinkers and writers Coleridge was ready to call a "Friend."

16. Martz, *The Poetry of Meditation* (New Haven: Yale Univ. Press, 1962) 168–174.

17. *The Saints' Everlasting Rest*, ed William Young (London: E. Grant Richards, 1907) 358. Unless otherwise indicated, passages cited are from this abridged edition, with page numbers indicated in parentheses or brackets.

18. *CL* I 237.

19. Ibid 238–239.

20. Not in Young abridgment. Quoted from Baxter, *Practical Works* (London: James Duncan, 1830) XXIII 57.

21. *LL* I 48–50 (24 Oct 1796) and 50–52 (28 Oct 1796).

22. *Coleridge* (New York: Macmillan, 1968) 134–138.

23. Cf. *Practical Works* 258: "Several ways will [a heart in heaven] preserve us against temptation; first, by *keeping* the *heart employed*" (emphasis added).

24. To William Godwin (3 Mar 1800) while Coleridge was visiting the Lambs: "The Agnus Dei & the Virgin Mary desire their kind respects to *you*, you sad Atheist—!" (*CL* I 580); to John Rickman (14 Mar 1804), whose dinner invitation drew this papal burlesque in response: "I will be with you by a quarter before 7 infallibly; and the Virgin Mary with the uncrucified Lamb will come with me" (*CL* II 1090).

25. Cp. *Practical Works* XXIII 55: "Consider also, that afflictions are exceedingly useful to us, to keep us from mistaking our resting place."

26. *CL* I 266–267.

27. Coleridge's "scathe of fire" may derive from Milton's comparison of the fallen angels "condemned / Forever now to have their lot in pain" to forest oaks that "heaven's fire / Hath scathed" (*PL* I, 607–608; 612–613). The excessiveness of the imagery in "This Lime-Tree Bower My Prison" may have appealed to a playfulness in Coleridge because Lamb a few months earlier had chided as a "lamentable" lapse in decorum an episode in a poem, "Visions of the Maid of Orleans," that Coleridge had high hopes for. The episode contained this description of a dying waggoner: "A miserable man crawl'd forth: his limbs / The silent frost had eat, scathing like fire." See Chapter 3 for a fuller discussion of the significance of Coleridge's poem and the context of Lamb's vexing criticism. Throughout this book, lines in Milton's poems are quoted from *The Poems of John Milton* ed John Carey and Alastair Fowler (London: Longmans, Green, 1968).

28. The strong resemblance in situation and tone between Coleridge's poem and Henry Vaughan's meditative elegy, "They are all gone into the world of light, / And I alone sit lingring here!"—a poem Coleridge could hardly have known despite some unusual affinities in expression—indicates the extent to which in substance and mode he perpetuates the tradition of seventeenth-century devotional verse. *The Works of Henry Vaughan* ed L. C. Martin (Oxford: The Clarendon, Press, 1957) 483–484.

29. Coleridge might also have read the following nearby passage in

'Saints' Rest with special attention to its analogical possibilities for his Nether Stowey situation: "Have not I after such an unsettled life, and after almost five years' living in the weary condition of war, and the unpleasing life of a soldier, and after so many years' groaning under the Church's unreformedness, and the great fears that lay upon us, and after so many longings, and prayers for these days; have I not thought of them with too much content; and been ready to say, soul take thy rest? Have not I comforted myself more in the forethoughts of enjoying these than of coming to heaven, and enjoying God? What wonder, then, if God cut me off when I am just sitting down in this supposed rest!" (194–195).

30. Durr 517.
31. "Systolic Rhythm" 316–317.
32. Mark Reed suggests the possibility that the Simplon Pass material was composed in 1799 (*Wordsworth: The Chronology of the Early Years* [Cambridge, Mass.: Harvard Univ. Press, 1967] 261). Coleridge's lines, as noted, were expanded to final form for publication in 1800.
33. *Osorio* IV i 13, 44, *PW* (EHC) II 563–565. Cp. IV i 18–20: "A jutting clay-stone / Drips on the long lank weed that grows beneath; / And the weed nods and drips."
34. *PW* (EHC) I 74. Cf. *CL* II 855.
35. *Lay Sermons* (CC) 72.
36. *C 17th C* 693.
37. *LL* I 99 (13 Feb 1797).
38. *WPW* I 93.
39. *CN* I 1512.
40. *CL* II 1053.
41. *Lay Sermons* (CC) 78. Cp. *CN* III 3406 and the similar imagery in the motto to the "Meditative Poems in Blank Verse" in *SL*, quoted as an epigraph to this book.
42. *Complete Works* IV 431–432.
43. 23 Oct 1833. *Complete Works* VI 491.
44. Durr 528 also notes this function of the humble bee image.
45. The momentary crossing of the "mighty orb's dilated glory" by the rook's black wing has an analogy in the earliest printed version (31 Dec 1796) of Coleridge's "Ode to the Departing Year," where England, despising peace and lacking Lamb's saving faith, sees a momentary setback for revolutionary France in terms of a similar natural phenomenon: "A cloud, O Freedom! cross'd thy orb of Light, / And sure he deem'd that orb was set in night." Similar language occurs in another apocalyptic context in lines that originally appeared in *The Watchman* (25 Mar 1796):

The early Year's fast-flying Vapours stray
In shadowing Trains across the orb of Day:
And we, poor Insects of a few short Hours,
    Deem it a world of Gloom.
Were it not better hope a nobler doom
Proud to believe, that with more active powers
    On rapid many-coloured Wing
We thro' one bright perpetual Spring
Shall hover round the Fruits and Flowers
Screen'd by those Clouds & cherish'd by those Showers!

PW (EHC) I 148, 163; *Watchman* (CC) 132.

46. *PW* (EHC) I 410.

47. In the draft of the poem Coleridge sent to Southey, the closing apostrophe was to "My Sister and my Friends!" (the "Sister" being Dorothy Wordsworth) and not to "My gentle-hearted Charles!" who is thus named only in the earlier passage when the "friends emerge / Beneath the wide wide Heaven." The exact repetition, twice, of that cumbersome but rhythmic phrase in the revised version, which undoubtedly added to Lamb's annoyance when it was published in 1800, was in all likelihood deliberately obtrusive, a gesture to take the reader beyond the meaning of the words themselves. What we probably have is neither compulsive repetition nor the evidence of embarrassingly artless sentimentality (as Lamb charged). Rather, the phrase may have been intended to function as a curious periphrasis, Coleridge's genial kenning, given odd prominence through repetition in order thus to call attention to the significant, concealed play upon the uninvoked surname of his friend.

2. Coleridge and "Intellectual Activity"

1. *CL* I 335n; 137. The burlesque context of the "compleat Necessitarian" remark is unmistakable when Coleridge continues: "Boyer thrashed Favell most cruelly the day before yesterday—I sent him the following Note of consolation. 'I condole with you on the unpleasant motions, to which a certain Uncouth Automaton has been mechanized; and am anxious to know the motives, that impinged on its optic or auditory nerves, so as to be communicated in such rude vibrations through the medullary substance of Its Brain, thence rolling their stormy Surges into the capillaments of its Tongue, and the muscles of its arm.'" J. D. Boulger, however, takes Coleridge's remark out of this antic context: "He adopted Hartley's theory that thought is corporeal, then Hartley modified by Priestley (at the time of "The Eolian

Harp"), next Berkeley's idealism, which should have occasioned a rethinking of the laws of association, *but did not*" ("Imagination and Speculation in Coleridge's Conversation Poems," *JEGP* LXIV [1965] 691–711). Boulger finds in the poems generally a struggle between imagination and abstract reason. On the problems inherent in philosophically oriented studies of the poems, with examples, there is a good discussion in G. N. G. Orsini, *Coleridge and German Idealism* (Carbondale: Southern Illinois Univ. Press, 1969) 37–40. See also the review of these tendencies by René Wellek, "Coleridge's Philosophy and Criticism: From 1956," in *The English Romantic Poets: A Review of Research and Criticism* ed Frank Jordan, Jr. (New York: Modern Language Association, 1972) 232–240.

2. A. R. Jones, "Coleridge and Poetry: The Conversational and other Poems," in *S. T. Coleridge*, ed R. L. Brett (London: G. Bell, 1971) 122.

3. See, for example, Kathleen Coburn, "Reflexions in a Coleridge Mirror," in *From Sensibility to Romanticism*, and Cleanth Brooks, "Coleridge as a Metaphysical Poet," in *Romanticism: Vistas, Instances, Continuities* ed David Thorburn and Geoffrey Hartman (Ithaca: Cornell Univ. Press, 1973). See also *CN* III 4073–4074.

4. *BL* (1907) II 11.

5. *Lects 1795* (CC) 34–35. Cf. *Friend* (CC) I 327–328.

6. *BL* (1907) I 20.

7. *Friend* (CC) I 124; *BL* (1907) I 21.

8. On the question of interpreting millennial language used by dissenters in the 1780's and 1790's and the problems of inferring literal belief in an apocalyptic scheme, see E. P. Thompson, *The Making of the English Working Class* (New York: Random House, 1963) 48–50.

9. *PW* (EHC) I 108–325; *CL* I 197, 203, 205.

10. *Watchman* (CC) 132. A similar hovering is part of Coleridge's version of the angelic activity in "Religious Musings":

> Contemplant Spirits! ye that hover o'er
> With untired gaze the immeasurable fount
> Ebullient with creative Deity! [402–404]

11. *CN* II 2064.

12. *Watchman* (CC) 132. On the coexistence in Hartley of concepts of determinist association and providential order, see J. A. Appleyard, *Coleridge's Philosophy of Literature* (Cambridge, Mass.: Harvard Univ. Press, 1965) 22–42.

13. *PW* (EHC) II 1136.

14. *Complete Works* IV 431–432; see above, pp 54–55.

15. *CL* II 1197; see below, pp 233–234.

16. *PW* (EHC) I 266–267.

17. *The Philosophy of Literary Form: Studies in Symbolic Action* (Baton Rouge: Louisiana State Univ. Press, 1941) 20, 61, and *passim*.

18. *Friend* (CC) II 18.

19. *Watchman* (CC) 31. In one of the early versions of "Dejection: An Ode," Coleridge hailed Wordsworth as a "great son of genius! full of light and love" (*PW* [EHC] I 366n).

20. *CL* II 1000.

21. *BL* (1907) I 59.

22. *PW* (EHC) II 1139.

23. Ibid 1098.

24. Ibid 1098–1099. Coleridge's language here resembles that in chapter 17 of the *Biographia* when, citing the Song of Deborah ("at her feet he bowed, he fell, he lay down; at her feet he bowed, he fell; where he bowed, there he fell down dead"), he wrote of "the *apparent* tautologies of intense and turbulent feeling, in which the passion is greater and of longer endurance than to be exhausted or satisfied by a single representation of the image or incident exciting it." With Deborah's song, of course, as with the odes of Pindar (Coleridge's favorite example of the sublime in poetry), there is no question of madness or of the perverse deliberation of a cruelly vengeful spirit. But his emphasis in both comments is on the insufficiency of a single use of the word or phrase to satisfy the passion. Wordsworth in a note to "The Thorn" (1800) also cited the Song of Deborah, calling its "repetition and apparent tautology . . . beauties of the highest kind." But his account is of a less turbulent passion: "The mind luxuriates in the repetition of words which appear successfully to communicate its feelings" (*BL* [1907] II 43; *WPW* II 513).

25. *PW* (EHC) II 1100–1101.

26. *CL* II 1000–1001.

27. *BL* (1907) II 56.

28. *CN* II 2396.

3. Wordsworth and Coleridge: Visions of the Ideal World

1. *BL* (1907) I 58–59.

2. Ibid II 5.

3. Wordsworth sent the revision in early March to Joseph Cottle, who gave it to Coleridge. *CL* I 216n.

4. *CL* I 309.

5. Ibid 297.

6. *LL* I 92.

7. Ibid 99.

8. *CL* I 309, 298.

9. Erdman, *Studies in Bibliography* XI (1958) 151–153. Line numbers refer to text of "The Destiny of Nations" in *PW* (EHC) I 131–148.

10. *CL* I 216n. Lamb's laconic remark, in a letter to Coleridge, that he had read Wordsworth's poem "not without delight" is inscrutable, though one might guess that it reflects his reluctance to encourage Coleridge's enthusiasm for the stranger from the north.

11. Text from *The Salisbury Plain Poems of William Wordsworth* ed Stephen Gill (Ithaca: Cornell Univ. Press, 1975). Numbering by stanzas indicated in brackets.

12. *WL* (*E*) 159; Gill, "*Adventures on Salisbury Plain* and Wordsworth's Poetry of Protest 1795–1797," *Studies in Romanticism* (1971) 48–65.

13. Bateson, *Wordsworth: A Reinterpretation.* 2d ed (London: Longmans, Green, 1956) 110.

14. *BL* (1907) I 62; *Sh C* I 188 (my emphasis).

15. *LL* I 99.

16. *The Watchman* (CC) 238–241 (19 Apr 1796). Cf. *RX* 104–109, 489n.

17. Legouis, *The Early Life of William Wordsworth 1770–1798* (London: J. M. Dent, 1897) 342.

18. Ibid.

19. *CN* I 186.

20. In this context one might also cite the passage from the sermons of Robert South (1634–1716) in a 1797 notebook entry: "Christ, the great Sun of Righteousness, & Saviour of the World, having by a glorious rising after a red & bloody setting, proclaimed his Deity to men & angels—& by a complete triumph over the two grand enemies of mankind sin & death set up the everlasting Gospel in the room of all false religions, has now (as it were) changed the Persian superstition into the Christian Devotion; & without the least approach to the Idolatry of the former made it henceforth the Duty of all nations, Jews & Gentiles, to worship the rising Sun." *CN* I 327.

21. *BL* (1907) II 5.

22. *Cornell Library Journal* XI (1970) 5–7.

23. Ibid 14.

4. *"Frost at Midnight": Coleridge's Companionable Form*

1. Abrams, "Structure and Style in the Greater Romantic Lyric," in *From Sensibility to Romanticism*, ed F. W. Hilles and Harold Bloom (New York: Oxford, 1965) 531, hereafter cited as "Structure and Style"; Humphrey House, *Coleridge* (London: Rupert Hart-Davis, 1953) 82, hereafter cited as House; cp. W. J. Bate, *Coleridge* (New York: Macmillan, 1968) 51, hereafter cited as Bate.
2. "Structure and Style" 532.
3. *PW* (EHC) I 240–241.
4. Ibid.
5. *Osorio* I i 97–99, *PW* (EHC) II 522.
6. *CN* II 2546.
7. House 82.
8. *PW* (EHC) I 242–243.
9. *PW* (EHC) I 211.
10. *CL* I 328.

5. *Coleridge's "Hymn Before Sun-rise: Mont Blanc, Mon Frère, Mon Semblable*

1. See *CL* II 865n for a summary by A. P. Rossiter of information relevant to the plagiarism charge. Brun's poem, and F. L. Stolberg's "On a Cataract," which may also have influenced Coleridge, are printed in *PW* (EHC) II 1131 and 1126 respectively. Coleridge's remark expressing his high opinion of the "Hymn Before Sun-rise" occurs in an 1819 letter to the *Blackwood's* reviewer, who had favorably noticed his poems (*CL* IV 970). It is quoted as an epigraph to Chapter 4.
2. In his recent reopening of the old plagiarism charge, Norman Fruman has added little except to place Coleridge's unacknowledged use of the Brun source in a broader context of concealment in order to gain immediate gratification of esteem for his poetic abilities. While acknowledging that none of Coleridge's close friends was likely to think he had in fact been to Chamounix, Fruman assumes that they would have read the poem, had they known of the Brun original, as a deceitful attempt on Coleridge's part to disguise his debt. This assumption, in turn, rests at least in part on the supposition that Coleridge's poem was primarily an attempt in the same vein as Friederika Brun's. As my reading of the poem in this essay will indicate, I would argue that in every important way the poem is "original," and that its originality is such that Coleridge would have had little to fear from exposure

of what was, after all, a casual or incidental source. See *Coleridge, the Damaged Archangel* (New York: George Braziller, 1971) 29–30, 451.

3. *Shelley's Mythmaking* (New Haven: Yale Univ. Press, 1959) 18.

4. *CL* IV 974. The line quoted by Coleridge first appeared in the 1812 edition of *The Friend*, indicating, if Coleridge's account is to be taken as accurate in such details, that it was at this time that Wordsworth expressed his censure (*Friend* [CC] II 156).

5. *CL* IV 572. See Chapter 7 below.

6. See Bate *passim*, esp. 46–51.

7. "Structure and Style" 551–557.

8. *CL* IV 974–975; *PW* (EHC) I 240.

9. *CL* II 864–865.

10. The essay is included in *BL* (1907) II 253–263.

11. "Reflexions in a Coleridge Mirror: Some Images in His Poems," in *From Sensibility to Romanticism* 416, hereafter cited as "Reflexions." On Richards, see Chapter 6.

12. *CL* II 851.

13. Ibid IV 974–975.

14. Bate, *The English Poet and the Burden of the Past* (Cambridge, Mass.: Belknap, 1970), *passim*, and *Coleridge* 50.

15. Quoted in "Reflexions" 429.

16. *PW* (EHC) I 408.

17. Ibid 133–134.

18. Ibid 124.

19. *Coleridge's Hymn Before Sunrise* (Lausanne, 1942) 110–111.

20. See also Coleridge's verse letter to Sara Hutchinson, 4 April 1802:

> The Bee-hive murmuring near,
> That ever-busy & most quiet Thing
> Which I have heard at Midnight murmuring.   [*CL* II 792]

21. *Shelley's Mythmaking* 17.

22. *CN* I 926.

23. It has not, I think, been noticed that "before sun-rise" constitutes a distinct, though subtle, adjustment of Friederika Brun's "beim Sonnenaufgang." Coleridge's *Morning Post* title emphasizes the time more clearly: "Chamouny The Hour before Sunrise A Hymn" (*PW* [EHC] I 376n).

24. *CL* II 1118.

25. To cite one example, Vicesimus Knox's widely circulated double volume, *Elegant Extracts . . . in Poetry* (London: Charles Dilly, 1770), which Christopher and William Wordsworth knew well and

which Coleridge was reading in 1799, includes "Milton's and Thomson's and [Psalm 148] the source of all three" in the first fifteen selections of its opening section, "Sacred and Moral Hymns." An indication, perhaps, of how naturally such texts would have come to Coleridge as models is an entry from Christopher Wordsworth's notebook in 1789: "Could I not introduce an Hymn in imitation of Milton's and Thomson's?" (*The Early Wordsworthian Milieu* ed Zera S. Fink [Oxford: The Clarendon Press, 1958] 86). Cf. Dorothy Wordsworth's letter to Catherine Clarkson, 12 Nov 1810: "William read part of the 5th Book of Paradise Lost to us. He read The Morning Hymn, while a stream of white vapour, which coursed the Valley of Brathay, ascended slowly and by degrees melted away. It seemed as if we had never before felt deeply the power of the Poet—'Ye mists and exhalations, etc., etc.!'" (*WL* [*M*] I 447).

26. *The Prose Works of William Wordsworth* ed Alexander B. Grosart 3 vols (London: Edward Moxon, Son, 1876) III 442.

27. *CL* II 842. For a different view of the genesis of the poem during the descent from Sca'Fell and an attack on the poem as both a betrayal of that experience and an instance of Coleridge's apostasy to the "spirits" of nature, see *Coleridge's Verse: A Selection* ed William Empson and David Pirie (London: Faber and Faber, 1972) 88–91 and 251–252.

28. "Reflexions" 419.

29. Cp. *CN* I 191: "In the paradisiacal World Sleep was voluntary & holy—a spiritual before God, in which the mind elevated by contemplation retired into pure intellect suspending all commerce with sensible objects & perceiving the present deity—"

30. "Reflections on the Evening Star," *New Perspectives on Coleridge and Wordsworth* ed Geoffrey Hartman (New York: Columbia Univ. Press, 1972) esp. 116–122.

31. *CL* V 109–114.

32. Ibid 104.

33. In his own letter to Oriel, Coleridge quoted the section of "Frost at Midnight" that begins "Dear Babe! that slumber'st cradled by my side" (*CL* V 111–112).

6. "Dejection: An Ode": The Old Moon's Effluence

1. The letter version was published by Ernest de Selincourt in "Coleridge's 'Dejection: An Ode,'" *Essays and Studies by Members of the English Association* XXII (1937) 7–25. Passages from this ver-

sion are quoted here from the text in *CL* II 790–798. The "incomparably greater" remark is in "Coleridge at the British Museum," *Times Literary Supplement* (21 July 1972) 852. Humphry House (133–139) agrees with the opinion "of many readers of the Ode, that brilliantly successful as most of it is, as *parts*, yet it fails to achieve complete artistic unity." He laments the self-pity of both versions but sees it is as an aspect of Coleridge's struggle for clear and mature self-analysis. Max Schulz argues for the unity of the final version, focusing on the storm imagery *The Poetic Voices of Coleridge* (Detroit: Wayne State Univ. Press, 1963) 33–38, 46. George Watson gives succinct expression to the debate by saying that the published form is "one of the oddest compromises in English poetry: an intensely, bitterly, almost indecently private poem of an unhappily married poet, cast into the most public of all forms, the neoclassical Pindaric." *Coleridge the Poet* (London: Routledge & Kegan Paul, 1966) 74. In Fields, *Reality's Dark Dream* (Kent State Univ. Press, 1967), see especially 119–167.

2. *PW* (EHC) II 1136.

3. *CN* I 1599 and 1601.

4. *Complete Works* IV 432.

5. Davie, *Articulate Energy* 69.

6. *Coleridge's Minor Poems: A Lecture at Montana State University on 8 Apr 1960.*

7. Influencing Coleridge's interest in the symbolic possibilities of this image may have been Milton's attention to earthlight in *Paradise Lost* VIII, in a passage charged with significance for one interested in reciprocal schemes of energy and in reflections of divine love and solicitude. Countering the unnecessary intricacies of Ptolemaic cosmology, Raphael notes for Adam's edification that such a system "needs not thy belief":

> If earth industrious of her self fetch day
> Travelling east, and with her part averse
> From the sun's beam meet night, her other part
> Still luminous by his ray. What if that light
> Sent from her through the wide transpicuous air,
> To the terrestrial moon be as a star
> Enlightening her by day, as she by night
> This earth? Reciprocal, if land be there,
> Fields and inhabitants: her spots thou seest
> As clouds, and clouds may rain, and rain produce
> Fruits in her softened soil, for some to eat
> Allotted there; and other suns perhaps
> With their attendant moons thou wilt descry

Communicating male and female light,
Which two great sexes animate the world,
Stored in each orb perhaps with some that live.   [136–152]

In a note to this passage Alastair Fowler cites an analogous discussion in Burton's *Anatomy of Melancholy* II ii 3: "If the earth move, it is a planet, and shines to them in the moon, and to the other planetary inhabitants, as the moon and they do to us upon the earth. . . ." *The Poems of John Milton* (London: Longmans, Green, 1968) 822. Coleridge's familiarity with the Milton passage may be indicated by his use of the unusual word "transpicuous" (*PL* VIII 140) in the 1802 version of the "Hymn Before Sun-rise" (8): "Deep is the sky, and black: transpicuous, deep, / An ebon mass!" *PW* (EHC) I 572.

8. *Reality's Dark Dream* 119. The canceled word is not recorded in Griggs's text.

9. *Lay Sermons* (*CC*) 30; *CL* III 305.

10. *Sh C* I 188–189.

11. *BL* (1907) I 86; II 51. Such emblems and figures may encourage readers to think of Coleridge's art in terms of the kind of biological metaphors for the process of inspiration referred to on p 10. But it should be kept in mind that Coleridge turns to such figures as that of the water-insect and those in "Dejection" to reinforce a view of the mind's conscious, voluntary activity.

12. *CN* I 1552.

13. *Complete Works* IV 434–435.

14. *CL* II 842 (emphasis added).

15. Readers who accept House's characterization of stanza six as "firm, sad honesty of self-analysis" are left to find another correlative for the "viper thoughts." Among the suggestions have been the unstated domestic anguish of Coleridge's marriage (that is, what he calls "afflictions") and the "abstruse research" undertaken as an anodyne to those afflictions. But such readings make the turn from those "viper thoughts" more agitated and hysterical than I think the evidence warrants, in spite of the proliferating exclamations in the seventh stanza.

To corroborate this reading one might cite the passage Coleridge added to his "Monody on the Death of Chatterton" in 1796. There a similar "turn" toward hope follows a veering of his own spirit toward desperate melancholy as he broods on Chatterton's courting of suicidal sublimity:

And here, in Inspiration's eager hour,
When most the big soul feels the mastering power,
These wilds, these caverns roaming o'er,

262   Notes: Pages 196 to 199

Round which the screaming sea-gulls soar,
With wild unequal steps he pass'd along,
Oft pouring on the winds a broken song:
Anon, upon some rough rock's fearful brow
Would pause abrupt—and gaze upon the waves below.

Poor Chatterton! *he* sorrows for thy fate
Who would have prais'd and lov'd thee, ere too late.
Poor Chatterton! farewell! of darkest hues
This chaplet cast I on thy unshaped tomb;
But dare no longer on the sad theme muse,
Lest kindred woes persuade a kindred doom:
For oh! big gall-drops, shook from Folly's wing,
Have blacken'd the fair promise of my spring;
And the stern Fate transpierc'd with viewless dart
The last pale Hope that shiver'd at my heart!

Hence, gloomy thoughts! no more my soul shall dwell
On joys that were! no more endure to weigh
The shame and anguish of the evil day,
Wisely forgetful! O'er the ocean swell
Sublime of Hope I seek the cottag'd dell
Where Virtue calm with careless step may stray;
And, dancing to the moon-light roundelay,
The wizard Passions weave an holy spell!

These lines were probably added under the stimulus of, and in re-sponse to, stanzas in Wordsworth's "Adventures on Salisbury Plain" which Coleridge read sometime in March or April 1796. On April 11, 1796, twelve days after writing to Thomas Poole that "my poems are finished"—he was making last-minute revisions for his first collection —he wrote again to Poole, noting, among other things, that "Chatter-ton shall appear modernized." See pp 198–200 below. *PW* (EHC) I 130; *CL* I 195, 203.

16. To argue the latter, that the abstruse research "suits a part" but now "infects the whole," is to perpetuate the long-standing miscon-ception that the philosopher in Coleridge was the fatal enemy of the poet, a misconception that has plagued popular accounts of Coleridge as a man of subterranean and antiintellectual genius who, thwarted by daemonic powers, sold out to philosophical prose. It is the use of *any* tactic to numb the exposed domestic feelings that Coleridge laments.

17. *CL* II 854.
18. *WL* (E) 328–329.
19. Ibid.

20. *CL* II 668–669.

21. *Reality's Dark Dream* 18–23, 146.

22. *Complete Works* IV 432.

23. "William's" is, of course, the reading of the letter version. The change to "Otway's" can only have been made out of a desire to transcend "personality" and avoid embarrassment (*CL* II 795).

24. House 165–166.

25. *Poetic Voices* 203–205.

7. *Wordsworth's Whelming Tide: Coleridge and the Art of Analogy*

1. See, for example, Schulz, *Poetic Voices* 132–134.

2. *CL* IV 572.

3. He had already written to Joseph Cottle and Lord Byron about the collection that became *Sibylline Leaves*. See *CL* IV 546–47, 551–552, 559–63.

4. *CL* IV 974.

5. *PW* (EHC) II 1144; *Table Talk*, 18 Aug 1833, in *Complete Works* VI 479.

6. *C 17th C* 579.

7. Quotations, with line numbers in brackets following, are from the "1805–6" text in *The Prelude* ed E. de Selincourt and H. Darbishire (Oxford: The Clarendon Press, 1959). This text is de Selincourt's collation of two manuscript copies completed by early 1806 and is the closest available approximation to the poem Coleridge heard.

8. *Sh C* I 181–82.

9. *PW* (EHC) II 1082–1083.

10. *CL* II 1197.

11. Ibid.

12. Ibid.

13. *CL* II 864.

14. *CL* I 425.

15. *Friend* (CC) II 193.

16. *PL* X 410–459.

17. *CN* II 3107.

18. *Table Talk*, 23 Oct 1833, in *Complete Works* VI 491.

19. *Complete Works* IV 432–33.

20. "Reflexions" 433.

21. *The Works of Jacob Behmen* (London, 1764) I 47. British Museum copy, C.126.k.1. A longer and more explicitly theological version of this passage forms the concluding paragraph of the *Biographia Literaria*.

Index

egotism, 12, 53-54, 76-77, 85, 181-182, 219-221, 230, 234-235, 238-240
Emmet, Robert, 88
Empson, William, 259n27
Erdman, David, 99
Estlin, John Prior, 136

Fenwick, Isabella, 205
Fields, Beverly, 180, 203, 259n1
Flower, Benjamin, 39-40
Fogle, R. H., 247n1
Fowler, Alastair, 260n7
Fricker, Sarah, *see* Sarah Coleridge
Fruman, Norman, 257n2

Gerard, Albert, 10, 249n3, 250n11
Gill, Stephen, 101
Godwin, William, 103, 248n2, 251n24
Goldsmith, Oliver, 100
Griggs, E. L., 151, 169

Harper, George MacLean, 247n1
Hartley, David, 28, 76, 192, 253n1
Hartman, Geoffrey, 168
Herbert, George, 66
House, Humphry, 10, 73, 127, 132-133, 194, 208, 259n1, 261n15
Hutchinson, Mary, 157, 167, 187
Hutchinson, Sara, 149, 150, 151, 157, 180, 194-195, 198, 218

imitation of Christ, 35, 39-40, 47-48, 65, 114

Job, Book of, 39-40, 160
Johnson, Samuel, 66
Jones, A. R., 254n2
Joyce, James, 66

Kant, Immanuel, 34
Keats, John, 70, 153
Knox, Vicesimus, 258n25

Lamb, Charles, 20-60, 65, 72, 84, 97-100, 102, 106-112, 131, 152, 223-224, 226
Lamb, Mary, 23
Leguois, Émile, 108-109
Leighton, Robert, 250n15
Locke, John, 63, 244
Lowes, J. L., 70
Loyola, Ignatius of, 28

Martineau, Harriet, 11-12, 56
Martz, Louis, 29
meditation, 9-10, 12, 28-47, 53-59, 77, 128, 192-193, 239
meditative play of mind, 11, 35, 45-46, 52, 56, 65-67, 74-89, 157, 168-169, 228, 233, 243-244
millennialism, 69, 72-76, 110, 156
Milton, John
    Coleridge's allegorical reading of *Comus*, 140; Coleridge's comparison of "Milton's 'Hymn'" and "Hymn Before Sun-rise," 146, 148, 153, 161, 258n25; Coleridge's defense of Milton's egotism, 219-221, 230; Coleridge's reverence for and dependency on, 52, 220-222; influence on Coleridge's poems, 47-49, 71-72, 96-97, 114-115, 118, 146, 148, 153, 161, 165-168, 197-198, 200, 205-206, 219, 221-238, 251n27, 258n25; self-portraits in Coleridge's sketches of, 68, 220
Milton's writings
    Comus, 140
    "Lycidas," 219, 221, q 222-223, 227-228, q 227, 230-233, 235-238, q 236, q 237, q 238
    "On the Morning of Christ's Nativity," 72, 97, 197, q 205-206, 233
    Paradise Lost, q 47-48, 51, 161, q 161, 165-168, q 165-166, q 167, q 197-198, q 226, q 234, 236, q 238, q 251n27, 258n25, q 260n7
    Paradise Regained, q 49, q 114, 118

Napoleon, 69

"One Life," 47, 60, 63, 73, 119, 154, 235, 238
organicism, 10, 26-27, 74, 248n2
Oriel College, Fellows of, 169-172, 259n33
Orsini, G. N. G., 248n2, 253n1

Pantisocracy, 21
personality and poetry, 64, 146-148, 150-156, 168-169, 180-181, 194-197, 201-207, 217-219, 232-235, 238, 242-244, 259n1, 261n15, 263n23
Pindar, 22, 255n24
Pinney, Azariah, 100

Coleridge's Meditative Art

Designed by R. E. Rosenbaum.
Composed by York Composition Company, Inc.,
in 11 point linotype Janson, 2 points leaded,
with display lines in Weiss.
Printed letterpress from type by York Composition Company
on Warren's number 66 text, 50 pound basis,
with the Cornell University Press watermark.
Bound by Vail-Ballou Press
in Columbia book cloth
and stamped in All Purpose foil.